INSIDER SEO SECRETS
Raise Your Business to the Top of Google Now

A Start-to-Finish Method to Rapidly Attract Thousands of New Customers Online in 11 Straightforward Steps

Karl zu Ortenburg, MSc
with Corinna Sturmer

AMI Publishing

No part of this book may be altered, copied, or distributed, without prior written permission of the authors or publishers. All product names, logos, and trademarks are property of their respective owners who have not necessarily endorsed, sponsored, or approved this publication. Text and images available over the Internet and used in this book may be subject to intellectual rights and may not be copied from this book.

First Published in Great Britain by Advanced Marketing on the Internet Ltd., trading as AMI Publishing

Copyright © Karl zu Ortenburg, 2010
All rights reserved.

ISBN 978-0-9563752-0-9

The contents of this book reflect the author's views acquired through their experience in the topics discussed here. The authors or publishers disclaim any personal loss or liability caused by the utilization of any information presented herein. The authors are not engaged in rendering any legal or financial advice. While the sources mentioned herein are assumed to be reliable at the time of writing, the authors and publishers, or their affiliates, are not responsible for any price changes or changes of offerings. Sources can only be confirmed reliable at the time of original publication of this book. This book is a guide only and as such, should be considered solely for information.

As with any business, your results may vary, and will be based on your individual capacity, business experience, expertise, and level of desire. There are no guarantees concerning the level of success you may or may not experience. Any examples used are not intended to represent or guarantee that anyone will achieve the same or similar results. Each individual's success depends on his or her background, dedication, desire and motivation. The use of our information, products and services should be based on your own due diligence and you agree that the authors, publishers, their affiliates or Advanced Marketing on the Internet Ltd are not liable for any success or failure of your business that is directly or indirectly related to the purchase and use of our information, products and services.

To my late dad, Alram Graf zu Ortenburg,
my family and friends.

Foreword

I advise you get started with this book - applying it to *all* your company web activity - as quickly as is humanly possible.

The reason is this:

Karl zu Ortenburg and Corinna Sturmer's *Insider SEO Secrets* is, thankfully and importantly, much more than just "another" system for optimizing web site performance. It is an intelligent, powerful yet simple method which, when applied diligently, has the ability to power your web site statistics, sales and profits far above and beyond the most optimistic goals set by competitors who are *unaware* of this method.

Karl and Corinna have done what everyone else seems to have overlooked - taken the single most powerfully effective SEO methods in the world today, created by the smartest minds in web optimization, and cleverly **combined** them in the right proportions to create a single MEGA STRATEGY able to geometrically propel your web site's performance by up to hundreds of percent in just weeks. Quite simply, there is not a competitor out there who will be able to keep up with you unless they own and act on the method exposed in this extraordinary book.

What I particularly like about Karl and Corinna is their insistence to get this technique 100% thoroughly and clearly explained before allowing it to be published. Yes, they could have "gone for the money" before they were a 100% satisfied with it, but instead they stuck like superglue to their work until the day it was truly ready to be made public.

That day is now!

Prepare yourself and your company for MEGA SEO RESULTS in the coming weeks and months. Keep a record of how rapidly your web site starts attracting new targeted customers or clients, how it helps prospective customers believe in your particular products or services, trust you, and honor you with their business - in volumes you've never witnessed until now - because your records will seem almost unbelievable to those who do not know the secret.

My advice: purchase and act on this book - this minute! It does not matter what product, service or treatment you sell, or how large, medium or tiny your enterprise is today. If you wish your company web site would perform dramatically better, *Insider SEO Secrets* contains a method so powerful that it will blow your statistics and sales charts through the roof, and do it quickly.

I take my hat off to Karl and Corinna! A powerful, important book that will help thousands of committed business owners, directors and professionals achieve significantly higher and wealthier SEO results than they ever could have done *without* this dynamite information.

Paul Gorman

Business Strategist and Author

Dear Reader - Business Owner, Professional and Entrepreneur

Welcome to attracting more customers to your website.

There are already over 1.8 billion users on the Internet today, and there are more to come since the Internet has only reached about 26.6% of the world population. With an increasing number of customers finding you or your competitors via the Internet, advertising budgets moving online and online ads becoming more and more expensive, Search Engine Optimization (SEO), is much in demand.

SEO simply means using techniques to get your website ranked highly on Google and other search engines in order to attract customers to your site. AOL's data shows that 89.92% of your potential customers only click on the first search results page, and almost half of those (42.13%) click on the first listing on that page. Therefore, getting your website listed as highly as possible is a necessity that no serious business owner can ignore anymore.

On the following pages, you will find a method for getting your website in front of the eyes and under the mouse click of many prospective customers, without having to pay for online advertising. Companies in a competitive market such as the loans industry could be charged up to $25 per click for their Google ads. Imagine if you had just a thousand clicks in a week, then this week's advertising could cost you $25,000. Optimizing your site for a high 'natural' listing on Google can be substantially cheaper and much more effective in the long run.

This book will give you an easily manageable SEO plan that you download and adapt to meet your needs. It is based on the most important search engine ranking factors to get you to the top of Google, Yahoo! Bing etc., agreed upon by 72 Internet experts, and in front of your target customer. The book will help you choose which techniques are right for your business, with hands-on advice and practical examples of how to implement them efficiently and quickly – or have them implemented for you. The book also includes a number of templates in the Appendix that you can download from the book's companion site at www.Internet-Experts-Live.com. Plus, you will get a good idea about future developments so you can stay on top of the game.

Last but not least, you will find some of the best, most effective and up-to-date resources on the Internet, put together for you. These SEO Tools will save you and your IT staff or webmaster countless hours, and make your online campaigns even more effective.

Enjoy your success.

P.S. With this book comes free access to a step-by-step course for some time, with practical help to immediately apply what you read in the book - the GROW Course. (**GROW** stands for **G**et **N**ew **C**ustomers **R**apidly **O**n the **W**eb). It is conveniently structured into easy-to-follow steps with useful tips and practical examples. It has 100 or more active links for further information you simply click on, and supporting pages you can instantly download.

My advice is: get it right now, use it in conjunction with the book. It captures the most important aspects of what's described in the book, brings it alive for you and helps you make improvements more quickly, if not even today, to benefit your business with.

Internet-Experts-Live
Ideal Customers Now — Questions? Call us: 020 7731 3077 — Mon-Fri 9am to 7pm

How to Get the SEO GROW Method FREE:

Business and Internet Strategist, Karl zu Ortenburg, MSc is allowing *free access* to his breakthrough SEO and Business Optimization Course! For a limited time only!

"Just Released: The Start-to-Finish Method that Attracts Thousands More Customers to YOUR Website and More Profits to YOUR Business."

SEO GROW Course

Get free access to the GROW Course on the membership site for a limited time, at www.Internet-Experts-Live.com/members/growcourse and use this code:

GROWCode0910.

Acknowledgements

I would like to express my deepest gratitude to the many people with whom I have had the pleasure to work in developing, discussing and refining the ideas and techniques presented in this book, as well as for all the generous support I have received in completing it.

To my beloved wife and partner Corinna, without her continued support and dedication to our family and business, this book would not have come into existence. Her drive, understanding and patience, her writing, editing and storytelling skills, as well as her ability to structure complex material were fundamental in getting this book in shape.

To Victor and Julius, our young and adored sons, who throughout the time of writing this book have seen less of me but have always imprinted a strong image on my heart, waving their 'goodbye' from the window. I hope we can spend more time together again, soon.

To all my friends and colleagues who have helped to get this book out of the door, namely Paul Gorman's relentless support and mentorship, Andrew Mather's wisdom, Nina Koenig's countless hours, Roshan Muthoora's true knowledge of the subject, as well as Sarah Williams' and Kate Snell's thorough proofreading.

To all our clients who, over the years, have put their trust in our ability to help them succeed and overcome the hurdles on the way. The more we have worked together, the more I have learned from you.

I would also like to thank the Internet and SEO experts who contributed to this book, especially Rand Fishkin for his great SEO study, Aaron Wall for his top SEO material, Chris Anderson, Editor-in-Chief of Wired Magazine, for his insights on 'long tails' and 'the value of free', Avinash Kaushik for his insight into Google and Web Analytics, and Wordtracker for their case studies.

And, finally, to you, the reader. I feel honored that you picked up this book and I hope you can use it to achieve your greatest success.

Thank you all.

About the Authors

Karl zu Ortenburg offers Search Engine Optimization (SEO) services through his company, Advanced Marketing on the Internet Ltd. (A-M-I Ltd). Karl sometimes takes on direct SEO consulting work and occasionally offers slots for 'case study' projects where he publishes SEO results in reports and in his courses. He has worked with companies such as Bertelsmann, Random House Publishing, Philips, Dow Chemical, to name just a few. He also works closely with Internet experts from Europe, North America and increasingly Asia in developing and implementing highly effective strategies for businesses, to create exceptional results and outperform larger competitors.

He redefines the way businesses achieve success by using marketing opportunities online, and it is Karl's passion to increase the number of companies who do outstandingly well in their business sector. In his efforts to help as many businesses and professions as possible in the current economic climate, he has agreed to make public his top Internet marketing techniques in the **GROW Method.** This Method or System has never before been released to the public. It allows you to reach 100s and 1000s of new customers.

Karl has the gift of taking you straight to the bottom line of exactly what works and what doesn't. He shows you how to optimize, in straightforward do-able language, every move you make on the web to attract significantly greater numbers of customers within your market place.

Corinna Sturmer is an accomplished TV producer/ director. She has directed and produced a range of highly successful documentaries and factual programmes for the most established television channels in the UK; such as the BBC, Channel 4 and Five.

Her credits include "The First World War", "Timewatch", "Changing Rooms", "Great Speeches", "A Place in the Sun" and many more.

Corinna was intrinsically involved in structuring and shaping the book and its contents. She has brought her writing and storytelling skills to the book to make this quite technical subject matter more accessible and digestible to the reader. Corinna is the company's video marketing expert and a partner in A-M-I Ltd.

Contents

Foreword v

Dear Reader - Business Owner, Professional and Entrepreneur vii
About the Authors xi
Contents xiii
Overview xxi

Introduction
How to Reach New Customers on the Internet 3
Your SEO Plan – To Get New Customers Online 4
What Will My SEO Plan Do for Me? 5
Developing Your SEO Plan 5
1. USP – What Makes Your Company Unique? 5
2. Business Goals 6
3. Search Engine Friendliness 6
4. Keywords 7
5. 'Natural' Listings (SEO) or Paid Listings (PPC)? 8
6. Competition 9
7. On-Page and Off-Page SEO 10
8. Follow-Up 13

Summary: The GROW Method in 11 Steps 15

PART I:
How to Get Your Keywords Right 17
Why Keywords Really Matter 19
Why Using Your Customers' Words Will Drive Your Business Forward 19
Understanding What Your Prospective Customers Really Want 20
Keywords are the Foundation of All Your Optimization Campaigns 21
Why You Want a 'Hungry Crowd' More Than Anything 22

GROW Step 1:
Choose the Best Keywords for Your Target Customers

1. Brainstorming Keywords into a 'Seed List' 23
2. Getting a Head Start – Courtesy of Google 25
3. Finding Your Competitor's Profitable Keywords 26
4. How to Discover the Most Lucrative Keywords 27
5. Evaluating the Market Value of Keywords for Your Business 29
6. Calculating the Return on your Investment 31

GROW Step 2:
Focus Your Campaign with 'Long Tail' Keywords

What is a Long Tail? 35
Think Global – But Act Local 37
    How Do I Get a Local Listing? 40
    Top Search Engine Ranking Factors for Local Listings 40
    Places to Build Local Links 42
Why a 'Phrase Match' Usually Gets More Business 43
Why You Want to Use 'Synonyms' 44
'Latent Semantic Indexing' (LSI) or 'Referential Integrity' 44
How to Test Before You Spend 45

Summary: Keywords – the Foundation of Online Marketing 47

PART II:
How to Outsmart and Outwit Your Competition 49

Competition Analysis 51
    Why Your Position On Google Is So Important 51

GROW Step 3:
Know Your Competition to Fast Track to the Top

The Good News about Competition Analysis 55
Top Ten Search Engine Ranking Factors 56

Contents

1. Keyword-Focused Anchor Text From External Links 56
2. External Link Popularity 56
3. Diversity of Link Sources 57
4. Trustworthiness of the Domain Based on Link Distance from Trusted Domains 57
5. Keyword Use Anywhere in the Title Tag 57
6. Existence of Substantive, Unique Content on the Page 58
7. Page-specific TrustRank 58
8. Keyword Use As The First Word(s) of the Title Tag 58
9. Iterative Algorithm-Based, Global Link Popularity 58
10. Use in the Root Domain Name 59

The Sign of Things to Come in the Future 60
   'Keyword Themes' or 'Theming' 60
   'Silo Structure' or 'Siloing' 61
   High Quality Links 62
Competition Analysis Tools You Can Use Right Now 64
   The Fast Track to Check your Competition – A Hands-On Example 64
Some Give and Take 74

Summary: Competition Analysis to Save Time and Effort 76

PART III:
How to Make Your Site More Competitive With 'On-Page SEO' 79

How to Get Your Own Pages fit for the Search Engines 81

GROW Step 4:
Place Your Keywords Where They Give You Most Power

Placing Keywords in Your Title Tags 83
   How to Write a Good Title Tag 83
   How You Put Your 'Title' in the 'Tag' 85
   Get the Click 85
Description Meta Tags 86
   How to Write a Good Meta Description 87

Keyword Meta Tags 88
Keywords in Your URL 88
Page Subtitles or Headings and 'Image Alt Text' 92
Keywords in The Body Of Your Text 93
    Where Should Keywords Appear in My Text? 93
    How Often Should Keywords Appear in My Texts? 93
Walking the Tightrope to Avoid Spamming 97

GROW Step 5:
'Theme' Your Content and Get Found by the Search Engines

How Theming Can Help You Beat Your Greatest Competitor - An Example 99
Arranging Keywords into Themes for a Google Page One Listing 100
How Minimal 'Theming' Can Give You Maximum Results 101
11 Important Pieces of Advice on How To Create a Well-Themed Page: 101

GROW Step 6:
Create a 'Silo Structure', Turning Your Store into a Goldmine

What is a Silo Structure 105
Why Does Google Favour Silo-Structured Sites? 107
Building a Silo Structure 107
Good Silo Categories 107
Sitemaps to Help Everyone Find What They're Looking For 108
    1. Site Maps for the Visitors 108
    2. Sitemaps for Search Engines 109

Summary: Making Your Site Search-Engine Friendly 110

PART IV:
How to Use Other Sites to Get Ranked Highly - 'Off-page SEO' 113

GROW Step 7:
Build Quality Links and Get Listed Highly on Google

What a 'Link' is and Why You Want it 117

Page Rank – The Essence of Getting a Good Listing on Google 118
Internal and External Links to Get a Good Page Rank 118
    a) Getting Quality External Links 119
    b) Using Internal Links Correctly 122
    c) How Not to Dilute Links 122
The Value Of Your Page Rank 124
Understanding Your Competitor's Link and Page Rank (PR) 125
The Top 15 Link Building Techniques for SEO 126
    Technique 1: Linkbait & Viral Content Creation 127
    Technique 2: Blogging and Engagement with the Blogosphere 130
    Technique 3: Classic 'Create Valuable Content' Strategies 131
    Technique 4: Public Relations (Beyond Just Press Release Publication) 131
    Technique 5: Direct Link Purchases from Individual Sites/Webmasters 133
    Technique 6: Widgets and Embeddable Content 136
    Technique 7: Conferences, Events and In-Person Networking 136
    Technique 8: User Generated Content 137
    Technique 9: High Trust/Authority Directories 137
    Technique 10: Niche Social Media Communities 137
    Technique 11: Local Link Building 141
    Technique 12: Social Voting Portals (Digg, Reddit, Mixx, etc.) 142
    Technique 13: Quizzes + Results Badges 142
    Technique 14: Social Bookmarking Services (StumbleUpon, Delicious, etc.) 142
    Technique 15: Contributing to Charities, Non-Profits Events, etc.
    to Earn Links 142
When Links Do the Most for You – Keyword Matching 143
    Keywords in Links Should Match Keyword on Target Site 143
    Keywords in Link Should Match Keyword on Source Page 143
What Kind of Links to Acquire 144
    Links from High PR Sites 144
    Links from Low PR Sites 145
Building Long-Lasting Quality Links Over Time 145
Do-It-Yourself or Get-It-Done 146
    SEO Consulting 147

GROW Step 8:
Promote Your Site Further with 'Social Bookmarking'

Why Being Social with Your Bookmarks Will Help You Build Links.....................149
What You Can Achieve with Social Bookmarking 150
    More Targeted Traffic to Your Site..150
    Faster Search Engine Indexing..150
    Higher Search Engine Ranking 150
How to Do 'Social Bookmarking'..151
Social Bookmarking Software to Save You Time 151
Outsourcing Your Social Bookmarking 152

GROW Step 9:
Use Articles as Your 24/7 Sales Agents

Article Marketing 155
    Direct Traffic through Article Marketing 156
How to Write Great Articles 157
    Using Keywords..157
The Copywriting Roadmap...158
    Element 1: Headlines - How to Grab the Attention 159
    Element 2: An 'Emotional' Style of Writing 160
    Element 3: The Rational Copy..160
Where to Send Your 24/7 Sales Agents 161
Web 2.0 Sites: 'Standing on the Shoulders of Giants' 161
    A Word of Warning 162
Getting Presence on non-Web 2.0 Sites That Matter...162
    Getting Offline Readership 163
    Submit Your Article to Blogs 163
    A Word about Duplicate Content..163
    Writing and Publishing Regularly 164

Summary: Off-Page SEO..166

PART V:
How to Turn Visitors into Customers 169
Converting Browsers into Customers 171

GROW Step 10:
Gain Customers' Trust Fast, Using Video

Videos Bring More Traffic to Your Site 173
Videos Increase Conversion 173
How to Produce and Optimize Your Videos So They Convert Well 174
    1. Video content 175
    2. Video to personalize your company 175
    3. Format 175
    4. Video script 175
    5. Keywords and competition 175
    6. Share 175
    7. Call-to-action 176
    8. Trackable 176
    9. Video player 176
Five Effective Ways to Publish Your Video on the Internet 176
    1. Keyword Placement 176
    2. Online Exposure 177
    3. Link Building 177
    4. Social Marketing 177
    5. Social Bookmarking 177

GROW Step 11:
Turn Searchers into Customers by Providing 'Free Value'

The Freebie Product 179
The Freebie Event 180
Why the Free Models Works 181
'Freemium' and the 1 Percent Rule 181
What Does All This Mean for You and Your Business? 182

Summary: Conversion 183

PART VI:
SEO Tools 185

SEO Tools For Your Keyword Research and Competition Analysis.................187
Tools to Maximize Your Business Profit Potential 188
   1. Keyword Tools – What Do You Use Them For? 189
      Which Keyword Tools Will Deliver the Results - For You?...................189
      Keyword Suggestion Tools and Keyword Selection Tools....................190
   2. Competition Analysis Tools..197
   3. Trend Analysis Keyword Tools and Keyword Popularity Tools 201
      Keywords Tools that Analyze Trends 201
      Social Media and Social Bookmark Sites That Tell You about Trends.................204
      Trendy Commercial Keywords 207
   4. SEO Toolbars..207
Take it With a Grain of Salt 209
   ... Where My Website Appears on Google 209
   … How Much Traffic a Site Gets 209

PART VII:
Conclusion..213

   The Long-term Benefits of Professional SEO 215
   Every Journey Starts With a First Step 220
Appendices 223
Glossary 241
Sources 263
Index 265
Publications from the Authors 275

Overview

This book - structured into seven separate parts – gives you a complete method from start to finish, to attract more customers to your business via the Internet. It starts right at the beginning with your USP and primary keyword, helps you get your site ranked highly on Google, shows you how to attract many more prospects, and eventually to convert new visitors into customers. To help you achieve this, the book takes you along **11 practical steps,** one by one. There are also a dozen or so **templates** and checklists to download, which will help you apply what you read to YOUR business.

Introduction: How to Reach More Customers on The Internet

Find out how SEO can help your business to achieve long-term growth and get the ball rolling with your SEO plan.

Part I: How to Get Your Keywords Right

This part shows you why keywords are the solid foundation for your online success and how quickly and easily you can select the most effective primary and secondary keywords and keyword phrases for your business.

Part II: How to Outsmart and Outwit Your Competition

Doing Competition Analysis can save you a lot of time and money by focusing your online campaign on where you can achieve the most realistic results. This part shows you exactly how to analyze your competition, and how to spot their weaknesses.

Part III: How to Make Your Site More Competitive with On-Page SEO

This part explains in detail which techniques to apply to your own site to get it indexed quickly and listed highly on the search engines, where to place your keywords on your site, how to use them effectively in your website text, and how to build a search engine-friendly site quickly.

Part IV: How to Use Other Websites to Get Ranked Highly - Off-Page SEO

Here you will see the most effective ways to increase the presence of your website across the Internet and get ranked highly on the search engines, using techniques like link building, keyword matching, social book marking and article marketing to grow your customer base exponentially.

Part V: How to Convert Visitors into Customers

In this section, I introduce you to two of the most effective conversion techniques to ensure that you can reliably turn the new visitors you have attracted to your site into customers.

Part VI: SEO Tools

Here, I suggest how you can save time and money by using the right SEO tools effectively. Mastering a handful of tools means you can cut many corners and increase the performance of your website much more quickly and efficiently.

Part VII: Conclusion

Finally, see all the techniques explained throughout the book working together in one powerful system, the GROW Method. This method will help you to rapidly and realistically secure your top spot on Google and the other search engines, and turn visitors into customers. When using these techniques in combination, they create a result exponentially greater than each technique working on its own.

Appendices

In the appendices you will find some valuable checklists and templates to support your online campaigns.

INTRODUCTION

Introduction

How to Reach New Customers on the Internet

Today, many of your prospective customers are online, even if you think your business has little to do with the Internet. To reach new customers, overtake your competition and differentiate your products and services from others, you need to use what works best for your online marketing campaigns.

Never before in history has one been able to reach over 1.8 billion people – the number of people who are on the Internet today - so quickly, so easily, and so cost-effectively. This means that, no matter what you are trying to sell, it is very likely that there are many people out there, right now, who want your product or service, if only they could find it.

A key factor for success in business is outstandingly effective marketing. How much will the best product in the market sell if nobody knows about it? No matter how good your products or services are, you will need to be able to convert them into sales, and if your potential customers continuously find your competition online rather than you, it will increasingly hurt your position in the market and your ability to expand.

This is where SEO comes in. SEO essentially helps you to reach your specific target market by ensuring that your website appears in high positions on search engines like Google, Yahoo!, Bing etc. Such unpaid listings are called 'natural' or 'organic' listings. Typically, the higher up your site appears on such listings, the more visits from potential customers you will receive. Professional SEO uses various 'on-page' and 'off-page' search engine rankings techniques and may target different kinds of search, including image search, local search, and industry-specific vertical searches. This gives your web site the online visibility it needs.

Therefore, with this book, I want to encourage you to grow your business online by using SEO even more effectively. The benefits will far outweigh the efforts you are putting in. The speed of technical developments on the Internet may be disconcerting and overwhelming for some, but as you can see from many online success stories, they offer vast and highly profitable opportunities, too. The good news is that you only need to understand the most effective SEO techniques to put your products and services in front of your future customers or clients.

 Think of the amount of people online today, how this figure is progressively growing, and how many of them could become your customers: Imagine what additional market share your business could potentially have online? If you multiply this amount by a standard visitor-to-customer conversion rate of 1% to 3%, and you multiply that by the lifetime value of your customers or clients – how much would that be?

> Use this formula:
> Your market share of 1.8 bn people online
> x visitor-to-customer 2% conversion rate
> x customer lifetime value = ... ?

When you add the fact that every day, **new** future customers come online, it just shows you the potential value of your time and money invested in optimizing your site.

The good thing about SEO is that it is a flexible process and you can scale it any way you like. Whether you are doing it yourself one hour a day or you are getting an SEO team to execute your SEO plan as quickly as possible, it's up to you. The more dedicated you and your team are, the better the results will be. And the book shows you where to set the priorities.

Marketing on the Internet is easier to scale and allows for faster tests than were ever previously possible. Plus, you can track your success directly and easily in ways that are not available in traditional advertising. For small to medium size companies, the real beauty of online advertising is that you can do a lot of the marketing yourself, and see exactly how things are improving. You can save yourself five figure sums, and still bypass the giants to attract new customers and pull in profits.

Your SEO Plan – To Get New Customers Online

Before you start optimizing your website, it's vitally important that you spend some time thinking about an SEO plan for your business. The SEO plan is an addition to your business plan and specifies how you aim to achieve your business goals with online techniques. Your SEO plan should include information about the current state of your site and pages, the goals of your site, your SEO efforts, cost, techniques to use, deadlines, follow-ups etc., taking into account what your competition is doing online today.

What Will My SEO Plan Do for Me?

a) Your SEO plan will help you get where you want to be online. After all, if you don't have a clear picture where you want to be, don't be surprised if you don't get there. Yes, a part of an SEO plan is "to be on Google's Page One." But clearly, there is much more to it. How will you actually get there, based on where you are now? How does the competition influence your choice of those keywords and keyword phrases that you want to get ranked highly for? Where should you start, what really works and what can give you the best leverage of your time and money investment?

b) Your SEO plan will help you to stay on track. On the Internet and in SEO, things can change quickly. New search engines come to light, such as 'Bing' recently did. Search engines change their algorithms and the way they rank and 'tank' websites, such as Google is doing with its new invention 'Google Caffeine'.

Your business or profession is unique and every SEO plan is unique, too. I am about to lay out the cornerstones of an SEO plan and how you can go about creating such a plan. Please adjust it to your needs since you know your business, profession and website or blog best. Here is a template that you can download to develop, set up, follow through and up-date your SEO plan. Download it from the book's companion website at: www.Internet-Experts-Live.com/members/templates.

The templates in this book are there to support the practical steps you will be taking, as you go through this book part by part, and step by step. They will help you to apply the information in the book to your particular business.

Developing Your SEO Plan

1. USP – What Makes Your Company Unique?

Your SEO Plan starts with your business goals and your Unique Selling Proposition (USP). Looking at your products and services and those of your competitors, think about what makes your company unique? What unique proposition can you make to a potential customer to convince him or her to switch brands and buy from you?

Your message to your prospect needs to say, "Buy this product or service, and you will get this specific benefit." Examples of unique propositions that were pioneers when they were introduced are:

- Domino's Pizza: "You get fresh, hot pizza delivered to your door in 30 minutes or less — or it's free."
- FedEx: "When your package absolutely, positively has to get there overnight"
- M&M's: "The milk chocolate that melts in your mouth, not in your hand"
- Wonder Bread: "Wonder Bread Helps Build Strong Bodies 12 Ways"

What makes your company special and your products or services unique in your prospective customer's mind is a vital question . But sometimes it is difficult to pin down what that uniqueness, that USP really is. This is why the majority of your competitors probably aren't clear about their USP. But if you work yours out, you are already a big step ahead *and* you will be able to use your USP for finding the most profitable keywords for your online marketing campaigns, too. I have, therefore, included a practical USP template in the online folder that you can download at: www.Internet-Experts-Live.com/members/templates (When you have downloaded and opened the worksheet folder, just find the 'USP' tab at the bottom of the page and click on it to open the USP page.)

2. Business Goals

Once you have formulated your USP, incorporate it into your specific and achievable **business goals**, pinning down your goals and how your SEO plan will help you to achieve them. Here are some sample questions to trigger ideas for your business goals involving your site:

- How can we improve revenue from our website by 15% over the next three months?
- What are our most productive website traffic streams?
- What does it cost us to earn an extra $1.00 on our website?
- Are we building brand value on our site?

3. Search Engine Friendliness

Use the downloadable template to assess your site for its search engine friendliness. Check the factors listed to see whether your site makes it easy for the search engines to index your pages. If the search engines can't read and index your site, you won't get much search engine ranking power, not a good listing, less traffic and subsequently less sales.

In your Templates folder that you can download from www.Internet-Experts-Live.com/members/templates, there is also a template to check your site for its Search Engine Friendliness.

4. Keywords

With the business goals in hand, and your site checked for its 'Search Engine Friendliness' it's now time to find the customers who will purchase your products and/or services. Or much better – let them find you. How? By brainstorming and researching what your prospective clients are searching for online and what kind of **keywords** and keyword phrases they are currently typing into the search engines.

Any serious SEO professional will tell you that once you have spelled out your USP and business goals, the choice of your keywords is *the* most important part of your SEO plan because it ensures that your business gets found online amidst thousands and thousands of other businesses.

It means you can put your offer right in front of prospective customers looking for *your* specific products or services. This is the foundation of all your online marketing efforts. Should you choose to skip keyword research and get your keywords wrong - your time and money invested will largely be lost!

> *Case Study*
>
> A good example of how keywords have tripled the sales for a vegetarian website is www.savvyvegetarian.com. Judy Kingsbury founded the website, which offers information and tips on vegetarian living. Judy receives an average of 60,000 visits to her site every month. So how has she been able to generate this level of traffic?
>
> "I can safely say that keywords are the basis for the growth of Savvy Vegetarian," she explains. Judy uses Wordtracker [the keyword tool] to discover which related keywords are relevant for her site. Her first stop was recipes - a popular resource on her site. "I started keyword research on tofu recipes and developed a tofu recipe section, with lots of tofu info, and, so far, about 20 tasty, tested, family friendly tofu recipes. I optimized page text and meta tags for that keyword phrase, and embedded links on other pages. ... When you realize how many people are looking for tofu recipes, see 1.8 million pages on Google, and then that I'm on the front page, I know I'm on the right track", she said.

> Thanks to this methodical approach Savvyvegetarian.com is above the fold on page one for about 50 search terms on Google. Without keyword research she says it would have been very easy to go off on the wrong tangent. "Once I started paying attention to keywords and optimizing my pages, I could see the benefits almost instantly. I think looking at keywords and researching them is really the basis of starting up and running a website - any website," explains Judy.
>
> By paying more attention to her keywords and optimizing her site, Judy says traffic through SavvyVegetarian.com has tripled in the past year. She has taken keywords and peppered them throughout her blog spots and her articles on living healthily. I will talk you through the techniques Judy used in great detail later on. For now, it's just important to remember how essential and effective keyword research can be. Judy Kingsbury shared her experience with Rachelle Money for Wordtracker.

5. 'Natural' Listings (SEO) or Paid Listings (PPC)?

Once you have chosen your keywords, what's the best online advertising for your business? Essentially you have two choices, and keywords are essential for both of them:

- Paid advertising, also called sponsored listings, such as Pay-Per-Click (PPC), for which the advertiser pays each time a visitor clicks, or
- Unpaid advertising, also called 'natural' search engine listings, also called 'organic' search engine listings, which you can achieve with SEO.

Currently, more advertisers use PPC rather than trying to achieve a top natural listing through SEO, despite the fact that customers are far more likely to click on their organic/natural listings than on their PPC ads.

Web analytics expert Avinash Kaushik says that 86% of clicks on Google are on organic search results, while only 14% of Google visitors click on paid search ads. This might be partially explained by the fact that – as Pennsylvania State University research reported (http://live.psu.edu/story/29879) - "…about 80 % of queries are informational and about 20 % are for navigational and transactional purposes." This tells you two important things:

a) You are far more likely to get 'the click', when you rank highly with a natural / organic listing; and

b) Your listing should address what the searcher is looking for, namely 'information'. This means offer them something of informational value, ideally free, to get their click and their visit to your site. After all, these are all potential future customers, even if they are not ready to buy right now.

Looking at the numbers above, the fact that more than 80% of searchers are clicking on natural listings makes it astonishing that so many advertisers still do only PPC advertising. They are missing out on 80 % of their market! One explanation for this might be that paid online ads are falsely considered to be an easier option than optimizing your site or blog. However, reading this book will make you realize that it is much more straightforward to achieve a top natural listing than you think. Remember two main advantages of SEO:

1) That you can address 80% of your target market and
2) That you will get traffic, visitors and prospective customers for months and years (whereas in PPC, when you stop paying the increasingly expensive cost, any traffic stops.)

However PPC advertising *is* very useful to test the keywords for your SEO campaigns and it can indeed deliver visitors faster than SEO, especially to a new website or blog. Nevertheless using PPC comes at a high price and only has a short-term effect.

According to Avinash Kaushik "PPC is also not ideal to build long-term relationships with your new customers, or to provide a sustainable advantage over your competition... In effect, you are only renting traffic. These effects, combined with an upward trend in user wariness, have put the focus on SEO... [However] although SEO strategies will yield long-term results, they also require investments... Hence, a combination of PPC and SEO will make for an effective search marketing (SEM) strategy... SEO is the right long-term thing to do for any business. With a small amount of investment, the benefits far outstrip any other [customer] acquisition strategy."

6. Competition

Once you know which keywords your prospective customers are using for their searches, you can find out who your competition is for these keywords. Which companies are listed high up on the search engines for these terms? Could you do better and beat them to their high listing on the search pages? Or are they so well optimized that they dominate a particular search term and it's pointless to try and target this term yourself?

Part II of this book explains in detail how to carry out 'Competition Analysis' and what to look for when you are checking out your competitors. In your downloadable templates folder at www.Internet-Experts-Live.com/members/templates you will find tabs and sheets for evaluating your competitor's pages. These template tabs are called 'Positive (Ranking) Factors' and 'Negative (Ranking) Factors'. Use these sheets to get a clear picture how strong or weak the competition is for certain keywords.

Once you have compared your pages to those of your competitors, you can make an informed choice as to which keyword or keyword phrase should become your main or primary keyword, which ones to target as secondary keywords and which ones to leave out completely. If you haven't built a page for a specific primary keyword yet, you can now decide whether you want to build such a page or rather re-focus one of your existing pages.

7. On-Page and Off-Page SEO

So, how can you start optimizing your pages? This is what Part III (On-page SEO) and Part IV (Off-page SEO) of the book deal with in great detail. If you have a large site, it might be overwhelming to apply SEO to all pages at once. Do it like climbing a mountain – one step at a time. One highly ranking page of your website can pull the rest of your pages up with it. The key in SEO is to prioritize:

    a) Which one of your selected keywords should you start with?
    b) Which pages should you optimize first?
    c) Which SEO techniques should you use?

a) Which one of your selected keywords should you start with?

Different businesses have different priorities. Some go for cash flow, others want to build their brand, others, their list of prospective customers, their long-term lifetime customers etc. Your choice of keyword depends on these priorities. And it influences your decision whether you want to start optimizing your site for a certain keyword, even if it is quite competitive, or whether you want to go for a less competitive one.

My advice is not to start with the most competitive keyword if you are relatively new to SEO. When you are just starting out, be careful. If you focus your efforts on really competitive keywords and your site has not yet got the power to compete successfully, it might take too long to achieve your desired results and you might get discouraged. That would be a shame. In SEO you will need patience and persistence. You can always take on a more competitive keyword once you are ranked for a less competitive one. Pages optimized for less competitive keywords that rank well on the search engines will help you to break into the more competitive keywords too.

b) Which pages should you optimize first?

When you start, optimize those pages first which already contain your primary keyword and those which are aligned with your business goals and strategy. Again, the ranking power of one well-optimized page will affect how the rest of your site gets ranked on the search engines.

c) Which SEO techniques should you use?

Search engines use over 100 factors to decide on the ranking for a certain site or page and these factors also change over time. It is, therefore, important to stay up-to-date about which SEO techniques give you the best return for your investment.

In this book, I list and explain the most widely-agreed search engine ranking factors in the industry, based on the wisdom and experience of 72 international SEO experts. This will give you a clear strategic plan for optimizing your website and selecting which techniques to use. If, so far, you have done more basic 'on-page' optimization like Keyword Placement on your site, you now need to add 'off-page' optimization techniques, such as Link Building, that promote your site across the Internet. Once this is done, you can also consider more sophisticated on-page techniques such as building a 'Silo Structure' and 'Keyword Theming'. These techniques and how to implement them are described in Parts 3 and 4.

Deciding which optimization techniques to choose and which ones to use first depends largely on your business goals, on how well your site is already optimized, and on what your competition has done to optimize their pages. To take over your competitor's position on the search engines,

1) analyze how they have optimized their site,
2) do what they have done to make sure you get to the same level and
3) choose techniques from the search engine ranking factors list that will give you a better ranking than they have achieved. When you rank higher, as a general rule, you will get more 'clicks', more visitors to your site and subsequently more customers.

The SEO templates folder will help you with this task. I have included the most important search engine ranking factors in order of importance so that they can be used like a checklist to analyze your competition. It also includes a handful of negative ranking factors so that you can look out for them, steer clear of them and avoid damaging your business.

> **Case Study:** *How Keyword Research can Multiply Your Traffic*
> This is a good example of how Keyword Research as the basis of your SEO campaign can multiply your incoming traffic. In the case of Caroline Blatchford's company SpottyGiftBoxes, traffic grew by 228%. When the business was barely a year old, Caroline was already reaping the rewards of building a search engine-friendly site from the get-go. Like most online business owners, Caroline has had a number of careers. A one-time lawyer, teacher and then fitness club manager, she found herself in a position where she had to stay at home to look after her young family. She soon struck upon the idea of starting up a gift site based on people's hobbies and interests.
>
> But she was faced with an SEO challenge – how do you optimize a site when your biggest keyword is also extremely competitive? Caroline says: "Because we wanted to compete well on search engines we didn't target words like 'gifts', because that's terribly competitive - we decided to focus on [keywords that centered around] hobbies and interests so we had 'gifts for cat lovers', 'gifts for gardeners', or 'gifts related to cooking'."
>
> It worked. Between September and March, traffic to the site increased by a whopping 228%. Caroline says the combination of creating each page with SEO in mind from the start, along with an increased depth of products has led to this incredible surge in visitors. While embarking on her first keyword research project, she was surprised by the range of keywords she discovered.
>
> "The one that [really got] me is that so many searches are for 'kid's' rather than 'children's'. That's the reason why I [always] use keyword research as a starting point because my brain is obviously geared towards the kinds of terms I am used to saying, but they don't necessarily match with the terms my customers are using.
>
> If I have a simple product for which I think the title is pretty obvious, once you start searching around you find people calling things by different names and searching in different ways. Once you get your mind around that, you can pick up all the traffic you want to." Caroline Blatchford shared her experience with Rachelle Money for Wordtracker.

As well as taking factors as the search level, competition, relevance etc. into account, your choice of keywords will depend on additional business factors such as your (time and money) budget, already-existing content and how quickly you can produce content for that keyword niche etc.

Try to put yourself in your competitor's shoes, too. What might drive your competitors and how well do you think they will do? If you know that their business depends on one particular keyword for example and yours doesn't than you can assume that they will do what it takes to outrank you on this one keyword. It is, therefore, probably not your best tactic to 'fight' for that particular keyword if you don't have to.

8. Follow-up

Your SEO Plan is not complete without having scheduled a follow-up. The ranking positions in the search engines will change over time since your competitors will try to catch up with you. The criteria that the search engines use to rank pages will change, too. The Internet is moving constantly and you simply need to adjust. Adapting to a changing world is nothing new. On the Internet, though, things happen faster and you will need to be quick, too. It won't take much of your time to go through your follow-up checklist once you have established the habit of doing so.

What is a good time frame for follow-up? This depends largely on how fierce the competition is in your niche and what kind of SEO techniques you are using. In general, I suggest a minimum of 3 months and a maximum of 6 months. If you leave too much time between your checks, your pages might have slipped from a number one position on Google's Page One with over 40% of all clicks to the 3rd search results page with almost no clicks.

However, following up on your SEO efforts too soon can also be counterproductive. Yes, you can get onto the first search results page within days, sometimes within hours, with modern SEO techniques, but it usually takes about three months to achieve sustainable long-term improvements with your SEO efforts. Let me add this:

Please take into account that a solid and effective SEO campaign hardly ever produces consistent results overnight. You are probably looking at a time frame of three to six months before you see your rankings, site visitors and thus profits improve considerably. But, this way, your site will have gained solid strength and presence for years to come.

There is no point expecting outstanding results in two or three weeks, just to get disappointed with SEO and to throw it all out. You will need to exercise some patience here. But let me assure you, you will benefit from your SEO efforts for a long time and it is worth it. Professional SEO is no 'quick fix' but it can deliver results for a long time, helping you to build an 'unshakeable' business that sits solidly on the search engine results pages and lets you sleep more deeply at night. Let me summarize your SEO plan here briefly:

1) Formulate your USP: What makes your products and services special, maybe even unique? You will need this for choosing your keywords, which are the basis of your SEO campaigns.
2) Align your business goals with your online plans.
3) Check your site for its search engine friendliness to see whether it can get indexed easily by the search engines. Remember, your site pages will need to get indexed first before they can pull in visitors and customers.
4) Decide on your primary and your secondary keywords. Keywords are where all SEO success starts.
5) Understand the long-term benefits of SEO over Pay-Per-Click.
6) Evaluate your competition for their strengths and weaknesses, in order to take over their top spots on the search engines.
7) Use the top on-page and off-page SEO techniques to optimize your site pages for consistent high search engine rankings and greater number of visitors and prospective customers.
8) Follow up on your SEO efforts, on average after between three and six months, to improve your results even further.

This is the template for your SEO plan. All you have to do is adjust it to your business situation and then carry it out, part by part, and step by step. It is really that straightforward.

Sometimes life gets in the way. That's not a problem. Even if you have been 'off the plan' for some time, just get back to it when you can and to carry out the next step of your plan. After all, it is most important that you don't get discouraged about moving forwards. Just stick to your plan and watch the results coming in.

SUMMARY
The GROW Method in 11 Steps

To put your SEO plan in place let's now roll our sleeves up. To give you all the essential and most effective techniques in one place, I have devised the '**GROW Method**'. **GROW** stands for **G**et **N**ew **C**ustomers **R**apidly **O**n the **W**eb. It takes you through the process of optimizing your site from start to finish in 11 practical and easy-to-follow steps, so you can start straight away to attract prospects to your site and turn them into loyal customers:

GROW Step 1: Choose the Best Keywords for Your Target Customers.

GROW Step 2: Focus Your Campaign with 'Long-Tail Keywords'.

GROW Step 3: Know Your Competition to Fast Track to the Top.

GROW Step 4: Place Your Keywords Where They Give You Most Power.

GROW Step 5: 'Theme' Your Content and Get Found by the Search Engines.

GROW Step 6: Create a 'Silo Structure', Turning Your Store into a Goldmine.

GROW Step 7: Build Quality Links and Get Listed Highly on Google.

GROW Step 8: Promote Your Site Further with 'Social Bookmarking'.

GROW Step 9: Use Articles as Your 24/7 Sales Agents.

GROW Step 10: Gain Customers' Trust Fast, Using Video.

GROW Step 11: Turn Searchers into Customers by Providing 'Free Value'.

Maybe some of the steps above don't make much sense to you right now. Not to worry. I will explain each step and how they are linked to the others throughout the book. Keep in mind that using just some techniques of this method alone can make your website exponentially more effective in ranking higher on Google than sites which don't use them, according to tests conducted by Themezoom (http://themezoom.com) and others. And, when all are combined, you begin to experience exponential growth in click-through enquiries, sales and profits.

PART I:

How to Get Your Keywords Right

Why Keywords Really Matter

Let me emphasize this: If you apply just ONE of the techniques that I provide for you on the following pages, make it **Getting Your Keywords Right**. If you don't, your investment into online marketing could be lost completely, or you will most certainly not make as much profit as you could do.

Keywords are the foundation of practically all cutting-edge SEO techniques. They can propel your website to a top listing on the search engines within days, sometimes within hours. When your pages show up on Google's front page, there is no need for you to look elsewhere for customers, because THEY will be finding YOU.

Choosing the right keywords changes the game from chasing potential customers, to customers knocking on your door, wanting to buy from you.

In this part of the book I will take you through the process of deciding upon the best keywords for your business. The aim is that you can develop a coherent and profitable strategy, based on those keywords. You will also understand how easily you can use keyword tools (see also Part VI: SEO Tools) to decide upon the competitiveness and profitability of certain keywords.

Secondly, you will see how to decide upon secondary, so-called 'modified' and synonymous keywords, and how to use them to increase the effect of your marketing campaign even further. When you realize how much leverage good keywords have, you will be able to grow your enterprise rapidly into a position of leadership within your market.

Why Using Your Customers' Words Will Drive Your Business Forward

The Internet is based on words. That's obvious. Words are what people use to communicate, talk, search and do business. Search words and keywords are the backbone of all search activity on the Internet, but very few companies capitalize upon this fact to its full potential.

Keywords give you a straightforward method to find out what your customers are wanting and thinking, what your competition is doing, and what you could be doing more effectively to bring hundreds or thousands or even tens of thousands more customers to your business. In other words, keywords help you to evaluate your chances of getting onto Google's Page 1 on the back of a specific term that most closely matches your products, services and business strategy.

Google says that, in general, keyword research is helpful in these situations:

- *When you are in the process of creating your **first** keyword list.*
- *When your current keywords are performing **badly** and you need to find better options.*
- *When you have one keyword that works really **well** and you want to find more like it.*

Understanding What Your Prospective Customers Really Want

Keyword research and competition analysis don't sound that sexy and this is one of the reasons why 95% of businesses don't do them correctly. This leaves huge swathes of the market place and its money to their competitors.

However, when you do research into the keywords your prospective customers use with search engines like Google, you'll be surprised how much better you understand what they're looking for. As a result, you'll understand better how to tailor your content to them, so that they keep coming back to your site again and again, and ultimately start buying from you. This is even more important in times of economic downturn, when prospective customers are even more careful where they spend their money.

You see, when you start using your keywords effectively, you turn yourself into a trusted resource for new customers, rather than a sales agent. When, through the proper use of keywords, your offer appears in the top ten listings of Google - or even better in the No. 1 position - you will gain credibility. Potential customers will not only find you online, but they will also feel - because Google has ranked you higher than your competitors - that you are a trusted and worthwhile supplier of the particular product or service they desire.

Case Study: How to Build Traffic by Knowing the Actual Words Customers Use.

Hearst Magazines is a good example of how to increase your website traffic by knowing the actual words your customers use to find what they want. Since using keyword research tools, Hearst Publication's Dan Roberts says that their online traffic has grown by 150%. Hearst publishes 15 of the world's most popular magazines such as Cosmopolitan, Esquire, Oprah's O Magazine, and Good Housekeeping, as well as five web-only magazines.

> Dan Roberts says that "…..for some of the women's titles, fashion is a big part of what they do, so early on, we made the decision that we'd instruct [our webmasters] to run some comparatives on the keywords 'fashion' and 'style'. In the print context, they like to use the word style, but I stressed to them that style is somewhat nebulous in that it can mean a number of things.
>
> People's behavior online is different, because when they are looking for content they tend to be much more literal, because they have to be. The Wordtracker [keyword tool] data showed us that 7:1 people were more likely to use 'fashion' than 'style' when looking for the kind of content we were promoting.
>
> We encourage editors to use keywords in the places we know will work: for example, by using keywords in the URL of a specific page. We have seen some pretty solid results because of that………In two and a half years we've seen well over 150% increase in traffic."
>
> "The data that's available gives you a better insight than ever before into your audience. Magazines for the most part have been all about guesswork, or they'll get focus groups to try to figure out what their audience wants. Online, we don't have to guess, we know what they're looking for and more importantly, how they're looking for it." Dan Roberts in an interview with Wordtracker's Rachelle Money.

Keywords Are the Foundation of All Your Optimization Campaigns

Keywords should be integrated in all your online material - be it as part of your own web content, your sales letters, your press releases, your articles, your blog, your video descriptions and video scripts, or your Twitter tweets - basically any text you put in front of potential customers online. Way beyond this kind of on-page and off-page content, keywords are also the foundation for building an effectively-**structured site** that shows up more easily on the search engines. I'll explain later on how this works. You will also see how fundamental these keywords are for a professionally-integrated **links campaign** to increase your site's ranking in a way which greatly influences your position on the search engine results pages (SERPS). And keywords are also the foundation of highly-effective and targeted **article marketing** and **video marketing campaigns** that can bring potential customers to your site for years to come. Plus, they can get you a higher search engine ranking.

Why You Want a 'Hungry Crowd' More Than Anything

When you are able to attract customers that are ready to buy, rather than those who just browse the Internet and gather information, your profits will go up significantly. A lot of businesses make the mistake of trying to get as much traffic as possible to their site. But a lot of traffic doesn't necessarily mean a lot of buyers!

In fact, when you are running a Pay-Per-Click (PPC) campaign on Google, browsers who click but don't buy can cost you a lot of money. After all, you pay Google each time a browser clicks on your ad! What you need is hungry, **ready-to-buy** traffic, not just any traffic; buying customers, not just information seekers. To find out how to get there, marketing guru Gary Halbert has asked his famous question:

"If you were to open a hamburger stand and could choose ONE key to maximize your success, what would it be?"
Gary Halbert

You might think that the most obvious answer might be a good price for the hamburger, a central location on a busy high street or top burger quality, right?

But Gary Halbert makes the point that the key to success is to place the hamburger stand right in front of a "starving crowd." It took Gary years to realize that the absolute, most important element in *any* marketing campaign is the **quality of your target market,** and the ability to reach these hungry **ready-to-buy** customers. So, how do you know where the starving crowds are or what people really want? By finding out which keyword phrases searchers use and what questions they ask.

Now then, let's have a look at how you can find out which words your prospective customers are searching for online, and how you can use exactly these words to put your offers right in front of their noses:

GROW Step 1:
Choose the Best Keywords for Your Target Customers

When you want to find the most profitable keyword for your business or profession, first think about what you believe makes your company, products and services special to your target market - your unique selling proposition or USP. Your USP is what makes your company, products and services stand out from the crowd. It makes your customers buy from you rather than from the competition. Being clear about your USP while choosing your keywords for your online campaigns can give you a huge advantage over your competitors because it focuses your SEO campaign from the start. To make the right choice, you need to weigh up how profitable and competitive a specific term is for you, so it works hard for you, selling your product or service.

1. Brainstorming Keywords into a 'Seed List'

Brainstorm an initial list of keywords you think your prospective customers put into the search engines. This is often referred to as building a keyword **"seed list"**. It should include keywords such as:

- Primary & secondary keywords
- Product / service terms
- Brand names
- Features & benefits
- Synonymous terms
- Problems / solutions

When you apply your business experience to decide which keywords to focus on, consider your **profit** margins as well as your marketing strategy. Some of your products or services will provide higher profit margins. Therefore, keywords that target these products or services are potentially worth spending more of your time and money on. However, you could also target keywords for low-profit products to initially attract potential new customers to your site. When people buy a low price product from you and understand the quality of your products and services, you then can send them your offers for more costly products afterwards. In the end, though, *you* are the best person to decide whether high or low profit margins suit your business strategy best.

Case Study:

This case study is a good example of how to find an audience for a radio show through keyword research. When Michael Laery and Michael Thomas launched their radio show, 'Technology For Business Sake (TFBS), the first thing they needed to do was to come up with a domain name that would be pretty easy to remember, and which would also bring some search traffic their way:

"After doing some keyword research, we settled on BusinessTechnologyRadio.com. It's a little long, but it contains some important terms that we thought would help us generate some hits to the site. We also wanted to include a few strategic words in the title of the site's homepage that we couldn't fit in the domain name, so we included "online small business radio podcast" there to help give us more opportunities to pick up some targeted search traffic.

Keyword research also played an important role in creating url text for the show pages when we were ready to post a new show. Having the right words in the url really paid off as show pages began showing up in relevant searches within a week. The other thing that helped move us up the results list was taking time to write thoughtful show summaries emphasizing strategic words for each page we put out.

Writing descriptive show summaries also proved important when putting together the RSS feed for the show podcast. Although it was critically important for us to have a solid website for the show, the majority of podcasts are downloaded from iTunes.

These folks probably wouldn't have found our site on their own, so we had to make sure our descriptions and tags caught the attention of people who'd be interested in our kind of content. In fact, we even tag the audio files with keywords so that people can find the mp3s without having to visit the show site. And we paid attention to how other people tagged links to our shows on sites like Del.icio.us and Digg.

But I think the most interesting way keyword research has added to the show is in how it aids us in finding interesting guests for our growing audience. For example, when we were thinking about doing a show on outsourcing IT projects, we decided to approach Elance.com CEO Fabio Rosati because there were a good number of searches for both Elance and Fabio. After talking to him we thought he'd make for an interesting interview and things worked out great.

We followed that same method a number of times and have had great results to show for it. In fact one of the extra benefits coming from this approach is a number of high quality links back from people who have been on the show. So in addition to getting great guests on with us, we also start showing up in search results in some important phrases, and pick up quality links that bring us quality traffic.

It really paid off for us to take time up front to figure out what small biz types were interested in, who they wanted to hear from, and what they searched on when they were looking for information on the web. It helped us be in the top 30 search results in Google, Yahoo! and others for terms like "business radio", "small business radio" and a host of others. And these terms have been a big factor in our little show being downloaded over 3,000 times last month." By Brent Leary, of CRM Essentials for Wordtracker quoting Michael Leary of TFBS.

2. Getting a Head Start – Courtesy of Google

If your site has already been up for some time, it is often easier to secure a head start on your competition by focusing on keywords that your site already ranks for. Ranking for a keyword simply means that Google has found these keywords on your site or blog.

But how do you find that out? Use Google's free Search-Based Keyword Tool to find out whether you rank for any keywords already. This is important because it is generally easier to get ranked highly for a keyword that is related to another keyword for which your site already ranks. Go to http://www.google.com/sktool. Put your URL into the box that says 'Website', then click on 'Find Keywords'. Google will return a list of keywords 'Extracted from Webpage'. You'll find these in the column to the far right in the search tool. The list is ordered by how many monthly searches a keyword gets.

PART I - Keywords

You can also consult your server logs and analytics programs such as Google Analytics, which also provide a variety of very useful keyword information. For example, they tell you which keywords your visitors already use to find your website or blog.

With this information in hand, you can reorder your list of initial keywords and start researching synonymous keywords that show profit potential for your business.

On a practical note, whenever you find a good keyword term or keyword phrase, write it down. I use an Excel spreadsheet to collect keyword ideas in one single sheet so I can sort them later on and apply formulas to them. Most sophisticated keyword tools allow you to export the keyword lists to Excel if you wish.

3. Finding Your Competitor's Profitable Keywords

With your ranked list of initial keywords in front of you, it's now time to check your keywords for these hard facts: search volume, competition and keyword value. Find out,

- how often these keywords are searched on the Internet: the search volume
- how many other web pages show in the natural / organic search results that contain the keywords you want to target: the number of competing pages
- how much PPC advertisers are going to pay for a single click on an ad that contains this keyword: the CPC rate (Cost-per-Click) and
- what this keyword is worth to you: the keyword's market value for you.

This information will help you decide which keywords could be the most profitable for you, which ones you should, therefore, target first, and which ones should be your secondary keywords. To get this information, go to Google's essential keyword research tool: https://adwords.google.com/select/KeywordToolExternal. It's free and great value. (For further keyword research and competition analysis tools, please go to the 'Resources' section at the back of this book).

When you arrive at the Google Keyword Tool page, put one keyword from your list into the search box where it says "Enter one keyword or…", and select these three essential columns of information under 'choose columns to display' to find out:

a) Which keywords get searched the most ('Approx. Avg. Search Volume')?
b) Which keywords have the most competition ('Advertiser Competition')?
c) How much people are willing to pay for a click on a certain keyword. ('Est. Avg CPC')?

The Google Keyword Tool screenshot below shows a search for the broad term 'golf' as an example. You will see some of the areas of the tool that you can customize for your own purposes.

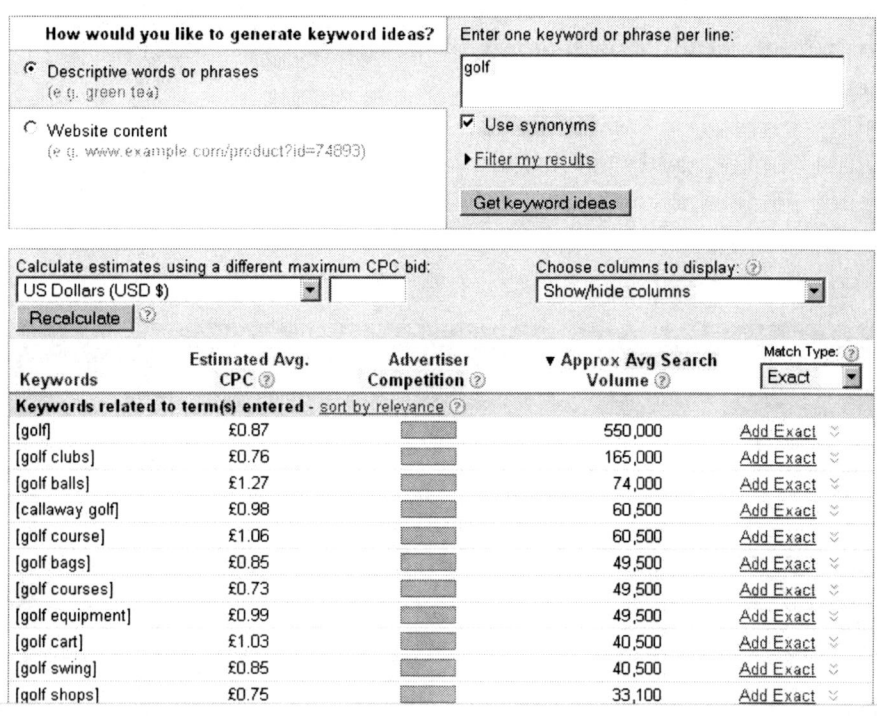

Keywords	Estimated Avg. CPC	Advertiser Competition	Approx Avg Search Volume	
[golf]	£0.87		550,000	Add Exact
[golf clubs]	£0.76		165,000	Add Exact
[golf balls]	£1.27		74,000	Add Exact
[callaway golf]	£0.98		60,500	Add Exact
[golf course]	£1.06		60,500	Add Exact
[golf bags]	£0.85		49,500	Add Exact
[golf courses]	£0.73		49,500	Add Exact
[golf equipment]	£0.99		49,500	Add Exact
[golf cart]	£1.03		40,500	Add Exact
[golf swing]	£0.85		40,500	Add Exact
[golf shops]	£0.75		33,100	Add Exact

Google's Keyword Tool (An updated version of this tool is now available)

1) In the 'Approx. Avg. Search Volume' column, you will see how much this keyword term is searched per month.

2) In the 'Advertiser Competition Column', you will see how much competition there is for your keyword, in terms of how many other web pages or blogs use 'your' keyword.

3) The column entitled 'Estimated Avg. CPC' tells you how much advertisers are willing to pay for a click (Cost-Per-Click).

4. How to Discover the Most Lucrative Keywords

If your competitor is prepared to pay a considerable amount of money for a click on a specific keyword, and their ad has been online for quite some time, then this keyword is likely to be profitable for them. They may have made money from their

PART I - Keywords

ad, and you could probably make money with this keyword, too, if you use it cleverly. But if the CPC number is low, that means the term is maybe too wide and not profitable enough, only attracting browsers but not serious buyers.

The keyword 'golf' obviously gets searched a lot, which you can see in the third column of the keyword tool. But, you can also see that it attracts major competition, and the chances of getting a high listing in the search engines for this term - at least for the average e-commerce website - is low.

For a **video tutorial** on how-to-use the Google Keyword Tool go to: www.youtube.com/watch?v=FCBwYZohgDA&fmt=18
[**Note**: Do not change the code, since it will give you higher quality on YouTube.com than you usually get].

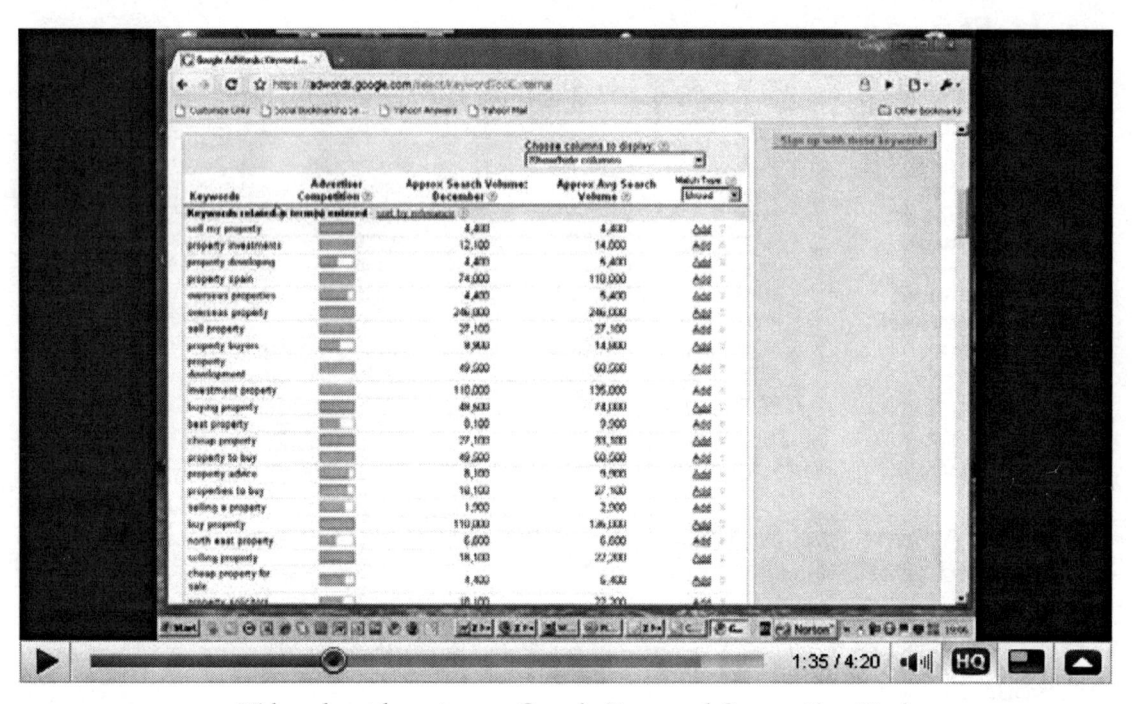

Video about how to use Google Keyword Suggestion Tool

Your task is to find keywords that are not too competitive but still get enough searches. In general, keywords or keyword phrases that attract a fair amount of searches per month will, in 99% of the cases, also attract a good number of competitors. This sounds like bad news but it is also good news since competition tells you that there is probably money to be made.

When you go through the process of researching keywords for their search volume, competition and cost (CPC) you will probably end up with quite a number of keywords that would be useful to target. How can you decide which ones to focus on? Which keywords promise to give you the best return on the money and time you are investing? To come to a decision as to which ones will be best for you, you will need to evaluate your keywords value to your business.

5. Evaluating the Market Value of Keywords for Your Business

Whether you are in a start-up situation or you have an established business, before you commit your time and some money to target certain keywords with your online campaigns, you need to know whether these keywords have enough value to support your business over time. That's easier said than done since tools such as the Google Keyword Tool cannot show us straight away how valuable keywords are for our business. But, we can do a simple calculation to see which keywords have the potential to support and grow our business. Let's now look at two short keyword formulas to calculate the value of keywords:

Example 1: Calculating the Value of a Keyword I

When you get figures like search volume, competition and CPC from Google's keyword tool, you can calculate a very basic 'market value' for a certain keyword. Simply take 'Approx. Avg. Search Volume' and multiply it with the 'Estimated Avg. CPC' number from Google. This gives you the Market Value in Dollars, Pounds, Euros, etc. for this particular keyword:

Search Volume x Avg. CPC' = Keyword Market Value

This calculation is useful to get an overall idea of whether the market you are targeting through that keyword or keyword group might have enough potential to support your business over time. But it is only a very general calculation, and you should not base your choice of keywords on it alone.

PART I - Keywords

Example 2: Calculating the Value of a Keyword II

Let's now look at how to use a slightly more thorough 3-step process to calculate the value of a keyword.

1. Advertisers: To find out whether the keyword phrase you are intending to target might have enough profit potential, see if there are a good number of Pay-Per-Click (PPC) ads above and alongside the natural search results for your keyword term. As a rough guide, if there are PPC ads above the natural (SEO) listings and you have at least ten PPC ads in the right column on the first page, it's safe to say there is competition. If there are PPC ads not only on the first but on the second and third page, you have even more certainty that others make money here and that the keyword seems to be profitable enough to attract this amount of advertising.

2. Traffic: If you already have a fairly constant ranking position and traffic stream to your site or blog, you will be able to calculate the value of any visitor and how much additional value you could add by increasing your search engine rankings with the formula below.

Tip: If your site is fairly new, you might not rank well in Google yet, but you might do on Microsoft's search results pages on Bing http://bing.com (formerly Live Search, Windows Live Search and MSN Search). Google usually takes longer to rank you if you are just starting out online.
You then take your Microsoft click-through numbers and estimate the Google click volume by looking at search market-share numbers from companies like **Comscore** (http://comscore.com/), **Hitwise** (http://hitwise.com/), and **Nielsen Netrating** (http://searchengineland.com/library/stats-popularity).
Tools such as **Google's Traffic Estimator** (https://adwords.google.com/select/TrafficEstimatorSandbox) and **Microsoft's Ad Intelligence** (http://advertising.microsoft.com/advertising/adcenter_addin) can also help to estimate the value of your traffic.

3. Visitor Value: Take your tracking data and try to establish the value of a single visitor for that keyword term.

> **Note**: Use free Google **Analytics** to track how many visitors come to your site, where they are coming from, what they do on your site.
>
> **What a Visitor is Worth**
> Let's say your tracking software (e.g. Google Analytics) shows that you are getting 5,000 impressions of your site in a day. These impressions have resulted in 200 unique visitors clicking through to your site and five of those visitors have bought something, together generating a total profit of $2,000. In order to find out what one of those visitors is worth to you, you divide your $2,000 profit by your 200 visitors. One visitor is worth $10!
>
> Now let me explain how your visitor value can help you better understand the value of one specific keyword: AOL some time ago accidentally 'leaked' some of their user data onto the Internet, which produced a big scandal and damaged AOL's brand (see www.jimboykin.com/click-rate-for-top-10-search-results/).
>
> However, the benefit from 'AOL's leaked data' was that various people used this data to calculate click rates for Google positions. We now know that when you get a Number one listing on Google, you get about 40% of the clicks. Let's postulate that this would result in you getting 2,000 visitors per day. 2,000 visitors per day times a value of $10 per visitor means that you would be looking at a keyword value of about $20,000 dollars per day or over $7 million per year in a very best case scenario.

Obviously, this calculation only gives you a well-informed guess about the value of a keyword, not a definite profit figure. But you can use these formulas to compare the keywords on your list and decide which ones you want to focus on.

6. Calculating the Return on your Investment

To get a better picture of what return on your investment (ROI) you could achieve, you also need to take other factors into account. For example, your company's ability to convert visitors into customers and the time and money you would be spending on your campaign.

To help you with calculating the possible return on your investment, Yahoo! offers **a free ROI calculator** (http://searchmarketing.yahoo.com/calculator/roi.php). This calculator measures the ROI (Return on Investment) of a PPC ad and helps you to estimate how much you can afford to pay for your traffic, plus it helps you calculate

PART I - Keywords

your potential monthly profit or loss based on:
>> Total Monthly Clicks (from Yahoo!)
>> x Estimated Average CPC in US Dollars
>> x Conversion Rate (CR) in percentage
>> x Average Profit-per-Conversion in US Dollars.

It is important to note that the formulas above are useful, but represent just one way of looking at the value and profit potential of a certain keyword. They ignore the fact that keywords can have additional value to build your brand and therefore have a greater impact on your bottom line at a later stage. In the end, how much of a particular keyword market value you will be able to capture depends on a number of other factors as well, such as:

- How many visitors you can convert into buyers.
- The price of your product.
- How much work you intend to put in.
- Your skills specific to that market.
- Your knowledge about that specific market.
- Your level of Internet marketing skills.
- The size of your sales force.
- Seasonal trends.
- How much content (text, image, videos etc.) you have.
- How much content you can produce quickly.
- Whether you have the time to grow your customer base gradually.
- Whether you need the income to support the business now.
- Access to resources like staff, funds, experts and software.
- etc.

To Sum Up:

There are a handful of tricks available to select the right single primary keyword and some very useful tools to help you assess profitability and competition for a particular keyword. Plus you can even calculate its value. Before you read on, apply what you have read to your business and take Step 1.

GROW Step 1:

Decide on your **single, primary keyword or keyword phrase** by brainstorming your initial keyword list and evaluating it with the Google Keyword Tool and others. Check your keywords for search volume, competition, CPC (Cost-Per-Click) and for keyword value. These powerful keywords allow you to target your ready-to-buy customers head-on so that they find you quickly and easily, despite competitors trying to gain their interest.

GROW Step 2:
Focus Your Campaign with 'Long Tail' Keywords

What is a 'Long Tail'?

If your main keyword has turned out to be too competitive, or you want to focus on a more specific group of customers, try using some modifiers to make your keyword more targeted towards a specific group of clients. Create a 'keyword phrase' consisting of two or more words. In case you are unsure whether you should go for the top keywords or some keyword phrases with a little less competition, ask yourself which one you would like to rank for? One keyword which sends you 5,000 visitors a day but only a handful are really ready to buy, or a keyword which sends you only 100 visitors, but a quarter of them really want to buy. Those definite buyers which your competitors have missed might come to you because of so-called 'Long Tail' keywords.

Modified or 'long tail' keywords describe a product or service, e.g. a golf-related product, more precisely, using three to four words. For example 'affordable golf hotels' or 'seaside golf resort hotels'. Such terms attract a smaller number of visitors, but go online and see how much higher the CPC price and how much lower the competition is (at the time of writing this book). The more competitive your market niche, the more modifier words you might need to find long tail keyword phrases that offer enough searches and less competition, thus giving you a chance to get on Google's Page 1, ideally into the Number one position there.

Numerous tests and examples have shown that a number of long tail keywords taken together, often **generate more sales than the top traffic keywords,** since top traffic keywords only make up less than 30% of all the searches on the web. The remaining 70% are what's called the 'Long Tail'. This Long Tail consists of hundreds of millions of searches that might be conducted only a few times in a day, but when added up, they comprise the majority of Internet searches.

Chris Anderson in Wired Magazine has a brilliant explanation of long tail keywords that deserves a longer than usual quotation here:

"What's really amazing about the Long Tail is the sheer size of it. Combine enough non-hits on the Long Tail and you've got a market bigger than the hits.

Take books: The average Barnes & Noble carries 130,000 titles. Yet more than half of Amazon's book sales come from outside its top 130,000 titles. Consider the implication. If the Amazon statistics are any guide, the market for books that are not even sold in the average bookstore is larger than the market for those that are (see " Anatomy of the Long Tail"). In other words, the potential book market may be twice as big as it appears to be, if only we can get over the economics of scarcity. The same is true for all other aspects of the entertainment business, to one degree or another.

Just compare online and offline businesses: The average Blockbuster carries fewer than 3,000 DVDs. Yet a fifth of Netflix rentals are outside its top 3,000 titles. Rhapsody streams more songs each month beyond its top 10,000 than it does with its top 10,000. In each case, the market that lies outside the reach of the physical retailer (the High Street) is big and getting bigger quickly.

When you think about it, most successful businesses on the Internet are about aggregating the Long Tail in one way or another. Google, for instance, makes most of its money off small advertisers (the long tail of advertising), and eBay is mostly long tail as well - niche and one-off products. By overcoming the limitations of geography and scale, just as Rhapsody and Amazon have, Google and eBay have discovered new markets and expanded existing ones.

This is the power of the Long Tail." (Source: Chris Anderson in Wired www.wired.com/wired/archive/12.10/tail.html)

Another example of the Long Tail in action is Google's new print-on-demand deal for two million public domain titles, (http://xrefer.blogspot.com/2009/09/google-signs-print-on-demand-deal-for.html) in which Google and On Demand Books, (www.ondemandbooks.com/home.htm) the maker of the Espresso Book Machine, have signed a deal to provide print-on-demand access to more than two million public-domain titles (essentially, those published before 1923). You can have them in your high street bookstore – digitally – without them taking up storage space.

The deal will also provide potential Print on Demand (PoD) access to millions more in-copyright 'orphan works' in about four minutes printing time, should the

Google Book Search settlement be approved. For any high street bookstore that can afford the cost of the Espresso Book Machine, this will provide the opportunity to offer books that are searched for far less than any current main selling title. These are titles which would be searched for using long tail keywords.

Think Global – But Act Local

A recent survey by comScore found that 60% of consumers use the Internet as their first choice to search for local businesses, and 60% of those searchers go on to make a purchase. Almost every online company today can benefit by building links to local information, locally available goods and conveniently-located services.

If you are targeting an audience that is specific to a geographic location, make sure to localize your keyword phrases accordingly. Place city, country, state or local references such as city districts or zip codes before or after each keyword phrase, like 'Golf Hotels Florida' or more location specific 'Golf Hotels Fort Lauderdale' or 'Electricians London W12'. After all, you don't want potential customers searching for you online but finding your competitor instead!

Localizing has become a major trend on Google and can help you get highly-targeted traffic to your site or blog. Plus, it reduces the cost of dealing with inquiries that are not in your geographical location and, therefore, outside your target market. Even though fewer customers search these terms, the ones that do have a specific interest and are much more willing to buy, and that's what really matters.

So, use the most popular keywords along with 'modifiers' or 'qualifiers', either geographic or sector specific. While it might be difficult to rank well for 'chocolate gifts', it is not such a challenge to rank well for 'Chocolate Gifts Buffalo', targeting a geographic area. Secondly, when searchers enter a local term like 'Golf Hotels Fort Lauderdale', what they see is quite different to the so called 'universal' natural search listings.

Any searcher adding a geographic modifier - such as the name of a city, district, region etc - to their keyword term, will now get a list of 10 entries that Google thinks are relevant to the search. This means that the searcher will get a list of 10 local Google entries next to a local Google map, which appears above or within the more universal listings. This does not work for every keyword phrase, and not yet for every town or country (at the time of writing) but, knowing Google (Yahoo!, Bing), it probably will do soon. This gives smaller businesses in a particular area a good chance to address their local target market. Opposite is a screenshot for local Fort Lauderdale listings in Google.

PART I - Keywords

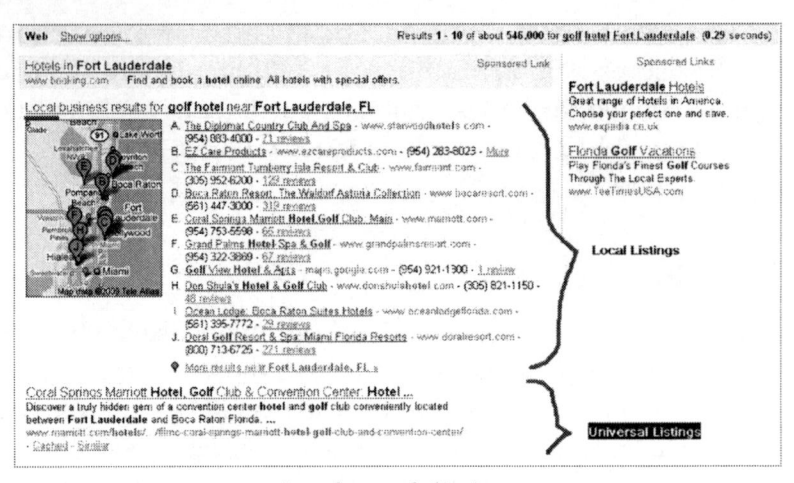

*Local search listings
for the location specific search term 'Golf Hotels Fort Lauderdale'.*

Notice that here the local listings appear before the universal natural listings. However, this is not a given. Sometimes, the local listings will appear **within** the natural listings. What I mean by this is that when you type simply 'plumber' into Google, you will probably see universal natural search listings before and after the local listings, as in the screen shot below:

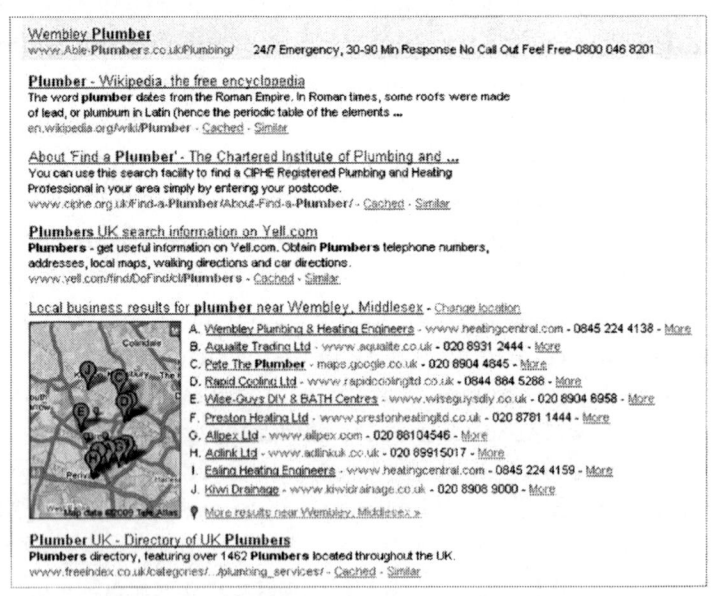

*Local search listings for the search term 'Plumber'
appearing **within** the natural listings.*

38

As you can see from the above, Google wants to give you local listings, like plumbers in Wembley, even though you have not requested it in your search. But they don't always get it right yet, since I generated this search from Fulham in London, not Wembley. These are probably the normal teething problems of a new service, but from my experience, I would expect it to improve quickly.

Let's make our search term a little more specific and add the location 'London' to it. Our modified keyword now has simply become 'Plumber London' and the search results listings don't appear in the same order anymore:

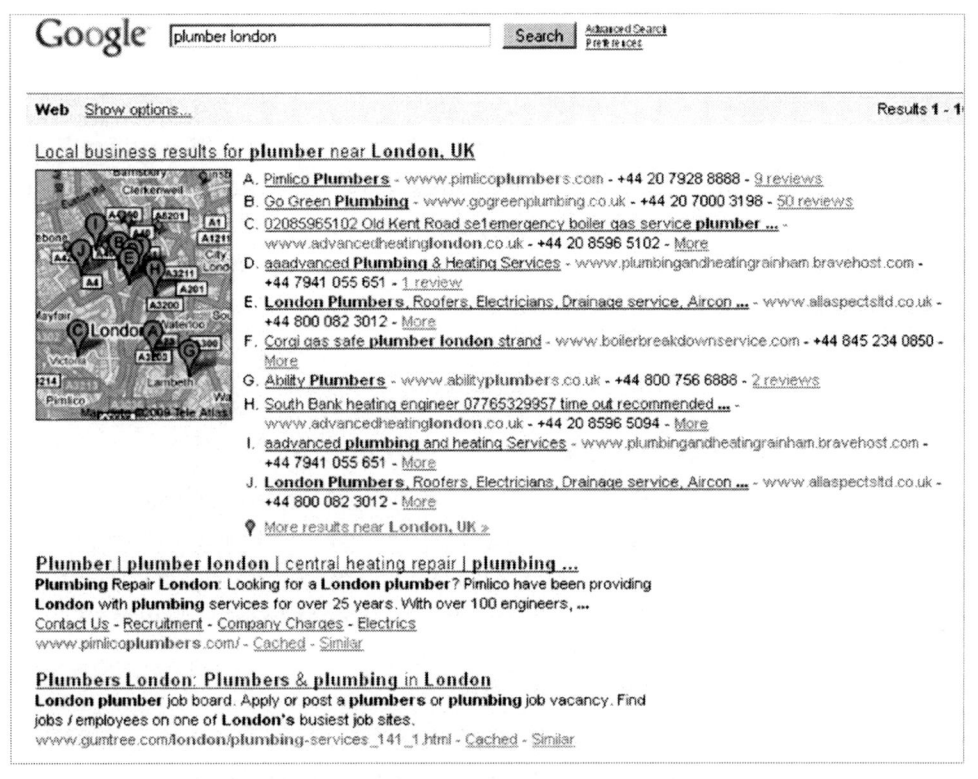

*Local search listings for 'Plumber London'
appearing **before** the Natural Listings.*

What you can see is that when prospective customers search with more specific keyword phrases, Google and the other search engines tend to lift your local listing to Google's top spot on its results page, just below the PPC ads. This is of fantastic value for a local business.

How Do I Get a Local Listing?

It's not difficult. Let me use Google as an example. Yahoo! and Bing work similarly. Basically, you create a business listing in e.g. Google's '**Local Business** Center' (www.google.com/lbc) and add the following:

- your business address
- opening hours
- a good description of what you do
- a map entry
- photos
- etc.

Next, you start promoting your local business listing (or listings if you can be found in more than one location). There are many ways in which you can optimize your local listing, and Google will actually help you with this by adding other entries to your local listing that seem relevant. For example, any company videos or reviews of your products. These additional items are called 'Citations' and are a great way of influencing Google to rank you high, locally.

Top Search Engine Ranking Factor for Local Listings

So, since you don't want to waste your time and money on things that won't give you much ranking benefit, below is a list of the top search engine ranking factors for local listings, also called geo-targeting factors. They are taken from a survey undertaken by Rand Fishkin, of SEOmoz. It is based on the experience of 72 industry experts and the factors are ordered by importance:

Very High Importance
Country code TLD of the root domain (e.g. .co.uk, .de, .fr, .com, .au, etc.)

High Importance
Language of the content used on the site
Links from other domains targeted to the country/region
Geographic location of the host IP address of the domain

Moderate Importance
Manual review/targeting by Google engineers and/or quality raters
Geo-targeting preference set inside Google webmaster tools
Registration of the site with Google Local in the country/region

Let's see briefly what these actually mean:

Very High Importance

Country code TLD of the root domain (e.g. .co.uk, .de, .fr, .com.au, etc.)
If your business is based in the United Kingdom and has a '.co.uk' domain extension, your site will get a local search engine ranking advantage over your competitor whose site has a '.com' domain extension.

High Importance

Language of the content used on the site
If you claim to be a business in Mexico and the only language that is available on your site is English, you won't get any local ranking benefit for that.

Links from other domains targeted to the country/region
Links from other sites in the local area will give your site a local ranking benefit.

Geographic location of the host IP address of the domain
If your site is hosted in the US but your local business is in Australia, you won't get any local ranking benefit either.

Moderate Importance

Manual review/targeting by Google engineers and/or quality raters
If you get a good review from respected reviewers, (a person, not a search engine robot!), the ranking of your listing will benefit.

Geo-targeting preference set inside Google webmaster tools
This is something you can influence yourself: Within the Google webmaster tools (www.google.com/webmasters/tools) you can set so-called 'Geo-Targeting Preferences' according to your local area, which will give your local ranking a boost.

Registration of the site with Google Local in the country/region
Registering your site with Google's Local Business Center (www.google.com/local) can also improve your page ranking for your local listing.

If you want to promote your local listing with links, here are some places to get links to your local listing:

Places to Build Local Links

- **Google Directory / DMOZ -** The Google Directory (http://directory.google.com/) is a good place to start since it is a human-reviewed and edited directory with imported DMOZ data, sorted by PageRank. It is well sorted by category and you should find your niche easily.

- **Local Business Organizations -** Business organizations are always an excellent source of local links. Some have member directories, others offer advertising space, and some will allow you to publish your articles. Add these to your list of places to send press releases and other newsworthy content that is of interest to your local market.

- **Newspapers, Journals, Independent News, Blogs -** You can get all sorts of links from these kinds of sites and a mix of links is not only the best for your search engine rankings, but will also give you extended exposure in your local market. On the Internet, people buy, on average, at the seventh contact, which means you have to get your (company's) name in front of your prospective customers as often as possible. This could be anything from getting mentioned in an article, to commenting on their blog, to buying advertising space. Also, find out what local media organizations are doing in your area and contact them to build a relationship with them. They can help you to build customers.

- **Other Popular Local Websites -** Find the most popular sites, such as message boards, event sites, chats, classified ads and blogs for your city or area. Think about what you can publish on these sites to get traffic and links to your site.

In Parts 3 and 4, I will describe in greater detail the most important things you can do to promote your universal natural listings, and you can apply these techniques similarly to promote your local listing(s), too. Local search is a massive opportunity for any business or profession now, since you can take your seat at the top of the local listings with a relatively small amount of work. Local search was only picked up about two years ago when Google lead the way and invested heavily in it. I suggest doing this sooner rather than later. Other businesses that target local customers will discover this too, and the space will get more crowded.

Why a 'Phrase Match' Usually Gets More Business

When you do your research for your long tail keywords on Google or more specialized keywords tools, make sure you are placing your search terms in "quotes" (parenthesis), for a 'phrase match', to get a more accurate idea of how many people are optimizing for your keyword phrase. There might be over 62 million webpages that contain the words golf, vacations and Florida. But when you search for "golf vacations Florida" within these quotes, the number of results drops to closer to 10,000 sites or fewer (at the time of writing).

This makes a huge difference, and for competitive keyword phrases, the difference might be even bigger. Three to five keyword phrases that have at least 50 to 100 daily searches and only 50,000 or fewer competing webpage / blog post results are usually good long tail targets, depending on whether your site is new or already has a Google PageRank.

With such a competition level, you should be able to reach a Google page one listing, and with some good copywriting in your Description Tag, you should be able to capture profitable traffic to make it worth your while. With more SEO experience and an increasing number of optimized links to your site, themed pages and a site silo structure in place, you can probably get top listings for keyword phrases with 100,000 or even 1 million competing pages. More on this in Parts III and IV.

To cut a long story short, do not just target two or three highly-competitive general keywords. Include a dozen or more easier-to-rank-for, long tail keywords too. On the other hand, don't focus entirely on the Long Tail either, since, if your target phrases are too specific, you might not get enough traffic to sustain your business initially. Ideally, have two legs to stand on and combine:

1. highly-competitive keywords, sending you large amounts of less targeted traffic.
2. less competitive long tail keywords, each sending you small amounts of highly-targeted traffic.

You might be asking: How can you combine these different sorts of keywords? It is easy, and it's one of the most effective SEO techniques that you can use with your content. It's called 'Theming' and it is explained in full in Part V of this book. Theming really is just an elaborate expression for grouping a number of different keywords on a page into one article. This is how you can group high traffic keywords and long tail keywords together.

PART I - Keywords

Now, let's look at another form of keyword that you also want to include into your keyword theme; 'Synonymous Keywords'.

Why You Want to Use 'Synonyms'

'Synonymous Keywords' are generally keywords that are related to your primary keyword, but without containing the original word. For a keyword such as 'golf clubs', related keywords would be 'ping driver' or 'golfing accessories'.

You will find these additional, related keywords in the field underneath the first results box, if you scroll down in Google's Adwords keyword tool under www.Google.co.uk/AdWords. As with long tail keyword phrases, these synonymous keywords are important because:

a) in highly-competitive market niches, it might be too costly to get onto Google's Page 1 for the 'most wanted' keywords. With synonymous keywords, you can target the same customers but with a higher probability of reaching them; and

b) you want to include a good number of synonymous keywords in your 'themed' pages to show Google that you know what you are talking about, that your page or article is seriously relevant for the keyword term just used by a searcher, and that Google should list your page/article highly on its search results page, so you get the click.

In Part III, I will explain in greater detail how including synonymous keywords and combining them into a theme can have a massive impact on your search engine listings to help you compete with more established companies who are not using primary, secondary and synonymous keywords in that fashion.

'Latent Semantic Indexing' (LSI) or 'Referential Integrity'

Google is always trying to improve its ability to understand what a certain webpage is really about. After all, Google wants to show a search results page that is relevant to the current search, and to be able to do that it needs to understand the content of the page.

The company, therefore, puts a lot of work into improving its indexing with so called 'Latent Semantic Indexing' (LSI) and 'Referential Integrity' (http://en.wikipedia.org/wiki/Referential_integrity); two indexing concepts that are currently much-discussed by SEO experts. These are quite technical areas and the detail of them is outside the scope of this book but, in essence, the fact that Google uses semantic concepts means that its capacity to understand the actual content of a webpage will continue to increase. Therefore, if you want to be ranked highly by Google, it won't be enough just to mention the same keyword five, six or seven times on a page.

As I stress in the part about 'theming', you will need to make sure that the content of your pages contains many variations of your primary keyword, such as related, modified and synonymous keywords. You will then have to incorporate all these keywords into a highly focused theme on one page, so that, when Google runs its semantic indexing technology over your page, it understands that, due to the wide range of relevant keywords that you are using and the focused theme of your text, your page is really relevant for the current search and thus should be ranked highly. If you want to read more on this subject, just put any of the terms mentioned here into Google.

How to Test Before You Spend

There are some tricks you can use to make sure that the keywords you use in your marketing campaigns actually convert visitors into customers. You can capitalize on these by running some quick and informative tests.

A straightforward way to test the profitability of your keywords is to run a small PPC campaign for the keywords you have chosen. Just point the PPC ads to your landing page and measure the response, as you did before when you calculated the value of a keyword. Once you have done that, you will know which keywords have made you the most money so far.

Let us say you are targeting the keyword phrases 'golf vacations', 'golf trips', 'golf courses', and 'golf books' on different pages of your site. After a couple of weeks and some traffic arriving, you notice you are selling more golf books than other products. This tells you that you are either ranking much better for 'golf books', thus bringing more traffic to your site, or that golf books just sell better to your target market, or both. Then you know that this is the keyword you want to focus on.

Now you can test related phrases such as 'books on golf', 'books about golf', 'golf instruction books' etc., supplementing your selling 'golf book' keyword with related keyword phrases on the same page. This will improve your page's ranking and, therefore, get you even more traffic and sales. How to do all this will become clear in the following parts when we look at 'theming'.

Note: When you are doing your PPC, test, just remember that your results will be

PART I - Keywords

influenced, not only by the choice of your keywords, but also by the quality of your landing page, and what kind of message or ad you are using. So, you need to make sure you understand where the results are coming from.

To Sum Up

Target not only two or three highly-competitive general keywords in your SEO campaign, but also include several easier-to-rank-for, long tail keywords and synonymous keywords too. Before reading on, make sure you have managed Step 2:

GROW Step 2:

Find **secondary keywords and keyword phrases,** modified/long tail keywords and synonymous keywords to target your specific product niche effectively.

SUMMARY:
Keywords – the Foundation of Online Marketing

Keywords are the foundation of your success online. I can't urge you enough – **Find Your Keywords**! Follow the two steps in this part to research, evaluate and even combine the right keywords and keyword phrases to give your website the best possible results on the search engines. Even in a crowded, competitive market place, proper use of your keywords will lift you far above the competition.

In the following parts, I will show you how to use your keywords most effectively. But first, DO TAKE THIS ESSENTIAL STEP! It's the basis for multiplying your customer numbers and profits. It will pay you back large dividends for the time you have invested.

GROW Step 1: Choose the Best Keywords for Your Target Customers

Decide on your **single, primary keyword or keyword phrase** by brainstorming your initial keyword list and evaluating it with the Google Keyword Tool and others. Check your keywords for search volume, competition, CPC (Cost-Per-Click) and keyword value. These powerful keywords allow you to target your ready-to-buy customers head-on, so that they find you quickly and easily, despite competitors trying to gain their interest.

GROW Step 2: Focus Your Campaign with 'Long Tail' Keywords

Find **secondary keywords and keyword phrases,** modified/long tail keywords and synonymous keywords to target your specific product niche more effectively. These secondary keywords will broaden your business's presence in the market place and strengthen your search engine ranking.

Next, let's discover what your competition is doing and how well they have executed their Internet marketing campaign, so you can outwit them and take their top spot on the search engines, their market share and their customers.

PART II:

How to Outsmart and Outwit Your Competition

Competition Analysis

To accelerate the speed of your online success and save money and time, you can analyze what your competition is doing – and how you can improve on their success. On the Internet, you can easily find out what keywords, strategies and tricks your competitors are using, and whether they are doing a good job in optimizing their site or blog. It is really astonishing that not more businesses use the fact that you can find this out easily and perfectly legally.

The great advantage of marketing on the Internet is that you can peek into your competitor's back office – and it's totally legal!

As in 'Musical Chairs' there are only so many 'seats' on Google's Page 1, and if you don't analyze how well your competitors have optimized their websites, your chances of beating them to a Page 1 listing are small.

Why Your Position On Google Is So Important

There is a big difference whether you have 50,000, 500,000 or 5 million other pages competing for 'your' keyword, but essentially, you want a listing on the first search engine results page (SERPS) of Google, Bing, Yahoo! etc. So, all that really matters to you is how good the others are that appear on that page. Even if 500,000 other web pages compete with 'your' keywords or keyword phrases, your real competitors are still those companies whose pages occupy the top 10 positions on the first results page.

It may be that some of the top ten sites have not done much page optimization at all. They might, for example, have had a Google page one listing for a long time and their competition is not doing enough to kick them off their top spot. If you search engine optimize your page better than they have, then there is a good chance that you will be able to take their place amongst the top ten.

The reason why you want to be on Google's first search results page is that only a small percentage of Internet users ever scroll down to Pages 2, 3, 4, and hardly any scroll down further. Page 2 gets about 10% of all clicks compared to Page 1, which gets almost 90%, according to Breakpoint, a former Earnersforum member who calculated leaked data from AOL (www.techcrunch.com/2006/08/06/aol-proudly-releases-massive-amounts-of-user-search-data/). AOL has a slightly different audience than Google, but these numbers are representative enough about search in

PART II – Competition Analysis

general, and they are currently the best figures available. The AOL data means that hardly any searchers click on listings on Pages 3 or more.

The position in which a site appears on a search results Page 1 is also significant. If you can't make position one, you ideally want to be listed in positions two or three, since the three top listings get over 60% of all click throughs, and automatically get displayed by other search engines as well. Have a look at the data below assembled by Breakpoint. The calculation shows how many clicks and visitors (meaning 'potential business') you can get if you have a listing on the first search results page.

Overall Percentages of Clicks on 1ˢᵗ Page	Relative Click Volume
Position 1 gets 42.13% of clicks	
Position 2 gets 11.90% of clicks	3.5 x **less** clicks than position 1
Position 3 gets 8.50% of clicks	4.9 x less clicks than position 1
Position 4 gets 6.06% of clicks	6.9 x less clicks than position 1
Position 5 gets 4.92% of clicks	8.5 x less clicks than position 1
Position 6 gets 4.05% of clicks	10.4 x less clicks than position 1
Position 7 gets 3.41% of clicks	12.4 x less clicks than position 1
Position 8 gets 3.01% of clicks	14.0 x less clicks than position 1
Position 9 gets 2.85% of clicks	14.8 x less clicks than position 1
Position 10 gets 2.99% of clicks	14.1 x less clicks than position 1

(Source: Breakpoint, Earnersforum, AOL 'Leaked' Data)

Competition Analysis - Introduction

The AOL data shown above can mean several things for you:

- When you get to Position one on the first search results page for a certain keyword phrase, you are likely to get over 40% of the total clicks on this phrase to your site or blog.

- If you are listed anywhere between Positions 2 and 10, you can hugely increase the traffic to your site by just going up a couple of positions on the results page. Clearly, Number one gets the lion's share of clicks, but even rising from Number 8 to Number 3 can triple your traffic.

- Search results Page 2 only gets 10% of the traffic Page 1 gets. So, in case your website is already listed on Pages 2 or 3, even a little bit of SEO to get you to Page 1 can increase traffic and clicks to your page significantly by moving you just a few positions higher.

You now know that your real competitors are the companies listed in the top ten, and more specifically the top three on Google and on the other search engines. Now, there are quite a few ways to **legally** spy on them and find out how well they have optimized their site, and where they left the loopholes so you could by-pass them and take their position on Page 1. To do this, take GROW Step 3:

GROW Step 3:
Know Your Competition to Fast Track to the Top

The search engines use ranking systems to categorize sites for their importance or relevance. They consist of over 100 ranking factors – factors which determine to which place your site is assigned on the search engine results pages. The million dollar question here is this: what are the most important factors Google and the other search engines look for when they analyze a site and decide where it should be listed? And which of those techniques have your competitors implemented effectively? Once you know that, you can start optimizing your website or blog pages accordingly and do better than your competition, achieving the best result with minimal time, effort and money.

The Bad News ...
...is that nobody really knows for sure what Google's criteria – or 'algorithms' as they are called in the industry – are, exactly. Firstly, Google does not tell you, and secondly, it changes them frequently. So, we can only find out what works and what doesn't from experience; from what we do, test, refine etc.

The Good News ...
...is that Internet Marketing and SEO experts such as us and others analyze search engine ranking factors all the time and are constantly testing what works best. Below, you will find the top search engine ranking factors to-date from a study undertaken by Rand Fishkin, of SEOmoz.org, representing and quoting the collective wisdom of 72 industry experts in the field of organic SEO. This study tells you what other experts agree to be the most effective search engine ranking factors to-date, and combined with our own experience, gives you probably the best method to get your website or blog listed highly on the search engine results pages:

Top Ten Search Engine Ranking Factors Against Which to Check your Competition

1. Keyword-Focused **Anchor Text** From External Links;
2. External **Link Popularity** (Quantity/Quality of External Links);
3. Diversity of **Link Sources** (Links from Many Unique Root Domains);
4. Trustworthiness of the Domain Based on **Link Distance** from Trusted Domains (e.g. TrustRank, Domain mozTrust, etc.);
5. Keyword Use Anywhere in the **Title Tag**;
6. Existence of Substantive, **Unique Content** on the Page;
7. **Page-Specific TrustRank** (Whether the Individual Page Has Earned Links From Trusted Sources);
8. Keyword Use as the First Word(s) of the **Title Tag**;
9. Iterative Algorithm-Based, **Global Link Popularity** (PageRank);
10. Use in the Root **Domain Name** (e.g. keyword.com).

Let's have a look at what these ranking factors actually mean:

1. Keyword-Focused Anchor Text From External Links:

The text part of a link pointing from another site to your website, called the 'Anchor Text', is currently the most important ranking factor for the search engines. Google, in particular, pays attention to the Anchor Text (also called 'Link Text'). Andy Beal says: "Keyword use in external link is one of the top SEO factors overall. I've seen sites rank for competitive keywords—without even mentioning the keyword on-page—simply because of external link text". For more details on how to use keywords in Anchor Text of inbound links, and how important it is that these keywords match, see Link Building.

2. External Link Popularity (Quantity/Quality of External Links):

This measures how many links your website gets from other sites and blogs and what the quality of those links is. The quality of the link is based on the following criteria:

- How established are these third party websites?
- How high is their authority rating?
- How many inbound links does the page your link is coming from have?
- How few outbound links does the page where your link is coming from have?
- How relevant is their site to your site?
- How relevant is the Link Text to your site from theirs?

3. Diversity of Link Sources (Links From Many Unique Root Domains):

With the arrival of social media sites, it has become more important that your links come from a balanced variety of domains. If all your links come only from article directories or from social media sites, Google will become suspicious and assume that you might have done some 'artificial' link building, meaning you got someone to build links to your site. This could decrease the value of those links to your site.

4. Trustworthiness of the Domain Based on Link Distance from Trusted Domains (e.g. TrustRank, Domain mozTrust, etc.):

This means that if you have a direct link from a trusted domain, you are one link away. If a trusted domain links to Domain A and Domain A links to you, you are two links away from the trusted domain etc. The less remote the trusted domain, the fewer links there will be in between your domain and the trusted domain, and the more trust and authority you inherit from that link.

5. Keyword Use Anywhere in the Title Tag:

This means placing the targeted search term or keyword phrase in the Title Tag of the web page's HTML header. Elisabeth Osmeloski, says: "Not only is [the Title Tag] one of your strongest chances to impact rankings, it is undoubtedly your BEST chance to convert a searcher to a visitor within the SERPS …" To find out how you can place your keywords in your Title Tags, see Part IV.

6. Existence of Substantive, Unique Content on the Page:

The more content you have on your site, the better. And yes, it can't be content scraped from other sites. Google and the other search engines will give the 'originator' – the site that showed that page first on the Internet – the most ranking juice.

7. Page-specific TrustRank (Whether the Individual Page Has Earned Links from Trusted Sources):

This is similar to No 4 except that here, it is the link to the individual page that counts, not the whole domain / website. How many links does the actual page you are competing with get?

8. Keyword Use As The First Word(s) of the Title Tag:

Above, we have seen that putting the keyword anywhere in the Title Tag is the 5th most important ranking factor. If you can move the keyword to the front so it becomes the first word of the Title Tag phrase, you will get more ranking power for your site. Chris Boggs says: "We have seen great and rapid results modifying the keyword use in the title, especially for large, branded sites that already have thousands of Inbound Links [IBLs]. Again, with everything, this is also dependent on the word's usage within content and IBLs. Additionally, the "prominence" of the keyword [the closer the keyword is to the beginning] seems to help incrementally, especially with sites that agree to place their brand name after the keyword."

9. Iterative Algorithm-Based, Global Link Popularity (PageRank):

Whereas No 2 and No 3 include quality factors of the links, this factor looks at the overall number of backlinks to your site. The assumption here is that the more links, the better. However, we have seen from the list above that the **quality** a link has, is becoming more and more important. This means that the actual number of links to your site – irrespective of their quality - will probably drop in importance in the future, and the importance of quality will go up.

Lucas Ng (aka shor) describes Global Link Popularity in a similar SEOmoz.org study: "Think of a web page as a town. If a city has freeways, airports, train stations, bus shelters and a port, that's a good indicator that it is an important hub. That orphaned web page with no links pointing to it? It may as well be a hidden tribe of Amazons that no one has discovered." (See Part VII of this book on how to create quality links to your site.)

10. Use in the Root Domain Name (e.g. keyword.com):

Including your primary keyword in the domain name is a good idea and the earlier in the URL the keyword appears, the better.

Note: Find additional search engine ranking factors in the 'Site and Competition Assessment' Template at: www.Internet-Experts-Live.com/members/templates. Download the folder to find the **'Positive Ranking Factors'** tab at the bottom of the page.

Assessment Sheet - Positive Search

(With this worksheet you can assess your own page and the competition for a keyword you want to ta[ke] down to see how well your competition has optimized their pages for that particular keyword. If your [page is missing] the additional ranking factors listed below.)

Top 10 Search Engine Ranking Factors	Your Page	Competitor Rank 1	Competitor Rank 2	Com[petitor] R[ank 3]
1. Keyword-Focused **Anchor Text** from External Links,				
2. External **Link Popularity** (quantity/quality of external links),				
3. Diversity of **Link Sources** (links from many unique root domains),				
4. Trustworthiness of the **Domain** Based on Link Distance from Trusted Domains (e.g. TrustRank, Domain mozTrust, etc.),				
5. Keyword Use Anywhere in the **Title Tag**,				
6. Existence of Substantive, **Unique Content** on the Page,				
7. **Page-Specific TrustRank** (whether the individual page has earned links from trusted sources),				
8. Keyword Use as the First Word(s) of the **Title Tag**,				
9. Iterative Algorithm-Based Global Link				

Tabs: Goals / Keywords / SE Friendliness / **Positive Ranking Factors** / Negative Ranking Factors / Local Li[nks]

Assessment Sheet with Search Engine Ranking Factors

PART II – Competition Analysis

Summary Search Engine Ranking Factors

The top ten search engine ranking factors listed above are the ones most widely agreed to give you a good idea of where to start when optimizing your pages. They can be summarized as follows:

- Keyword relevant, high quality links to your site and within your own site are a priority for top search engine rankings.
- Rich, fresh, keyword-rich content earns search engine trust and high rankings.

The Sign of Things to Come in the Future

You might ask: If these are the factors that work best now, where are we going over the next couple of years? There is no easy answer since Google, Bing etc. are only giving us glimpses of what's going to come. However, we can see one development starting to happen that will have a major effect on rankings. Google is spending a lot of time and money researching and developing concepts and improvements in the area of 'semantics' – the science of understanding the meaning of text (as I touched on earlier in the paragraph about Google's indexing techniques, LSI and Referential Integrity).

Google and the other search engines always want to display the most relevant webpage for a particular search, and for that reason it needs to understand what the various pages are really about. The better Google understands the subject of a specific web page, the better the chance for that page to get listed for a specific search.

Due to Google's advances in 'semantics', on-page optimization factors - the ways to optimize your own page by putting content with keywords on it - will become increasingly important in achieving a good ranking on Google. Two techniques will start making a greater and greater difference: so called 'Silo Structure' or 'Silo-ing' and 'Keyword Themes' or 'Theming'. I will, in the following parts, describe in more detail what these are and how you can use them for your business or profession, so your site gets ranked highly. For now, let me explain briefly what they are.

'Keyword Themes' or 'Theming'

In a nutshell, 'Theming' means grouping keywords into a single focused theme on a web page. It works like this: Once you have done your keyword and competition research, and you have decided on your primary and secondary keywords, you group keywords into a specific theme – like members of one family grouping together. For example, this could be 'Affordable Golf Holidays in Scotland'. You can build a whole website / blog with this theme or you can use it for just a single page of your site or blog.

The key here is to stay true to your theme by featuring only information, products, services and treatments that are relevant. So, if your company offers 'Affordable Golf Holidays in Scotland', 'Affordable Golf Holidays in China' or 'Affordable Golf Holidays in Florida', you take only one of those holiday packages and stick to it on your page. Do not mention expensive holidays, or scuba-diving holidays or golf equipment etc. on the same page. This doesn't sound like big news and it is rather straightforward to do. But you will be surprised how many websites do not focus on one theme per page. This alone can already make a big difference to how your site or blog gets ranked on the search engines, and will become even more important in the not-so-distant future. (For more information on Keyword Themes see Part V.)

'Silo Structure' or 'Siloing'

'Siloing' is an advanced strategy that can give your site and pages a real ranking boost. The following will probably sound a bit technical, but it's straightforward really. In essence, it is a way of structuring your site to appeal first and foremost to the search engine robots, and most of the times your site visitors will benefit from the clear structure, too.

This is how it works: You divide the content of your website into different containers or so called 'silos' of content in distinct categories. One silo consists of a top page called a landing page and various content pages that all focus on one subject. A structure is only called a silo if its content pages are clearly distinct from another silo. It is important that the links from one silo to another must only go to the top or landing page of the other silo, not to the inner pages. That's it.

This is a way of making clearer to the search engines what your various pages are about. Indiscriminately linking from one page to another would dilute the organizational theme of your site, thus making it harder for your pages to be relevant to specific search terms. (For more information on Silo Structure see Part VI.)

High Quality Links

Apart from these two on-page developments, Google and Bing etc. will ask for more and more quality in the links you are getting to your site. Years ago, a decent number of links gave you search engine ranking power, no matter what these links were. Then, we saw links from no-authority sites such as duplicate content, affiliate sites

PART II – Competition Analysis

etc. starting to be discounted for ranking power. Next, keywords in the Link Texts needed to match your page content.

Today, the authority of the pages where your links are coming from counts towards whether you will be getting any 'link juice', and how much. Tomorrow, keywords in the link or Anchor Texts will not only have to match the keywords on your page but also the page from where these links are coming from, at least to a certain extent. Plus, the authority of the site from which your link originates will be of even greater importance. So, if you want to assess your competition's ranking power and their links, you will need to assess the pages they are getting their links from too. I will be going into more detail about links and link building in Part VII, but for now, let me give you the most important facts about your competitor's links in a nutshell:

First of all, you need to find out the link information of any of your competitor's pages that rank in the top ten for your main keyword. At this point you don't need the link information for their entire site but want to know about the quality of the links go to the particular page(s) listed in the top ten. Internal links usually don't have much ranking power. What you really want to find out is what kind of inbound links they are getting to the page with which you want to compete.

Links only count for a better ranking ...
- if they come from another website that is trusted. Links from 'Link Farm' sites or duplicate article content don't count much, but links from authoritative sites such as .gov and .edu and directories such as DMOZ and the Yahoo! Directory with a PageRank of about 7, count a lot.
- if the Link Text (Anchor Text) carries at least a keyword variation. 'Click Here' won't give the page a lot of ranking power.
- if the topic of the site where the link comes from is relevant to the topic of the page the link is pointing to. If the keyword and subject have to do with 'Golf' and the site where the link comes from is about 'Dating', the page won't get much link juice.

Links don't count for a better ranking ...
- if the source page (where the link is coming from) links to hundreds of other pages.
- if the link source page sits four, five levels or even deeper in its site.

○ if they don't get any links from web 2.0 sites. This could mean that your competitors haven't looked after this page recently, or that their webmaster is unaware that bookmarking links from Delicious.com etc is an indicator for Google about a site's social authority and popularity.

These are the first things you want to find out about the links going to your competitor's pages, to get an idea of how strong their position is. The SEO ranking factors shown above will help you to find weak spots of your competitor's page optimizations and to beat them to their listing on the search engines.

Note: If you want up-to-date information for your competitive link research, don't use Google's PageRank Toolbar info since it is incomplete. Use Yahoo!'s! Site Explorer (http://siteexplorer.search.Yahoo!.com/) instead, or use tools such as SEOElite.com or MarketSamurai.com.

In the future, Google will probably give inbound links slightly less ranking. The chart below shows that almost half of the SEO experts consulted here believe this to be the case. Instead, On-page SEO factors such as **'Keyword Content Theming'** and **'Silo Structure,'** which I introduced above, will gain importance.

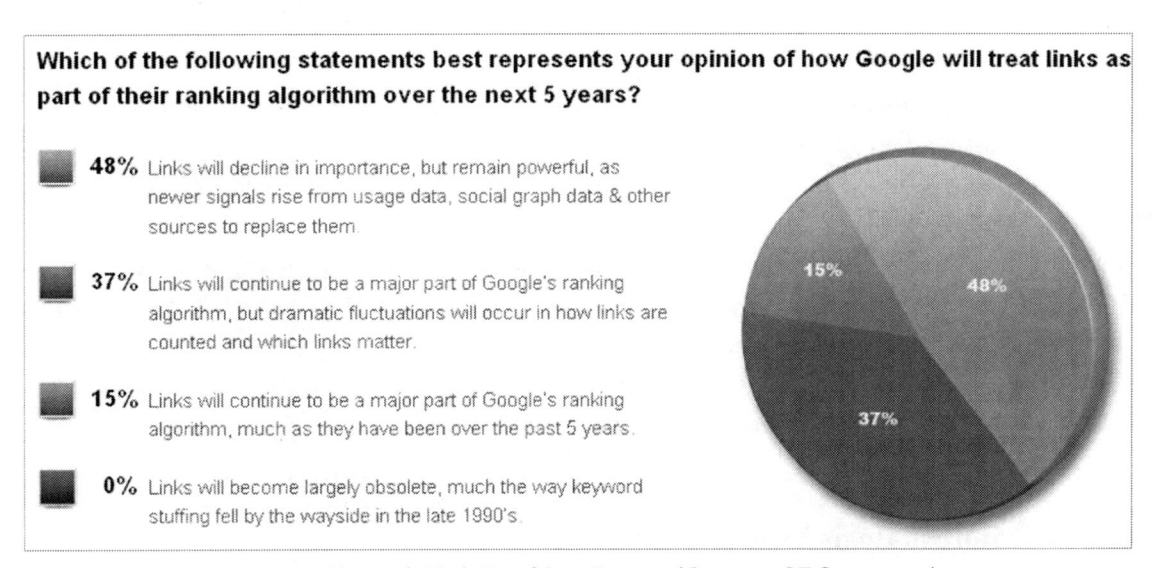

Which of the following statements best represents your opinion of how Google will treat links as part of their ranking algorithm over the next 5 years?

- **48%** Links will decline in importance, but remain powerful, as newer signals rise from usage data, social graph data & other sources to replace them.
- **37%** Links will continue to be a major part of Google's ranking algorithm, but dramatic fluctuations will occur in how links are counted and which links matter.
- **15%** Links will continue to be a major part of Google's ranking algorithm, much as they have been over the past 5 years.
- **0%** Links will become largely obsolete, much the way keyword stuffing fell by the wayside in the late 1990's.

Future Inbound Link Ranking Power (Source: SEOmoz.org)

PART II – Competition Analysis

Competition Analysis Tools You Can Use Right Now

To 'spy' on your competition - totally legally - you can use a number of competition analysis tools. There are quite a few tools out there, but I have put together a handful that I think are the most useful ones to get you started. See a list of them in the 'SEO Tools' section in Part VI of this book.

The Fast Track to Check your Competition – A Hands-On Example

Let's look at a fast way to identify your competitors for your chosen keyword and how well they have optimized their pages. Plus, how you can beat them to their listings and, therefore, win over their prospective customers to you. This generally works for any product or service and can be done in **5 simple steps**. With every step, you will get a more detailed view of how strong your competition is or, in other words, how well they have optimized their pages. The picture that will evolve tells you whether it is worth your time and effort to target a specific keyword before you spend anything on it. I'm doing this with the help of an extensive example, so that you see:

a) how much valuable information about how well your competitor has optimized their site you are able to access relatively quickly.
b) how much time and money you can save. It is not complicated to do keyword and competition analysis online, and it is absolutely worth doing before you commit any budgets.

Now, let's see how you can find out what your chances are to overtake your competition for certain keywords. If, for example, you are considering an additional line of business such as printing company logos onto golf balls to sell the balls online as presents or for corporate branding, you would want to be found online for the keyword "Golf Ball Logo". To quickly see whether this keyword phrase would be worth your time and money, here is what you can do:

Competition Analysis Example: Step One

First check the demand for the keyword "golf ball logo". If there is not enough demand, meaning searches, there is no point of spending more time on it, at least not as a main keyword. Put the keyword phrase "golf ball logo" into Google's free keyword tool at https://adwords.**google**.com/select/**KeywordTool**External and see what the demand is like.

At the time of writing there were an average of 1,900 searches over the last 12 months, there is not maximum competition (the box under 'Advertiser Competition' is not filled in completely) and advertisers are willing to pay a considerable amount of $2.53 per click on their "golf ball logo" ads. This means there's a market out there but there is not too much competition for the keyword you want to target.

Keywords	Estimated Avg. CPC	Advertiser Competition	Global Monthly Search Volume	Match Type: Phrase
Keywords related to term(s) entered - sorted by relevance				
"golf ball logo"	$2.53	▭	1,900	Add Phrase

A search for "golf ball logo" in Google's free Adwords keyword tool.

Competition Analysis Example: Step Two

We can now find out where the demand for that keyword is coming from. Since golf is such an international sport, one would probably guess that demand comes from all over the world, right?

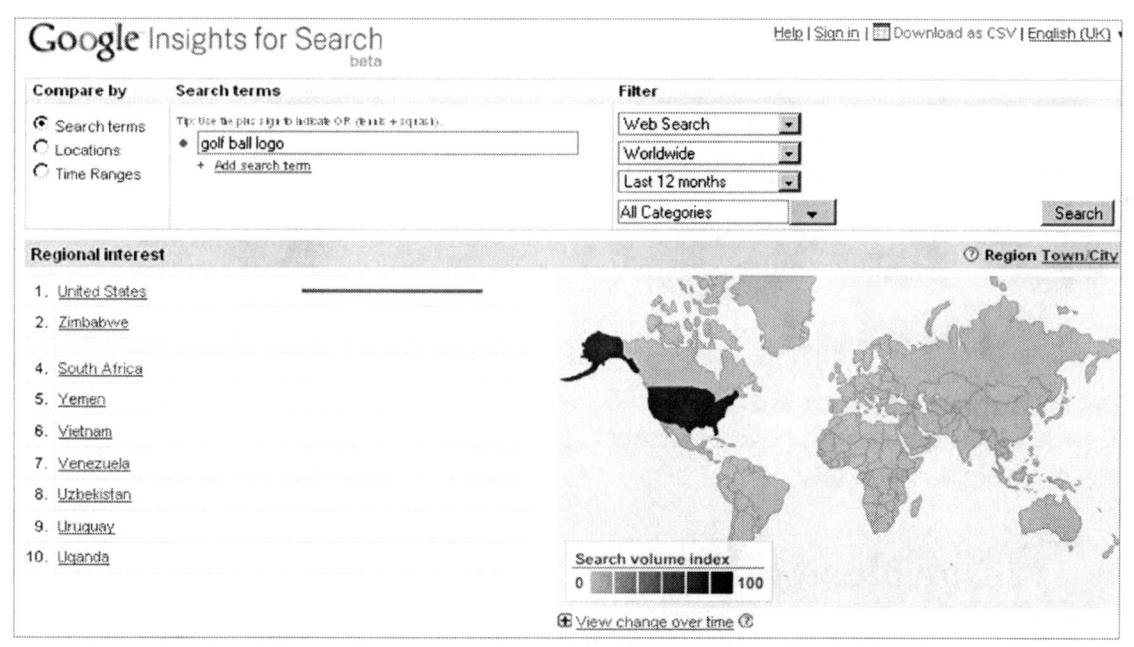

Regional demand in terms of searches for the keyword "golf ball logo"

PART II – Competition Analysis

When we have a look in Google's Search tool (www.google.com/insights/search), we see that the searches for our keyword "golf ball logo" came exclusively from the US. Which, besides other commercial considerations, tells you that you might have a slight disadvantage over a US based firm to get the No 1 listing on Google if the server of your site is located outside the US.

Also if you are based in Australia and only interested in the Asian market, this might not be an ideal keyword for you. But if you want to market this product or service to the US market, then let's have a look at what the competition is like for that keyword.

Competition Analysis Example: Step Three

To get an overview over how the competition is doing for our keyword, download the free SEO For Firefox tool at:

> http://tools.seobook.com/firefox/seo-for-firefox.html and install it on your PC. This will give you a range of SEO data about other companies targeting this keyword.

SEO For Firefox Tool Download Page

Competition Analysis Example: Step Four

Once you have installed and activated the SEO For Firefox tool on your PC, put your keyword "golf ball logo" into Google search. Here is what showed up in the top four positions (at the time of writing).

The top 4 listings for "golf ball logo" in Google

In the screenshot above you see three **text** listings and one **image** listing. The first text listing reads: 'graphicPUSH: The Golf Ball Logo Test'. Below it you can see a number of lines with SEO data by the SEO Tool. The three interesting bits of data:

a) **Title Tag:** In the first listing, the keyword is part of the headline saying 'Golf Ball Logo'. The second listing has a slightly different version of our keyword in the Title Tag, namely 'Logo Golf Ball' and the other two don't feature the keyword in their headlines. So, out of the top four listings, only two have used the Title Tag to optimize their site. This tells you that if you optimize the Title Tag on your page, you have got a chance to get listed here, too.

However, it is not enough to just get the Title Tag right. Remember, the more competition there is for your keyword the more ranking factors you need to get right.

b) **PageRank**: You can see the PR (Google PageRank) highlighted in grey half way down each listing. The PR gives you a good general indication how competitive the niche is that you want to target. The higher the PR number (it can go up to 8 or even 10), the stronger the site.

In this case the PR is 0 for the first listing and 2 for the second and third. This shows you that this keyword does not attract high PR sites (yet), that the competition is not very well optimized and, therefore, it should not be too difficult to beat them to their listing.

Also note that listing 1 with its PR of 0 managed to overtake listings 2 and 3 with their PR of 2. This shows you something else, namely that the PR value of your site or blog is not the only deciding factor as to whether you will get ranked above or below your competition.

c) **Links:** Earlier on in the part, we saw how important quality links to your site are. Let's have a look now at the number of links the top four listings show. When you look at the first listing ('graphicPUSH: The Golf Ball Logo Test'), you will see a section that reads Y! Links: 283,000 | Y! .edu Links: 822 | Y! .gov Links: 1 | Y! Page Links: 23

> graphicPUSH: The **Golf Ball Logo** Test
> Good logos should be able to be read at small sizes, look good in one color and be able to withstand weird printing., In other words, it should look good on ...
> www.graphicpush.com/the-golf-ball-test - Cached - Similar
> #1 | PR: 0 | Google Cache Date: Sep 7 2009 | Traffic Value: ? | Age: - | del.icio.us: ? | del.icio.us Page Bookmarks: ? | Diggs: ? | Digg's Popular Stories: ? | Stumbleupon: ? | Twitter: ? | Y! Links: 283,000 | Y! .edu Links: 822 | Y! .gov Links: 1 | Y! Page Links: 23 | Y! .edu Page Links: 0 | Technorati: ? | Alexa: 274,242 | Compete.com Rank: 394,819 | Compete.com Uniques: 3,472 | Trends | Cached: ? | dmoz: 0 | Bloglines: ? | Page blog links: ? | dir.yahoo.com: - | Botw: ? | Whois | Sktool | Yahoo position: ? | Majestic SEO linkdomain: ?

SEO Toolbar information

What Does All This Mean?

'Y! Links:' means that Yahoo! found 283,000 links to this domain.
'Y! .edu Links:' means that Yahoo! found 822 links from educational sites (universities etc.) to this domain.
'Y! .gov Links:' means that Yahoo! found 1 link from a government site to this domain.
'Y! **Page** Links:' means that Yahoo! found 23 links to the page listed here as No 1 listing.

What Is Important Here?

First of all, as we have seen in the search engine ranking factors section, when a site or blog gets a lot of quality links, Google will consider the site an authority and give it ranking credit for those links. Links ending with .edu and especially .gov links carry even more ranking value, since .edu and .gov are usually considered authority sites themselves and the more authorities that link to you, the better.

    Secondly, it is important to check how many of these links actually point to the one individual **page** of your competitor's site that is directly competing with you, since not all of the ranking power of the entire site will spill over to a particular page. The SEO tool gives you a number for links to the entire site ('Y! Links:') and links to the specific page ('Y! **Page** Links:'). The number of links to the page competing with your page is the more important one here.

    The more quality links from authority sites that a certain single page gets, the more ranking power it will have and the more difficult it will be to take this page's place in the listings, or even get listed above it.

When you look at these numbers, you will have to use some common sense to spot any possible glitches in the information given (See Part VI: SEO Tools - 'Take it with a Grain of Salt' for more information on the limitations of SEO / keyword tools.). For example, looking at the number of links quoted for the 'graphicPush.com' domain – 283,000 – this number seems high for a blog established in Oct 2003. If in doubt, you can take your investigation one step further and evaluate certain listings in more detail, using the SEO tool and other tools.

    For now, let's just remember that with the SEO tool installed, you can quickly get a fairly **good overview** over the competition for a certain keyword or keyword phrase that you might want to target.

    Ok, now let's find out whether you have a chance of taking the first listing position on that page. This could bring over 42% of searchers to your site. To achieve

PART II – Competition Analysis

this we now need to learn a little more about the No 1 page listing 'graphicPUSH: The Golf Ball Logo Test'.

Clicking on its link, you can see that the website page actually doesn't offer any golf ball customization products or services such as printing your company logo on a golf ball. The page is about the design of graphic design icons and does not directly compete with your product or service. This is good, since you might want to strike some kind of partnership with them and get a link from their site by leaving a comment on the page.

Now, let's see whether, from a SEO point of view, there is any chance of taking this site's seat in the top ten. (Please note that I am just using this site as an example, searches from other PCs might show a different No 1 listing).

Competition Analysis Example: Step Five

To get a far more detailed view of the optimization of any top ten competitor, you now switch over to another SEO tool that is not free but affordable for most businesses. It's called 'Market Samurai' and you can download a 12 day free trial from www.marketsamurai.com/.

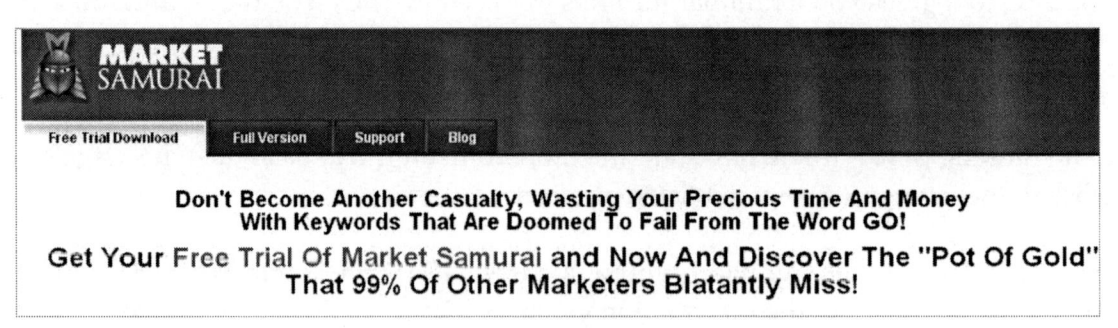

MARKET SAMURAI

Free Trial Download | Full Version | Support | Blog

Don't Become Another Casualty, Wasting Your Precious Time And Money With Keywords That Are Doomed To Fail From The Word GO! Get Your Free Trial Of Market Samurai and Now And Discover The "Pot Of Gold" That 99% Of Other Marketers Blatantly Miss!

www.marketsamurai.com

MarketSamurai gives you access to a wide variety of data about your competitors. For fast insights, this is what you can do: Create a 'New Project' by typing in "Golf Ball Logo", and generate the results. You will get a screen like this:

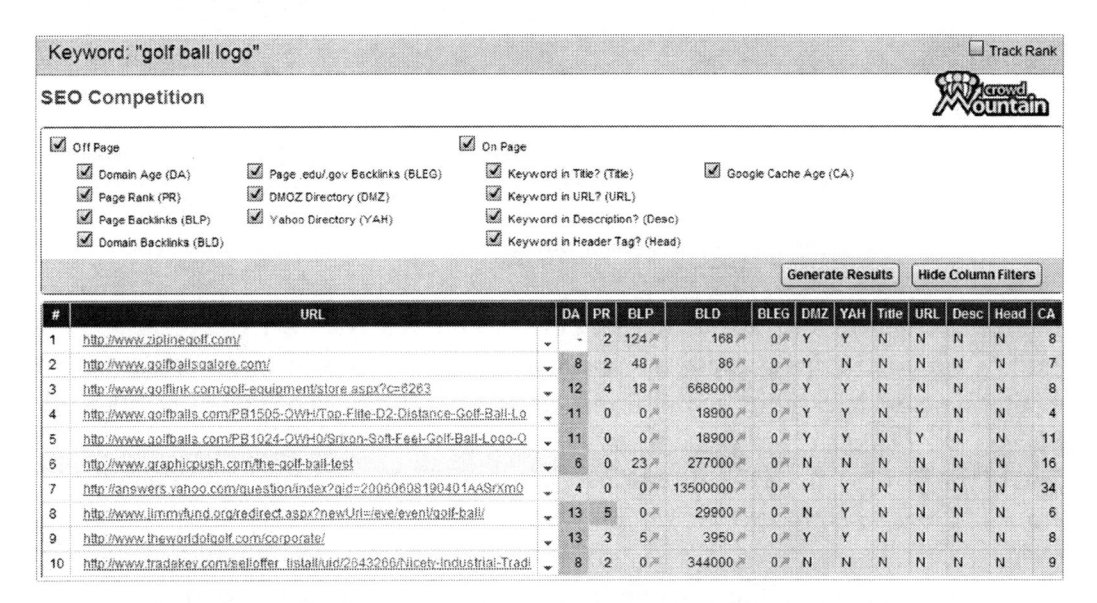

SEO competition for "Golf Ball Logo" as shown by MarketSamurai

Note that the page 'graphicPUSH: The Golf Ball Logo Test', which I have highlighted, is listed in position No 6 here and the number of links to the domain shows as 277,000. (You will regularly find different competitors in different listings, since they often change positions).

I now want to show you how you can analyze the 'PR' and the 'Anchor Text' for each of the sites listed in the top ten. Combining these two factors with the data you already know will give you a pretty good idea of how strong the competition is for your keyword.

In the screenshot overleaf, I placed a little arrow pointing to a triangle next to a company listing. In this case, I have chosen listing 6. Clicking here reveals the 'Additional Analysis Field', which shows you a lot of data including the PR Analysis, Anchor text Analysis, Google Trends etc.

PART II – Competition Analysis

#	URL	DA	PR	BLP	BLD	BLEG	DMZ	YAH	Title	URL	Desc	Head
1	http://www.ziplinegolf.com/	11	2	132	174	0	Y	Y	N	N	N	N
2	http://www.golfballsgalore.com/	8	2	50	86	0	Y	N	N	N	N	N
3	http://www.golflink.com/golf-equipment/store.aspx?c=6263	12	4	17	668000	0	Y	Y	N	N	N	N
4	http://www.golfballs.com/PB1505-OWH/Top-Flite-D2-Distance-Golf-Ball-	11	0	0	18900	0	Y	Y	N	Y	N	N
5	http://www.golfballs.com/PB1024-OWH0/Srixon-Soft-Feel-Golf-Ball-Logo	11	0	0	18900	0	Y	Y	N	Y	N	N
6	http://www.graphicpush.com/the-golf-ball-test	6	0	23	276000	0	N	N	N	N	N	N

PR Analysis | Anchor Text Analysis | Google Trends | Whois Information | Quantcast | Alexa

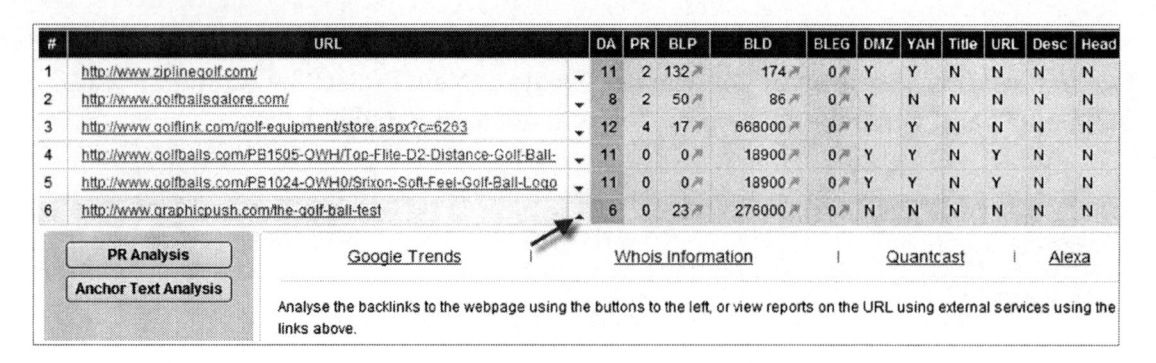

Analyse the backlinks to the webpage using the buttons to the left, or view reports on the URL using external services using the links above.

Additional analysis field within the MarketSamurai top ten listings.

(It might take the software some time to perform the Anchor Text Analysis, depending on your software settings and your Internet speed, but the result is worth the wait. You can check your actual Internet speed beyond what your provider tells you, at: www.speakeasy.net/speedtest/)

One of the things you will find out is how many links with the right keyword in the Link Text or 'Anchor Text' there are. Why is this important? Because you can pretty well assume that, if a page has dozens or even hundreds of links pointing to it with the right keyword in the Anchor Text, this is not by chance, and your competitor has done a good job optimizing his/her site.

To get the keyword into the Anchor Texts of all incoming links is a time-consuming task, and, if your competitor has optimized his/her page to that extent, you can expect a serious fight for the top listing regarding that keyword. This might influence your decision as to whether to spend money and time targeting this search term. For our example keyword 'Golf Ball Logo', this doesn't seem to be the case. How do I know this? Read on:

SEO Competition Analysis: http://www.ziplinegolf.com/

PR Analysis | Anchor Text Analysis | Google Trends | Whois Information | Quant

Anchor Text	Total
[preview]	1
buy logo golf balls	1
click to open in a new window	1
go to ziplinegolf	1
golf ball	6
golf ziplinegolf.com	8

ANCHOR TEXT: golf ball
http://funkyfinds.blogspot.com/2006_05_28_fun
http://funkyfinds.blogspot.com/2006_05_14_arc
http://funkyfinds.blogspot.com/2006_05_21_fun
http://funkyfinds.blogspot.com/2006_06_01_arc
http://funkyfinds.blogspot.com/2006_05_14_fun
http://funkyfinds.blogspot.com/2006_05_21_arc

ANCHOR TEXT: zipline golf offers many choices
http://www.ehow.com/how_4525309_buy-perso

Number of Inbound Links with the Keyword in the Anchor Text

The previous screenshot shows a part of the Anchor Text Analysis, for the No 1 listing in MarketSamurai, which is www.ziplinegolf.com (not www.graphicPUSH.com). Ziplinegolf.com is a really serious competitor who also wants to sell imprinted golf balls. So, let's look at them instead of www.graphicPush.com for more details. In the screenshot, you can see that ziplinegolf.com has only one link with a similar Anchor Text in it. It says 'buy logo golf balls' and, since the words are not even in the same order as your keyword phrase, that's promising!

You can now find out what 'PR' the site from which this link comes has. Remember, the quality of a link is very important, and that is hugely influenced by the quality of the site it's coming from.

In the screenshot below you can see that www.ziplinegolf.com gets a 'Total' of 134 links (133 without matching Anchor Text). 122 of them, the majority, come from sites with a PR 0. This is not good news for Ziplinegolf.com, but it's good news for you. In the 'Anchor Text' field, we see that the one single link to the site that **does** have a partially matching Anchor Text 'buy logo golf balls' also comes from a site with a PR 0. Even better news for you!

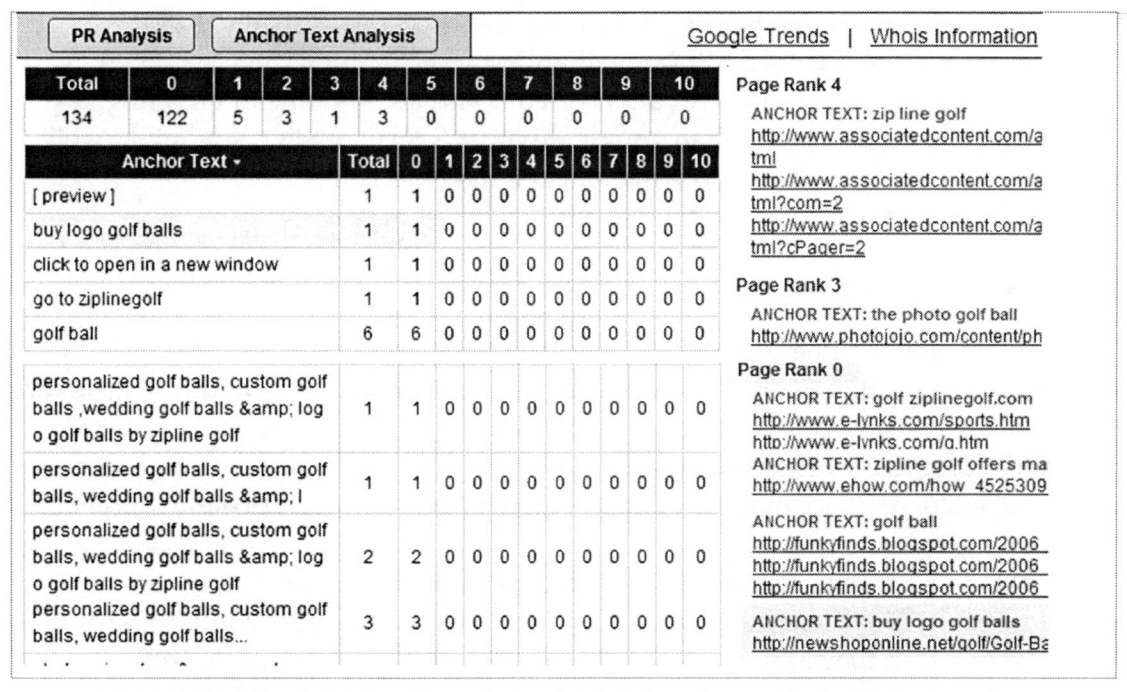

Total	0	1	2	3	4	5	6	7	8	9	10
134	122	5	3	1	3	0	0	0	0	0	0

Anchor Text	Total	0	1	2	3	4	5	6	7	8	9	10
[preview]	1	1	0	0	0	0	0	0	0	0	0	0
buy logo golf balls	1	1	0	0	0	0	0	0	0	0	0	0
click to open in a new window	1	1	0	0	0	0	0	0	0	0	0	0
go to ziplinegolf	1	1	0	0	0	0	0	0	0	0	0	0
golf ball	6	6	0	0	0	0	0	0	0	0	0	0
personalized golf balls, custom golf balls ,wedding golf balls & log o golf balls by zipline golf	1	1	0	0	0	0	0	0	0	0	0	0
personalized golf balls, custom golf balls, wedding golf balls & l	1	1	0	0	0	0	0	0	0	0	0	0
personalized golf balls, custom golf balls, wedding golf balls & log o golf balls by zipline golf	2	2	0	0	0	0	0	0	0	0	0	0
personalized golf balls, custom golf balls, wedding golf balls...	3	3	0	0	0	0	0	0	0	0	0	0

Page Rank 4
ANCHOR TEXT: zip line golf
http://www.associatedcontent.com/a tml
http://www.associatedcontent.com/a tml?com=2
http://www.associatedcontent.com/a tml?cPager=2

Page Rank 3
ANCHOR TEXT: the photo golf ball
http://www.photojojo.com/content/ph

Page Rank 0
ANCHOR TEXT: golf ziplinegolf.com
http://www.e-lynks.com/sports.htm
http://www.e-lynks.com/g.htm
ANCHOR TEXT: zipline golf offers ma
http://www.ehow.com/how_4525309
ANCHOR TEXT: golf ball
http://funkyfinds.blogspot.com/2006
http://funkyfinds.blogspot.com/2006
http://funkyfinds.blogspot.com/2006
ANCHOR TEXT: buy logo golf balls
http://newshoponline.net/golf/Golf-Ba

PR Analysis and Anchor Text Analysis showing the number of links to a site, where the links are coming from, the PR of the sites where the links are coming from and the Anchor Text in the links

PART II – Competition Analysis

The right part of the screenshot tells you from which page the link is coming. So, you can easily see whether you would like to approach that site and maybe get a link to your site too – with Anchor Text that matches your keywords, of course!

You now know that you have a pretty realistic chance – with all other parts of your site being equally search engine friendly - to overtake www.ziplinegolf.com. As they are your most direct competitor, it's likely that you could achieve a top search engine listing without too much effort. You have now just saved yourself a fair amount of the time and effort that would have been needed for a non-targeted site optimization.

So far, you have only checked out one competitor to your keyword, www.ziplinegolf.com. In that fashion, you can check the other competitors that are listed on Google's Page 1. This will tell you whether you can do better than their level of SEO, and get you a top listing on Google page one.

Summary - Competition Analysis Example

You now have some understanding of how to use three powerful SEO tools (Google's Free Keyword Tool, SEOToolbar and Market Samurai) and to quickly check demand and competition for any keyword you are thinking of targeting. If you can do just slightly better than your competitor's level of SEO, you might well take their spot in the top ten, Top Three or even the No 1 listing.

Some Give and Take

Competition analysis does not dictate your optimization techniques entirely, but it influences them and can help you to be focused and targeted. It is hugely helpful to know the box of tricks and techniques others are using, and you can use these tricks yourself to promote your own business. However, SEO also requires a good amount of testing and experience until you can be sure which technique or combination of techniques got you to No1.

For example, search engines do not update all their local databases simultaneously. This means the listings, for example, on Google's results page and the order in which they appear on Google can sometimes vary from PC to PC, town to town, or country to country. This leaves a certain amount of give and take in all competition analysis. If you find that your page is in Position 3 on Google's first results page on your PC, it might be in another position on someone's PC in another country, or town, or occasionally even next door.

Don't be put off by this. The benefits of being able to analyze your competition – even if the answers reveal a certain amount of grey area - and to search engine optimize your site effectively, far outweigh the amount of uncertainty that there is.

A Word of Caution: Copying exactly what your competition is doing is not a good idea. Instead, use their success and what they do right to inspire you. Adjust the techniques that work for them to suit your needs. Also, be aware that competitors sometimes include false keywords, tags and other elements to mislead and keep their competition at bay…

SUMMARY:

Competition Analysis to Save Time and Effort

Deciding which Internet marketing techniques to use, and which one to start off with, is no longer overwhelming. If you can quickly pinpoint the weaknesses in your competitors' campaigns you can outperform them by optimizing your business where it really matters.

In a nutshell – competition analysis helps you to be focused and to achieve maximum results with minimum time and effort. So, before you move on, take this step so you know who you are up against in order to win more customers and profits:

GROW Step 3: Know Your Competition to Fast Track to the Top

When analyzing your competition in the way we have just seen in the example, start with the first listing on search engine results Page 1 – the place where you would ideally like to have your page listed. Then, if you think the competition is too strong, work your way down the nine consecutive listings on Page 1.

Use competition analysis tools such as Market Samurai and others (see 'SEO Tools') to **check your competitors** so that you focus your campaign at the points where you can achieve the greatest advantage over them

In Part III, let's see how to boost the ranking of your site and to achieve a top listing on the search engines,

- ○ by placing keywords in the most essential places on your website – URL, Title Tag, Meta Tag, headline, sub-headline etc;
- ○ by grouping your keywords into Themes to make your site even more relevant to the search engines and your customers alike; and
- ○ by 'Silo-ing' your site in such a way that the search engines immediately detect you as important and relevant, and list you in top positions on their results pages.

Using even just one of the techniques can increase your online success significantly.

PART III:

How to Make Your Site More Competitive With 'On-Page SEO'

How to Get Your Own Pages Fit For the Search Engines

You have now decided on your primary keywords. You also know – after having analyzed your competition - where they have left loopholes in their optimization campaign and where you can now use your target keywords to the greatest effect. Let's now apply these keywords to your website or blog to make it more competitive. This is called on-page SEO because it optimizes all necessary aspects of your own site. Off-page optimization – the technique you use across the Internet to promote your site and create links to it - will be covered in Part IV.

An important reason for optimizing your website is to up its PR. This in turn affects the way you are listed on Google. Let me explain the term PR because it will come up again and again in this book. Google uses PR to categorize sites for their importance or relevance, and optimizing your site cleverly has a massive impact on how Google ranks you. The higher your PR – it can go up to 10 - the more likely it is that you can get a top listing on Google's results page. Since, on average, 80% of prospective customers come to a business via the search engines, this is imperative.

"Good rankings start at home." Leslie Rohde, Stompernet, STSE2

Building your PR and optimizing your website starts with positioning keywords strategically in several places on your website, from the Title Tag to the full article (Part IV). You can improve this by presenting content according to themes (Part V), and by structuring your website accordingly (Part VI). Let's get on with on-page SEO.

GROW Step 4:
Place Your Keywords Where They Give You Most Power

Knowing where to place your primary keywords and how to use your secondary, modified and long tail keywords effectively on your site can make or break your online campaign. A lot of this work is relatively easy to do. Get ready to take GROW Step 4:

Placing Keywords in Your Title Tags

The 'Title Tag' is the headline in bold of your listing as it comes up on the search engine results pages Google, Bing or Yahoo! etc. It is the most eye catching text on the results pages and contains the first words a searcher reads when coming across your entry. Therefore the Title Tag has the very important function in 'selling the click' to any searcher: If you write the Title Tag like an interesting, informative or compelling headline for an ad, your chance of getting the searcher to click on your listing instead of that of your competitor is far greater. Plus when you **combine** the Title Tag with the 'Meta Description' tag – the piece of text right under your 'Listing Headline' – both pieces of text combined will be a great ad for your site, and you further increase your chances to get the click.

Secondly, Google usually ranks pages well for the keywords that are positioned in these places like the Title Tag. Search engine experts agree that placing your keyword in your Title Tag has been one of the most important SEO techniques for years. (see the Top 10 SEO Ranking Factors discussed in Part II of this book). If your competition has not done this, you have a good chance of taking their spot on Google, other optimization factors being fairly equal. If they have done it already, it's best to do it too, since it doesn't involve much work.

How to Write a Good Title Tag

Here's how to write the Title Tag well and where to put keywords:

- First write the Title Tag text containing your main keyword. Remember, it has to be written for your future customer, in their words, not for the search engine

PART III – On-Page SEO

robots. Keep it short, compelling and relevant. Treat it like a headline that has to sell a product. The Title Tag's job is to get a customer to click on your listing, not elsewhere.

○ Have a look at competing pages that are listed in top positions and ask yourself, would I click on their listing, when I read their Title Tags? And why would I? What's good, compelling, intriguing?

○ In the Title Tag, don't use more than **eight** words or so because you don't want the end of your sentence to clip off. So-called 'ellipsed' title texts that end in '…' put people off and will get you fewer clicks and income: Research has shown that a listing in Position one on a Search Engine Results Page ('SERPS') with a poor title will get you a lower click through rate than a Position 2 listing with a great title! Google allows for **70 characters** including spaces and punctuation. These are the official numbers. However I have found that these change and I recently had to shorten the Title Tags in a site with over 20,000 pages … It is always best to check how much words and characters get shown in the major search engines, then make your Title Tag way shorter to stay on the save side.

○ To get to the top ten on the SERPS, you do have to keep in mind what the robots like of course. You will have to find a fine balance between Keyword Density, Keyword Prominence and Keyword Proximity in your Title Tag.

Let me briefly explain what this means:

Keyword Density here means how often you use your primary keyword in the Title Tag. This depends on how well you can write the title, including your primary keyword several times. With only 70 characters to choose from, there is not much room for mentioning your keyword more than two or three times.

Beware of keyword spamming your Title Tag. This means putting your primary keyword in many times like 'Discount Golf Equipment, Discount Golf Equipment, Discount Golf Equipment'. This may hurt your ranking, not improve it! Plus, it puts your customers off and you probably won't get the click to your site.

There is no absolute rule, but you should weave no more than three keywords into your Title Tag to keep it flowing naturally and to avoid getting penalized by the search engines and any searcher reading your Title Tag.

Keyword Prominence means how close to the beginning of the Title Tag your keyword appears. The rule here is, the earlier you mention your keyword in the title, the better.

Keyword Proximity describes how close the keywords appear to one another in the tag.

How You Put Your 'Title' in the 'Tag'

Once you have decided on the Title Tag you want to use, simply go to the source code of your site and type your text between the <title> ... </title> tags.

```
<html>
<head>
<title>Video Marketing Report for Download</title><br>          Title Tag
<meta name="description" content="This fr.ee Video Marketing Report reveals 4 important video marketing techniques
<meta name="keywords" content="Internet Video Marketing Report, Video Marketing Report, Internet Video Marketing,
<meta http-equiv="Content-Type" content="text/html; charset=iso-8859-1">
</head>
```

A Screenshot of a Title Tag

You can also check how many other pages have placed the same keyword in their title and are currently optimized for your keyword. Just put the following command into Google: 'allintitle:' plus the keywords you want to check for. An example would be 'allintitle: golf hotels Florida'.

Get the Click

When you type your main search word into Google you will find out that many Page 1 listings don't actually contain the main keyword for which they are listed in the title tag. In fact about 50% of the top sites on Google don't show the primary keyword in the title. However, I still advise you to put it in and to write a great title for ALL of your pages. It makes it easier to beat upper listings and makes it more likely that potential customers click through when they see their chosen keyword right in front of their eyes. You can't rely on the title tag alone to get you to Google's Page 1, but you shouldn't leave it out.

If you want a word other than your main keyword in the headline of your search engine listing - for example a buzzword that's too competitive to base your campaign upon, but would grab your future customers' attention – then use your main keyword in other ways to optimize your page as I describe later in this book.

PART III – On-Page SEO

Description Meta Tags

Search engines often display this text on their results page as a description of what your site is about, right underneath your bold Title Tag. So, it's like a sub-headline, and it is key to persuading a prospective customer to click through to your site. Writing a good description is an important part of your search marketing strategy, and in getting prospective customers to your site. If the description includes your keyword, it will reassure potential customers that you have the information they are looking for, and that you are their best choice.

For example, if you put "Wedding Favors" into Google.com, these listings which you see in the screenshot below are displayed on Google's first search results page at the time of writing.

These results are an example of good 'Meta Description' copywriting:

Screenshot of three different Google search results listings for 'Wedding Favors'.

See how the Title Tag together with the Meta Description are combined, as would be the case, for example, in a Google Adwords ad. Now, let's look at the elements which the webmasters who wrote these tags used:

Listings No. 1 and No. 2 have the same Title Tag, but differ as to which elements they use in their descriptions.

- **Listing No. 1** uses the keyword phrase 'Wedding Favors' twice, early on in their description (meaning with high prominence). Plus, the webmaster has added a telephone number and a price guarantee. This is good description writing.

- **Listing No.2** doesn't use any of the keyword phrases from the Title Tag in the description at all. Instead they rely on the 'trust' which they have built up since they started in this business, and their URL which does contain their keyword 'Wedding Favors'.

- **Listing No.3** puts the keyword more often in the Title Tag and mentions it twice in their description, once right at the beginning. Plus, they provide a map to their location with their address.

How to Write a Good Meta Description

Putting keywords in the meta description is certainly important, but it is also imperative that this text reads like good informative sales copy, not like hype, so you get the searcher's click. You do this by:

- writing a unique, compelling and relevant description that appeals to the searcher, not a general description.

- include 'facts and figures' if you can, i.e. freebies, offers, sales, guarantees, a clear Call to Action, even a phone number, if it makes sense.

- do not exceed 156 characters, which is about 25 words, (check in Google whether this figure remains up-to-date). You don't want your description to end mid sentence with ...", making it incomplete and unappealing (except if you want to make it intriguing on purpose).

There is no real guarantee that search engines will always display the text you put into your Description Tag on their results page. This is unfortunate, but, as testing has shown, by putting your keyword in the description, you can sometimes persuade the search engines to put it on the SERPs. If you don't provide a good description text, Google might use another, less relevant, text extract from your page, for example, the text which surrounds the keyword on your site that matches what the searcher has put into Google's search line. This text can be drawn from the following

locations:
- First 'alt' image text found on the page.
- First text found on the page.
- Additional heading tags on your page.
- Additional Alt text on your page.
- Navigation bar on the left hand side of the page.
- Copyright information on the bottom of the page.
- Wherever the keyword phrase is found on your page.

So, place your keywords strategically into the copy of your site to influence which text might show up on Google's results page to describe your site.

Keyword Meta Tags

Spammers used to pack 'Keyword Tags' full of keywords they wanted to get ranked for. Yahoo! and Bing might still index this tag but you won't get much ranking power from it and Google has disregarded the Keyword Tag altogether.

If you still want to place keywords here, put only low priority keywords in. Why? Because you potentially are giving your tricks away to your competitors. These days, there are excellent keyword tools that let you scrape all the keywords from your competitors' sites, simply by going through the Keyword Tag. You can use these tools to find those keywords at your competitors' sites that you might have forgotten in your campaign. But don't give away all of **your** keywords in your Keyword Tag.

Keywords in Your URL

The URL - the web address for a certain page on your website or blog - has great value for marketing to searchers. On the search results pages it appears underneath your meta Description Tag and in the browser window as you can see in the graphic opposite.

Search engines display URLs on the results page for certain keywords, like, for example, when you search the keyword 'Free Video Marketing Report' as you see opposite. The first listing has the keyword in the URL.

The wording of your URL, also influences whether a searcher thinks your listing is the most relevant one for his or her search. When you use descriptive text, including the searcher's keyword, in your URL, it can simply reassure the searcher that your site will have what he/she is looking for. Additionally, URLs are often used as links by other websites or blogs, and your URL can then become the description text, the 'Link Text / Anchor Text' of your link. Later on in Part VII of this book, we look at having the same keywords which you have on your page also in the Anchor Texts of your links. This is important to get ranked highly on Google, and it is another reason to write a good, short, descriptive and compelling URL containing your keywords.

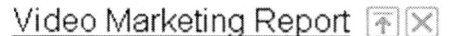

URLs as they appear on search engine results pages.

Here is a good guideline from Rand Fishkin, of SEOmoz.org on how to construct good URLs. I have extended some of the points made:

- **Employ empathy**
  Place yourself in the mind of a user and look at your URL. If you can easily and accurately predict the content you'd expect to find on that page, your URLs are appropriately descriptive. You can't spell out every last detail in the URL, but a clear name or summary in a handful of words, explaining what the site is about is a good start.

PART III – On-Page SEO

- **Shorter is better**
  While a descriptive URL is important, minimizing length and trailing slashes will make your URLs easier to copy and paste (into emails, blog posts, text messages, etc), and will be fully visible in the search results.

- **Keyword use is important (but overuse is dangerous)**
  If your page is targeting a specific term or phrase, make sure to include it in the URL. However, don't go overboard by trying to stuff in multiple keywords for SEO purposes - overuse will result in less usable URLs and can trigger spam filters (from email clients, search engines, and even people!).

- **Go static**
  With technologies like mod_rewrite for Apache and ISAPI_rewrite for Microsoft, there's no excuse not to create static URLs. (A static URL is a page that is always present in its entirety on the Internet, whether you open it or not, whereas with dynamic pages the content get pulled up from a database when a visitor clicks on the URL).

  Even single dynamic parameters in a URL can result in lower overall ranking and indexing. When SEOmoz.org switched from dynamic URLs - e.g. *'www.seomoz.org/blog?id=123'*, to static URLS - e.g. *'www.seomoz.org/blog/11-best-practices-for-urls'*, in 2007 it saw a 15% rise in search traffic over the following six weeks.

- **Choose descriptives whenever possible**
  Rather than selecting numbers or meaningless figures to categorize information, use real words. For example, a URL like *www.thestore.com/hardware/screwdrivers* is far more usable and valuable than *www.thestore.com/cat33/item4326*.

- **Use hyphens to separate words**
  Not all of the search engines accurately interpret separators such as underscore "_,", plus "+," or space "%20,". So, use the hyphen "-" character to separate words in a URL.

- **Canonical URLs**

  In essence canonical URLs can create problems for your site in the sense that some of your pages might get indexed twice. The search engines don't like duplicate versions of content on your site and therefore will punish your search engine rankings if they find more than one copy of the same content on your site. This is one of the most common SEO problems for sites and can be fixed so easily.

  Below is an extended explanation of how to test your site for 'duplicate content' problems plus how to fix it. If you are not so much interested in the technical side of it – which I completely understand – hand this task over to your IT or SEO person.

  Here is the technical explanation: Some webmasters use inconsistent link structures in their sites that will get the same content indexed twice or even several times under various URLs. The canonical version of any URL is the most authoritative version indexed by major search engines. Webmasters should always use consistent linking structures all through their sites to make sure they direct the maximum amount of PR to the URLs they want indexed.

  When you are linking to the root level of a site or a folder index, it is best to end the link location with a forward slash ('/') rather than including the 'index.html' or 'default.asp' filename in the URL. Be aware that the search engines consider the following URLs as different pages and therefore would probably index them twice or more times:

  - http://www.Internet-Experts-Live.com/
  - http://www. Internet-Experts-Live/index.shtml
  - http://Internet-Experts-Live.com/
  - http://Internet-Experts-Live.com/default.asp

  If you want to see whether your site suffers from this common problem, open the Firefox or Internet Explorer browser and type your site URL with and without the 'www' suffix. If the URL redirects to one single version, you are fine. The next step is to do the same test with standard file extensions such as 'index.htm(l)', '/index.php' or '/default.asp'.

All these versions, including your internal links, should point to the same URL version that you have chosen. Then, get your IT / SEO people or webmaster to set up 301 redirects to always point to your preferred version. Log into your Google Webmaster Tools account and set up your preferred URL. There is now a so-called 'Canonical URL Tag', supported by the major search engines to help webmasters and site owners eliminate self-created duplicate content in the index so your webmaster or SEO expert can sort the issue for your site.

Page Subtitles or Headings and 'Image Alt Text'

'Page Subtitles' and 'Paragraph Headings', defined in HTML as <h1> and <h2> …, are a way of getting your primary, secondary and related keywords in key places on your page. You simply write a subtitle for a paragraph and put the relevant keywords in it.

Also, emphasize certain words with subtitles and font styles like 'bold', 'underline', 'italics' etc. Google understands that these words seem to be important for your content and, therefore, your page might be more relevant than others for that particular word.

The 'text alt image' - the text which holds the place of an image on your site when the image can't be seen - is yet another way of getting keywords mentioned on your page. But, beware if you use only your primary keyword everywhere on your page, the search engines will not like it. Instead use variations of your primary keywords and your secondary keywords, too.

Make sure that your online images load fast, otherwise they can slow your page down. When you put all the right keywords in the right places but your page doesn't load within six seconds, all your other optimization work might have been lost. Why? Simply because, if the page loads too slowly, your potential customers will have left before they can even see your products and services. Therefore, optimize your images for best quality and smallest file size to ensure quick loading times.

Plus Google has just announced that 'page loading speed' will become a SEO ranking factor with the release of its new search engine infrastructure Google Caffeine. So, the slower your page loads the less likely it is to rank highly on Google.

Keywords in The Body Of Your Text

When you write your text, make sure to avoid **'keyword stuffing'** – which means don't use too many keywords that break the natural flow of a text. Of course, the longer your article or text, the more keywords you can put in, which is fairly obvious. Again, when you put your keywords/phrases in bold, italic, bulleted lists, or in other text that is specially formatted, the search engines pick up those keywords more easily.

Where Should Keywords Appear in My Text?

Ken Evoy of Sitesell.com says "When you apply your keyword to your texts and articles, spread keywords and keyword phrases in an hour-glass like shape across the page." This means using more keywords in the beginning of the text, whereas the middle part would have fewer keywords, and towards the end you would increase your keywords again. In general, an even natural spread of keywords throughout the text with mild hour glass shaping, in most cases brings you the greatest success with prospective customers and search engine robots.

How Often Should Keywords Appear in My Texts?

Business owners, SEO experts and webmasters have, for some time, tried to find **one** formula that would explain how often you need to include a keyword into a certain size online text to get a good listing on the SERPS. You might hear that the 'Keyword Density' (which means how often a keyword should be used in a text) should be about 2% - 3%. That is not really the case, and a lot of SEO experts frown if you mention Keyword Density since there is not one single formula that fits all sites in relation to how often to use keywords in a text.

    However, you can use Keyword Density to evaluate your competition and what you have to do to get a top ranking for a specific keyword. At least to a certain extent. Let's say you are interested in targeting the keyword phrase 'tailor made golf bags'. Now, you want to know whether you could compete for a top ten listing in Google for that keyword phrase? From looking at Google's keyword tool for that term, we can guess that with the amount of searches per month (~ 5,000 / mth) and our own site not being one of the biggest golf sites on the Internet, we would be happy to secure a Top ten listing. Let's see how we could get onto the first search results page.

PART III – On-Page SEO

When you put 'tailor made golf bags' into Google, you get something like this (at the time of writing):

Taylor Made Golf Bags at Compare Store Prices UK
Compare Prices of **Taylor Made Golf Bags** at Compare Store Prices UK. ... Compare prices and read reviews for **Taylor Made Golf Bags** then buy online and get a ...
www.comparestoreprices.co.uk/by.../**taylor-made-golf-bags**.asp - Cached - Similar

Taylor Made Golf Bags at GlobalGolf.com
Taylor Made golf bags. GlobalGolf.com golf store offers superior selection, service, and quality for your golf bag equipment needs.
www.globalgolf.com/gallery/.../-/bid.../taylor-made.aspx - Cached - Similar

taylor made golf bags - offers from taylor made golf bags ...
taylor made golf bags manufacturers directory - over 3000000 registered importers and exporters. **taylor made golf bags** manufacturers, **taylor made golf bags** ...
www.tradekey.com/ks-**taylor-made-golf-bags**/ - Cached - Similar

Taylor Made, Taylormade, Taylor Made Golf, Taylormade golf, R7 ...
Taylor-Made Golf Accessories Accessories · Taylor-Made Golf Apparel Apparel · **Taylor-Made Golf Bags** Bags · Taylor-Made Golf Balls Balls ...
https://www.golfcircuit.com/Taylor-Made-Golf/_5_.html - Cached - Similar

Taylor Made - Golf Bags
Offering golf equipment, golf gifts, and golf accessories including personalized golf balls, used golfballs, logo golf balls, golf shoes, golf bags, ...
www.golfballs.com/B1-9933/Taylor-Made-.html - Cached - Similar

Taylor Made Irons - Mens Drivers - Mens Cart Bags Utility / Hybrid ...
We have Taylor Made Golf Clubs, **Taylor Made Golf Bags**, Taylor Made Putters, Taylor Made Hats and much more. Taylor Made Golf equipment features the latest ...
www.discountgolfworld.com/brands/taylormade - Cached - Similar

Natural listings in Google for 'tailor made golf bags'

Place Your Keywords Where They Give You Most Power – GROW Step 4

Once you know who the top ten listings, (the top ten pages) are for 'your' keyword phrase, you can check how well the pages are optimized for the most widely agreed search engine rankings factors to-date. (See PART II: Outsmarting and Outwitting Your Competition; top ten Search Engine Ranking Factors 2009)

If you believe that you can indeed beat at least one of them to their spot, you then find out what the Keyword Densities of your competitor's pages are. This simply means how many words they have used and how often they have they included the target keyword phrase 'tailor made golf bags' into the text of their pages. As you will quickly see, some include the actual term more often on the page than others. See the No1 listing which is 'www.CompareStorePrices.co.uk/…'below:

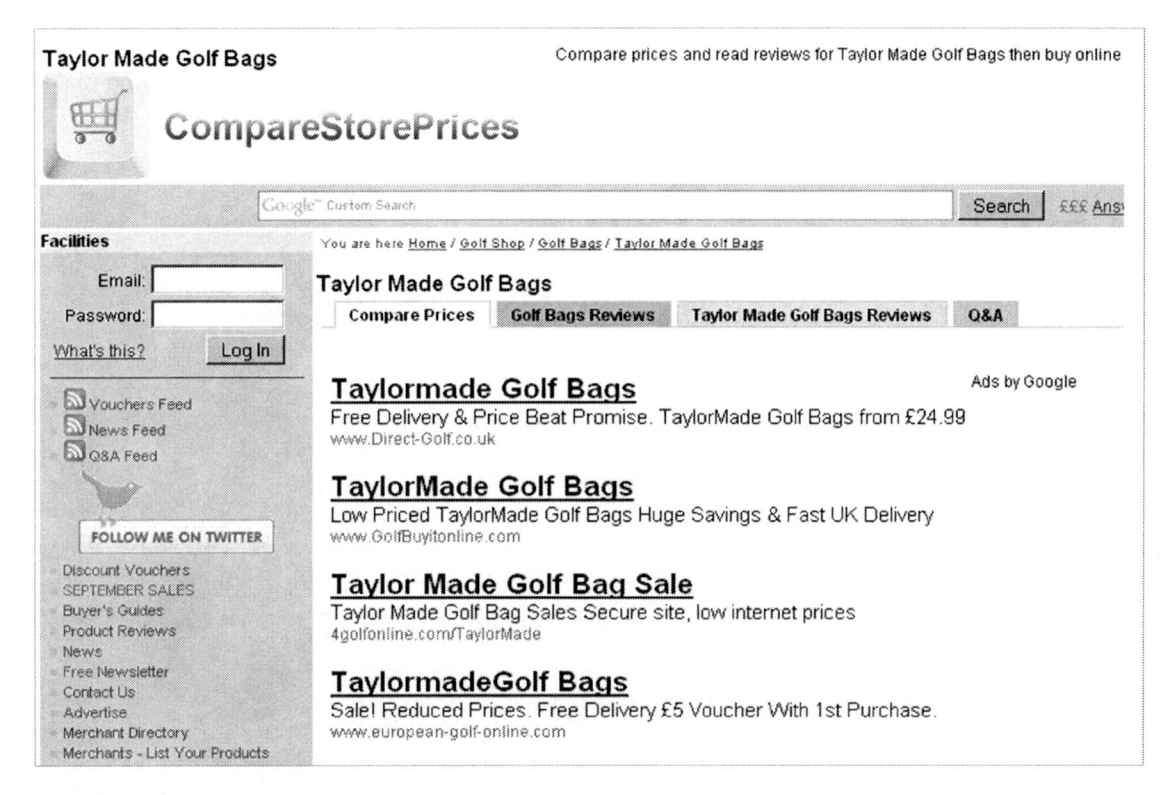

Shopping comparison site 'CompareStorePrices.co.uk' is using the keyword phrase 'taylor made golf bags' several times in the body text. ('taylor' might actually be the wrong spelling but even this spelling produces some results.)

PART III – On-Page SEO

And the listing in position 2 on Google is 'GlobalGolf.com':

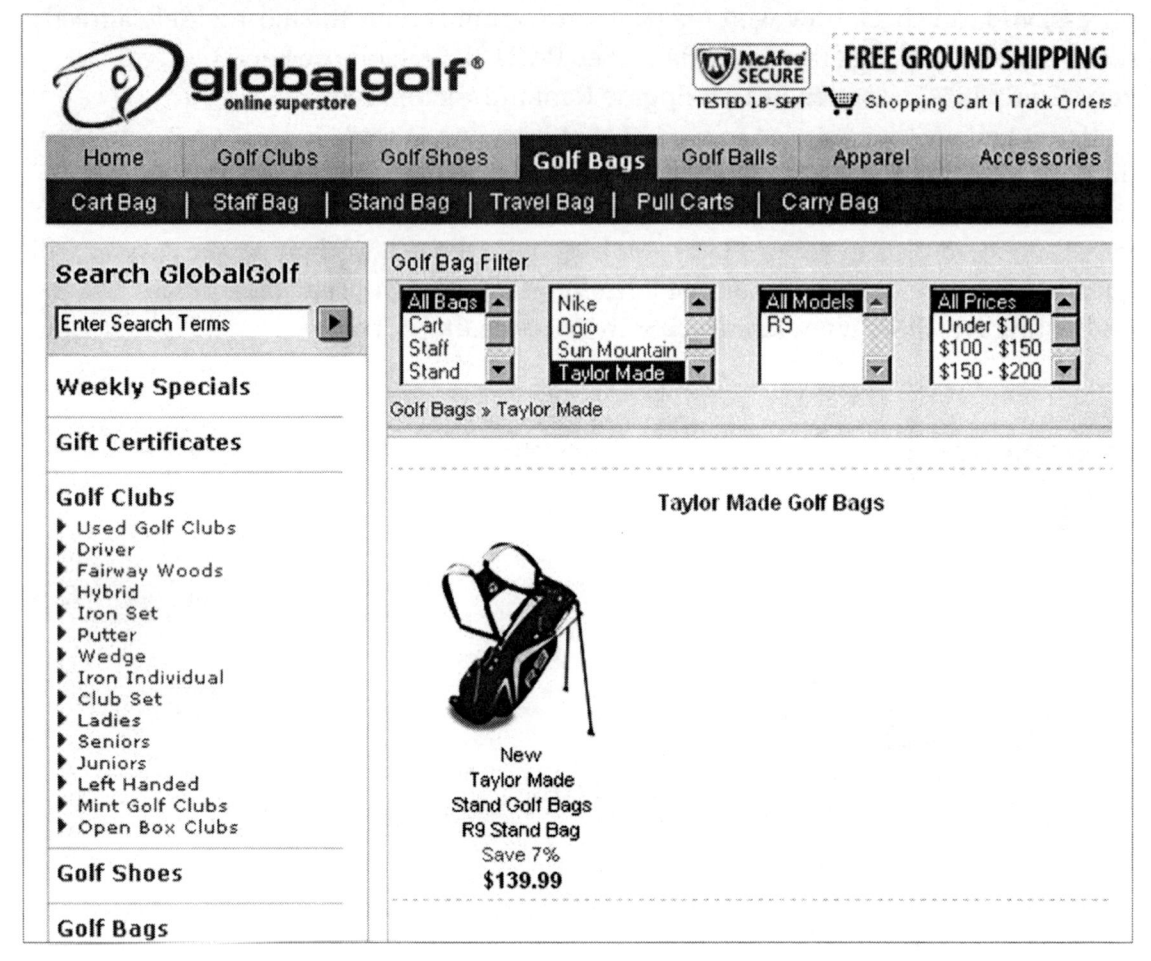

E-commerce site 'GlobalGolf.com' is using the keyword phrase 'taylor made golf bags' rarely in the body text.

You will have a good chance to take one of the top ten spots on Google if you...

- ○ are on equal search engine ranking terms with your competitors and
- ○ you place an equal amount of unique pages (or more), optimized for the search term, on your site or blog
    - ❏ using more text words;
    - ❏ a higher keyword density; and
    - ❏ a more focused keyword theme, with primary as well as secondary keywords

The real power in ranking for your keyword comes not so much from simply repeating your keyword in the text, but from grouping your primary keywords with a number of highly-relevant, secondary keywords into a so-called 'keyword theme', which I'll explain on the next pages.

Walking the Tightrope to Avoid Spamming

If you do your keyword optimization too well, and the exact same keyword appears everywhere on a specific page - in your URL, in your Title Tag, your Meta Tags, in your page subtitles and in the text - the search engines might get suspicious.

For example, it might make them wary if you have the same keyword in your URL and Title Tag. Since the Title Tag is one of the first things the search engine robots check to see what your page is about, you should put the exact keyword in the Title Tag and in some of your page headings, but **not** in the URL at the same time. But, you could place variations of your keyword in the URL. For example, if your primary keyword is 'Golf Vacations Florida', use something like 'Florida Golf Vacations' or ' Florida Golf Vacation Packages' in your URL.

To Sum Up:

You now have a pretty good idea in which places to position your keywords on your site, how often to put them and what to avoid. Before I move on to show you very effective ways of 'clustering' or 'theming' your keywords in your online copy, I urge you to make sure you have mastered GROW Step 4:

GROW Step 4 :

Place your primary and secondary keywords in the most essential places on your website – URL, Title Tag, Meta Tag, headline, sub-headline etc. Avoid keyword spamming and keep your text compelling, readable and informative, so you get the click of the visitor who has found you on the search engines.

GROW Step 5:
'Theme' Your Content and Get Found by the Search Engines

'Theming', in simple words, means grouping only related material and keywords together onto a single page on your site or blog, and leaving all non-related information out. Google and other search engines are looking for clusters of semantically-related words that demonstrate expertise in a certain topic, so they can safely send searchers to your website and be sure they will be satisfied with what they find. Professional theming makes your site relevant in their eyes, because all the answers and information to a particular question are in one place.

"Build a Theme Park – not a Shopping Mall" Rosalind Gardner

Even if you have fewer links pointing to your site than your competitor has pointing to his (links are one of the most important factors to increase your page listing with Google– see Part VII), your site might still overtake your competitor's just by using proper theming. This is a powerful optimization technique, and straightforward to do.

How Theming Can Help You Beat Your Greatest Competitor - An Example

Here is an example of a website that ranks better for 'theming' competitive keywords than many of its bigger competitors: Adam Pick set up the site heart-valve-surgery.com a couple years ago because at the age of 33, he had to have double heart valve surgery. He then wrote a book to support patients and caregivers through the entire heart valve surgery process. Heart surgery is not a subject that anyone can write about in detail, so you can imagine that only educational sites (.edu) and very authoritative sites tend to rank for keywords about heart surgery. However, Adam's site ranks Number one in Google for over 60 such keywords and currently, over 1,400 other keywords (at the time of writing). You can check this yourself with tools such as Semrush (www.semrush.com/info/heart-valve-surgery.com).

This is an example of how theming of primary, modified / long-tail and related keywords in expert theme articles can help you to overtake larger competitors. Google is ranking Adam Picks' site above WebMD (www.webmd.com), Merck

PART III – On-Page SEO

(www.merck.com) and Cleveland Clinic www.clevelandclinic.org (one of the most respected heart institutes in the world). How could you achieve something similar yourself? Let me talk you through it in Step 5:

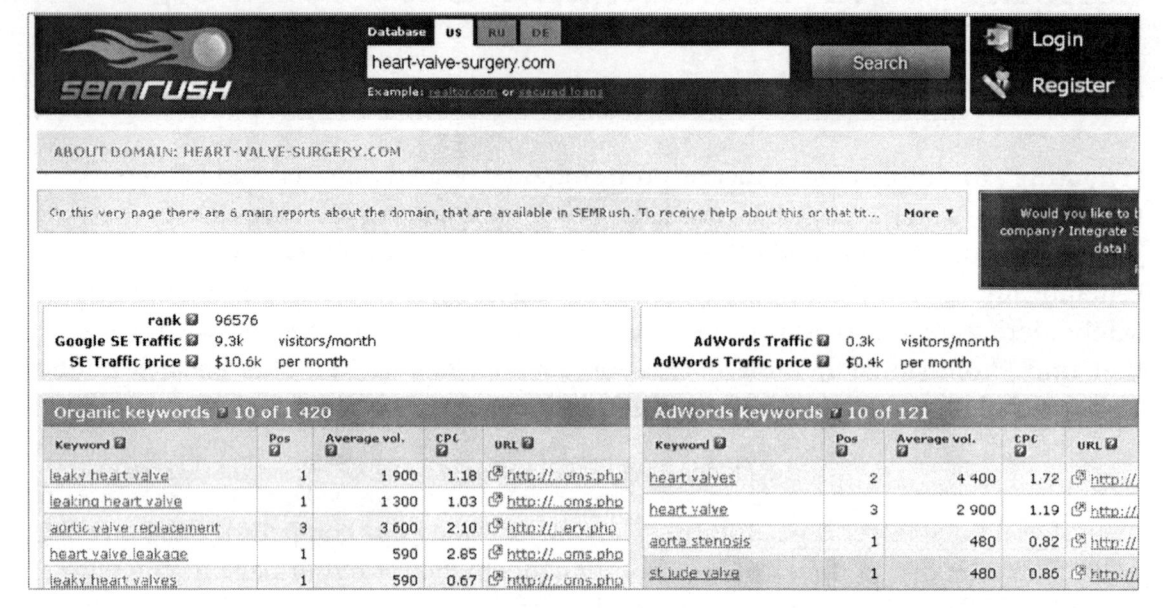

Semrush: Organic / Adwords Keywords for 'heart-valve-surgery.com'

Arranging Keywords into Themes for a Google Page One Listing

> *"It is important to use the keyword phrase throughout the page where it makes sense. As engines get more sophisticated, it's not just the targeted keyword phrase that counts, but the mix of all the words on the page that help to determine what the page is about."*
> Scottie Claiborne

Scottie Claiborne's quote indicates how important it has become to theming your keywords. To do that, you simply order your content so that related material stands together, and you keep it separate from other material. You 'group' your primary, secondary, modified / long-tail and related keywords together into one specific theme on a certain page so that these words co-occur on the same page.

Of course, you are not just 'theming' for the search engines alone. By creating one theme per page, you are doing yourself and your site visitors a favor too. Clearly, visitors do not want to see all sorts of unrelated content on your page that they just found, they want answers to their specific questions and information to hand, so they can stop searching. If the visitors don't like your page, Google does not rank it highly either.

For example: If you are selling sports vacations and sports equipment, don't put your 'cycling holidays' on the same page as the 'golf equipment' you are selling. This wouldn't achieve top rankings for either, since the two are essentially different products and most likely appeal to different visitors. Keep them apart. Create one page - or if you have the time, one site or blog - for golf equipment, and a separate one for cycling holidays. This sounds obvious but check your own site to remind yourself where you may have placed only slightly-related products or services on the same page that, taken to separate pages, would achieve higher rankings on their own.

Grouping your products and keywords into one theme is really straightforward. However, not many companies do it properly to the extent that they get a top ten listing, including some of your competitors. This is a great opportunity for you.

How Minimal 'Theming' Can Give You Maximum Results

It might sound like a tall order to theme all the content on your website. So, just start with one or two pages. When they start to rank well with Google, they will lift other pages of your site up too. Google has recently given content theming and related keywords a lot of attention. Individual web pages seem no longer to get ranked based only on their own content, but also based on the content and rank of other web pages within that website. So, when one page of your site gets a high ranking, it can pass some of its ranking power on to other pages of your site or blog.

11 Important Pieces of Advice on How To Create a Well-Themed Page:

Now let me give you a list of mini-steps about how you can create a well-themed page from scratch:

1. First, choose the general subject for your theme from your market research.
2. Put your primary, most important keyword into Google's free keyword tool to find modified / long tail and related keywords, and combine these into one group per page.

3. For each keyword phrase, find some variations that go onto the theme page. Variations are usually plurals, single, or add-ons such as "ing", "ed", etc. In many cases, you can change the order of words in keyword phrases too.
4. Use the top ten listed websites or blogs in Google (Yahoo! and Bing) to extract the most common keywords used within that theme.
5. Go to an article site like Ezinearticles.com and select the top 10/20 articles written by experts on your chosen theme. Go through each article and extract 350-500 words and phrases commonly used in the articles.
6. Cross reference your selection of themed keywords with keywords on web 2.0 sites like Hubpages.com, Squidoo.com, Propeller.com etc. which are considered to be authorities.
7. Select titles and text sub-titles for your theme which have a good volume of search traffic and moderate competition.
8. Write a 500 -1000 word piece of text on your chosen topic for your page theme, or get someone to write it for you. (Ideally create two unique themed pages for each of your themes to allow for 'double listings' on Google's Search Results Pages.)
9. Finally, integrate the top most commonly-used modified / long tail and related keyword search phrases into your text and put it onto your site, in your blog, or on an authoritative web 2.0 site.
10. Promote your own piece of text with Social Bookmarking and other link - building techniques.
11. Monitor how your page is moving upwards in the rankings with tools such as Marketing Samurai, and improve its performance as you see fit.

This list was inspired by Dr Andy Williams and is easier to do than it sounds. If you feel unsure about your writing skills, you can always outsource the content writing to a professional writer and focus on the marketing part.

To Sum Up:

Before moving on to how to consolidate your themed pages in your site structure, make sure you have taken Step 5 and have created a themed webpage or site:

GROW Step 5:

Organise your site content according to **themes**. You do this by placing distinct products or pieces of information on separate pages and use primary, secondary, long tail / related keywords accordingly, so the search engines consider your site well-themed and rank it highly.

GROW Step 6:
Create a 'Silo Structure', Turning Your Store into a Goldmine

We have just learned that 'themed' content is very popular with the search engines. Let's now look at how you can multiply this effect with the search engines, by constructing your whole site according to the same principle. The result is called a 'Silo Structured Site'.

What's that? – you might ask and I don't blame you. It's a funny term and most people probably think of farming methods in the American Midwest, but that's not what we mean here. It is actually pretty straightforward: It means using specific categories for your products or services, and linking from one product or service category to another in a special way.

> *"After more than 6 years… I have not met a site where I could not create ranking improvements from internal linking changes alone"*
> *Leslie Rohde*

Silos connected only at the top – like the landing pages of a silo structured site.

PART III – On-Page SEO

You have probably deduced that we are using the term 'silo structure' in a similar way to the word 'categories'. However, we use the term 'silo structure' because we want to emphasis that, with silos, your main connection is between the top level pages of each category or silo. This means you don't connect the different sub-pages of different silos to each other.

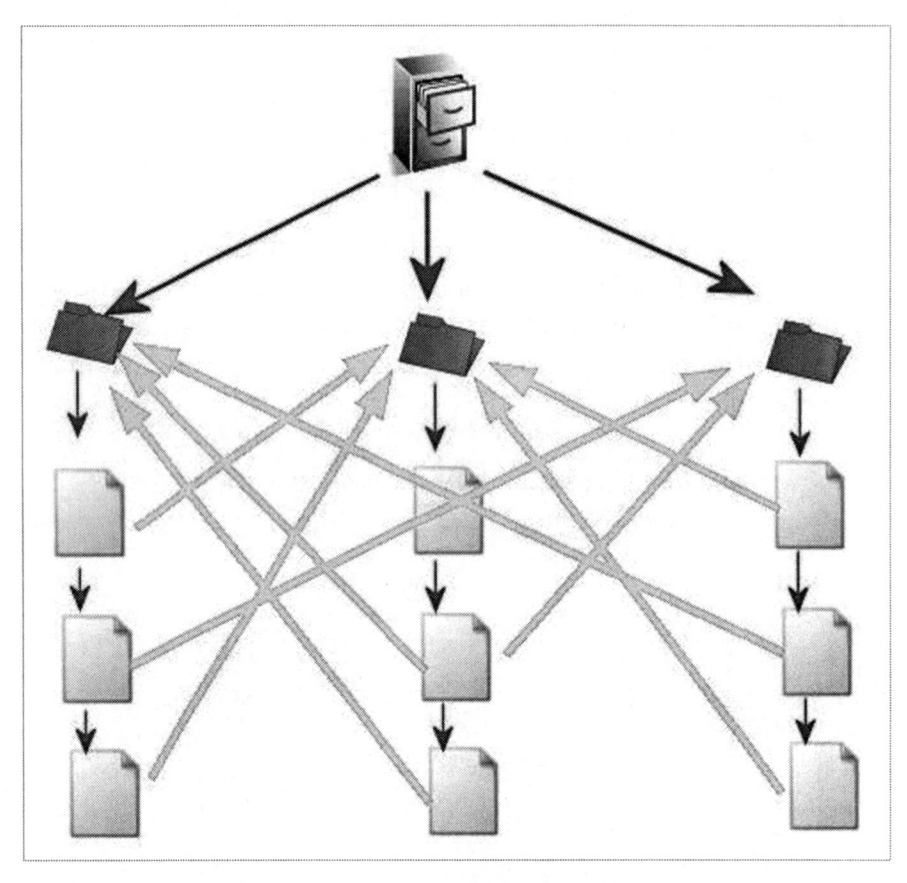

Silo Structure Illustration by ThemeZoom.com,
[Copyright © ThemeZoom.com]

When you want to connect one sub-page to another category, you simply point to the top level page of the other category, not to another sub-page, just like in the graphic above. That's the most important feature of this step. Imagine it like a grain silo where the wheat is stored separately from the barley and there is no connection between the two containers so the grains can't get mixed up! Basically, it is a way of keeping related information in one silo container - or in our case on one webpage or blog category - separate from others.

Google and the other search engines prefer you to structure the information on your site or blog in this kind of a way and, if you do so, will a) index your site quickly and b) give you a higher ranking than those of your competitors that are not using this structure.

Why Does Google Favour Silo-Structured Sites?

Google wants to make sure that if someone searches for a certain product online and clicks on a link, that searcher then finds only information on the page he/she is taken to that is highly relevant to what he/she is looking for.

In that sense, a silo structure helps the search engines, the visitors and you too, since visitors find such a well-organized and relevant site very satisfying. Tests conducted by J P Schoeffel, have shown that visitors stay longer on such a site and follow call-to-actions more, such as subscribing to lists, buying e-books etc.

Therefore, a search engine optimized silo structure, built with profitable niche keyword themes, will get your pages indexed quicker and give you a better search engine ranking than those of your competitors who don't do this, bringing you more traffic and more prospective customers. Get started and take step 6 - it's effective and relatively easy to do:

Building a Silo Structure

In the paragraph on **'Theming'**, I've explained that if you have a 'Golf' website, selling a range of golf related products, it's advisable to place 'golf equipment' on different pages than 'golf vacations' or 'golf tournaments'. To take this further and build a Silo Structure, you would create separate category silos on your website with pages for each category, i.e. one page for golf equipment, golf tournaments etc.

What turns your site into a silo structure is how these sub pages are linked to each other. Don't connect them horizontally; keep the 'golf tournament' silo totally separate from the 'golf equipment' silo. The links coming from one individual page or 'silo' should only link to the top pages or landing pages of the other silo. This will give your website the greatest SEO and PageRank effect.

Good Silo Categories

If you have quite a large site that already ranks for a number of lucrative keywords and you want to compete successfully with bigger companies, then it would be a good idea to categorize these pages with a silo structure. You can use Google's great free 'Search-Based Keyword Tool' to see which categories to use with your keyword. I will put up a video explaining how to go about finding categories that Google thinks are relevant for your keyword. To watch the video, just go to: www.Internet-Experts-Live.com to GROW Step 6.

However, if you don't have an extensive site yet, you could transform your site into a blog site, which makes categorization easier. A blog can look just like a website, but also has the advantage that it is generally indexed more quickly than a website.

When you set up a blog, either as a 'stand alone' or with your website, you can use the Wordpress.com blogging platform, since it is the most popular and flexible platform. Plus, it allows for the easy integration of search engine optimized blog themes, like the professional version of Semiologic [see the **'Resources'** section at the end of this book]. This can give you an additional search engine ranking advantage over your competition.

Sitemaps to Help Everyone Find What They're Looking For

Sitemaps in general will help your visitors and search engine robots to find things more easily on your site. There are two types of sitemaps - one for your site visitors and one for the search engine robots (and you can also include keywords in these site maps):

1. Site Maps for the Visitors

These site maps help your visitors to find their way through your site to the pages they are most interested in. In general, a site map links to all pages of your site but it might be better to show only the most important pages; those that you really want your visitors to see.

If you put up all pages on your site map, a visitor can get overwhelmed and might not be able to find the landing page they look for. If this happens, he/she won't be able to follow the path to conversion you had designed for him or her. Have a look at other sites' sitemaps for inspiration, and don't forget that even on your sitemap, you can optimize for keywords, using compelling text that entices your visitors to click on the actual links.

2. Sitemaps for Search Engines

Sitemap type 2s are so called XML Sitemaps, e.g. a Google Sitemap. They allow you to submit URLs and additional page information directly to the search engines. They increase the search engine visibility of your site by providing search engine robots with links to index all of the pages of your site. This helps particularly when you have dynamic pages or others that are difficult for the search engine spiders to reach. To find out how to create such a XML Sitemap, you or your webmaster can access information on this site: http://sitemaps.org

To Sum Up:

A well-organized site is good value for your visitors and appreciated by the search engines. This technique is very effective but not complicated to put in place. You have now almost mastered off-page optimization techniques, but before you move on, make sure you have taken GROW Step 6:

GROW Step 6:

Organize your site well using a **Silo Structure.** This simply means you keep the 'themed' pages separate in different categories. Interlink them only from one sub-page to the top page of another silo category, not horizontally.

PART III – On-Page SEO

SUMMARY:

Making Your Site Search-Engine Friendly

Placing your keywords in strategic positions on your website, 'theming' your content and giving your site or blog a 'silo structure' are important ways to make your site search engine friendly. This will give you a serious advantage over your competition and will have a substantial impact on the ranking of your site. It means getting increasing numbers of prospective customers coming to your site where you can then win their business.

    These techniques persuade Google and other search engines that your site is particularly valuable for a specific keyword and keyword theme. This, in turn, gives it the chance to rise to the highest positions on the SERPS.

And just in case you missed anything, let me recap on PART III of this book; to optimize your own site effectively, take these three GROW Steps:

GROW Step 4: Place Your Keywords Where They Give You Most Power

Place your primary and secondary keywords in the most essential places on your website – URL, title tag, meta tag, headline, sub-headline etc.

GROW Step 5: 'Theme' Your Content and Get Found by the Search Engines

Theme your site **content** using primary, secondary, long tail / related keywords and place separate themes on separate pages.

GROW Step 6: Create a 'Silo Structure', Turning Your Store into a Goldmine

Organize your site well using a **silo structure.** This simply means you keep the 'themed' pages separate in single categories. Interlink them only from one sub-page to the top page of another silo category, not horizontally. This makes your pages specific to what prospective customers are looking for. As a result your site becomes very user-friendly, searchers like it and search engines rank your site highly.

So far, we looked at SEO techniques that you can apply on your own site; so-called 'on-page' SEO factors. Now, let's switch to the outside world. In other words, what you can do on other people's websites to further improve the search engine optimization of your own site or blog.

In the next part, find out how you can use link building techniques to propel your site or blog forward to the first search engine results page.

PART IV:

How to Use Other Sites to Get Ranked Highly - 'Off-page SEO'

Off-page SEO

In the previous part we looked at what you can do on your site to optimize it for the search engines. Now let's focus on other sites on the Internet, many of them being 'Social Media Sites', to see how you can use those to further optimize your own site or blog.

Methods to promote your site using third party sites – such as link building and article marketing – are very effective with the search engines, particularly with Google. Google pays a lot of attention to how other Internet sites rate yours, and if they rate yours highly, Google will also give it a high ranking. If others appreciate your output, Google will do the same.

So, if you want to outsell your competition and take their customers, discover here how you can make your site appear very popular across the Web, by combining a handful of essential optimization techniques into a power strategy. This will give your website a massive boost, and your business exponential growth.

In this part, I will give you tools to apply the most powerful so-called 'off-line SEO' techniques, and I will show you how to put them in place, step-by-step. Even just employing one or two of these powerful techniques can increase the profitability of your online business significantly. Here's the first one – link building.

GROW Step 7:

Build Quality Links and Get Listed Highly on Google

Google says:

> *Everybody "…can improve the Rank of their Sites by increasing the Number of high-quality Sites that link to their Pages."*
> *(Google Webmaster Center)*

Links from other websites pointing to your site or blog are amongst the most important factors that search engines take into account when deciding how important and relevant your site is, and where it should be listed on their results pages. This is particularly important for a Google listing. Links tell Google that you are relevant for your chosen subject, and the more good quality links you have, the greater the chance to get ranked highly.

What a 'Link' is and Why You Want it

In a piece of text on a website or blog, so-called "click here" links are built in to take you to relevant content on other websites. You have probably seen them many times. They are usually in blue ink and underlined. When such a link points to your site and has the right keyword instead of 'click here' in the blue underlined text (the so-called Link Text or anchor-text), this link provides a boost to the ranking of your webpage.

However, there is a difference in the quality and ranking-power of individual links. If the page that links to you is popular and ranks highly itself, then this link is worth more in the eyes of Google, and as a result Google ranks your site higher too.

The more good quality links there are pointing to your website, the more popular it is for Google, which in turn ranks your site highly and gives it a better listing. All this leads to more customers finding your site.

PART IV – Off-Page SEO

Page Rank – The Essence of Getting a Good Listing on Google

Let me take a little detour here and explain the important online phenomenon of 'Ranking'. I have already explained in Part III that search engines 'rank' websites to categorize them for their importance or relevance. Google (and only Google) uses a technique called PageRank to do this. The higher your PR – it can go up to 10 - the more likely it is that you can get a top listing on Google's results page. Optimizing your site professionally has a massive impact on how Google ranks you, and even just using one of the techniques explained in the upcoming part can increase your online success significantly.

It's important for you to know that Google treats the single pages of your site individually. For Google, each page gets a distinct PR, which is probably different from your homepage's PR. For starters, this PR needs to be high enough for your page to at least get indexed in Google, since if it doesn't get indexed, your page won't show in the search engines at all!

Ok, lets assume that all your important pages have indeed been indexed in Google and show up on the search results pages. First hurdle overcome. Now you will see how to increase your PR so you get a higher position in the listings and prospective customers come to your site, bringing profits to you, not to your competition.

Internal and External Links to Get a Good Page Rank

For this part of the book, let's conceptualize the extra ranking power, that you will get as you move up the results pages, as PR 'juice'. Imagine a good helping of PR juice, flowing to your website from another site that links to you. This gives your page a massive boost, and you can influence it by building these links. You can also direct those links to where you need this boost the most. For example, you can make sure that the greatest amount of juice flows to your most important pages, maybe where you want to sell something or advertise a special offer. You get this juice through 'external links', which you could picture as canals. leading from other big lakes to your lake, increasing its size as the juice flows. Let's see how they can be created.

a) Getting Quality External Links

The most immediate, but probably also the most costly way to build links, is to buy them. The higher quality a link is, the more expensive they are. This quality, and therefore the price of an incoming link, is determined by several factors, but the most important factor is the PR of the site where the link is coming from. If you choose this route, here are some criteria that will help you to get value for money when buying links:

- The site from which you get your links must be **relevant** to your site or blog, otherwise the link value will be small.
- The page from which you are buying your link should have a good PR.
- Also, this page shouldn't have too many other links going out. This will dilute its linking power.
- Make sure that the keywords in the Link Text / Anchor Text are matching the keywords on your page which the link is pointing to.
- Also, keywords on the source page where the link comes from should match the keywords in the Link Text (more on this later).
- Make sure Google is actually spidering that page by checking the page's last cache date. Spidering means that the search engines send out a robot that crawls all webpages on the Internet. If the page hasn't been spidered for more than three weeks, this is a concern. If it has not been spidered for a couple of months, move on to another site. Why? Because the less the site has been spidered, the less important it is to the search engines, which means the less ranking power you might get from that site.
- Check in Google whether the site has been attacked / hacked by spammers using this command: '**site:thesiteinquestion.com** [check for spam words like sex, porn, Viagra etc. e.g. '**site: thesiteyouwanttocheck.com sex**']. You can tell whether they have been hacked when you find a good number of links with spam words in them. The more adult, gambling, etc. words appear on their site, the more it is likely that the site has been hacked.
- Do not buy links from 'bad neighborhood' sites as this can easily reflect badly on you. In general, search engines regard sites that spam a lot as bad neighborhoods. This can be any site from any industry, but they are most likely to be sites that are aggressively spamming because the financial rewards are high. In addition to the usual suspects, sites that have been hacked and spammed can also become bad neighborhoods.

If you want to build links yourself, you have several options. Some of the most widely used ways of building links are:

1. Submit your website to **directories** with a link pointing back to your site/blog.
2. Write and submit unique articles to **article directory** sites such as EzineArticles.com with links back to your site/blog included. (I will explain article marketing in detail later on.)
3. **Web 2.0 Sites**: Create content on so-called 'content sharing sites' with text, video, images etc. Examples are Hubpages.com, Squidoo.com or Propellor.com. Include text links to your site/blog.
4. Write comments on relevant **blogs** with highly-searched discussions, including a link back to your site in the comments you make.
5. Upload **videos** with search engine optimized descriptions which include your URL to video sharing sites like YouTube and others, and get at least one link to your site or blog (more about this later in this part).
6. Upload images to **image sharing sites** like FlickR.com with a link to your site/blog. Add keywords to the ALT attributes of your images but remember search engines don't weigh ALT text as highly as Link Text. (The ALT text of any picture is simply the text that you get asked to write when you put up a picture anywhere on the web.)
7. Put together packages for webmasters at relevant **websites** which makes it easy for them to link to your site. This package contains all the necessary information about your site, where to link to, what Link Text to use, etc. so webmasters can install what you want from them in one, single, convenient click. If it takes more, then they rarely do it.
8. Ask other **relevant websites** whether they are willing to give you a link, by offering them content, such as writing an article exclusively to their site.
9. If you are going to **buy links** from well ranked sites, make sure you get value for your money (see above) and make sure you do not get seen as someone buying links all the time, everywhere, on a large scale and at bad quality since Google might penalize you for it.

There isn't really a formula for how many links you can buy, since this depends very much on your specific business situation. For example if you have a brand new site with 20 pages, you are not a celebrity or the latest, hottest start-up on the Internet and you show 1,000 links mainly from non-relevant sites after one month only – Google and other search engines might get a little suspicious.

Once you are on their 'in question' list it can go downhill quickly from there. One of the next steps might be to send a human investigator round and if they don't like what they see, your site might get even banned from their search engine, which in turn would mean that prospective customers wouldn't be able to find your site anymore.

For example Google penalized BMW, the car maker some years ago. They had to give a lot of explanations why they had optimized their site in the way they had, and why Google should re-instate their site. If this was pretty hard for such a well established company, how difficult might it be for a less well known company?

In essence you need to use your good judgment of what kind of links might appear to be relevant for your site and in proportion to its size, how well your site is established on the Internet and how many links you already have.

So how can you arrive at such a judgment? To get a benchmark figure of how many links you can have to stay under the search engine's radar, see how many links the top ten sites have that are competing with you. Then use Alexa.com's 'Go-Back' Machine to see how many links they had a year ago, two years ago etc. That gives you an idea of how many links they built over what time. If you don't go massively over that range and your links don't all come from 'bad neighborhoods' there is no reason for why Google should get suspicious.

Much better than buying links would be to use your (or your SEO expert's) creativity and come up with ways how you can build links. Yes, it might take a little more use of your mind but in the end this approach often gets you the most valuable kind of links which you should aim to get anyway: Links from websites that are relevant to what you do and that contain keywords in the Anchor Texts that match the keywords on your site.

For example, instead of buying links, Flowers Direct created a directory on their website, listing details of Flowers Direct's network of florists and affiliates, targeting search terms such as London florists Manchester flower delivery etc. The site then was able to generate quality natural backlinks from these florists' sites to the Flowers Direct site which helped them rank well in a very competitive niche.

PART IV – Off-Page SEO

Some of what I have highlighted in this section might be unfamiliar to you if you have never built links or bought links from other websites. But there is nothing to worry about. As with most new things, if you take one step at a time, matters become more familiar and you quickly will see that they are not rocket science.

I will go into more detail on links and building links to your site later on in this part and will explain how you can do all this in simple, manageable steps. Before I do that, I want to briefly touch on 'Internal Links', links within your website. Picture them as pipes leading from one page of your site to another page. Why are we at all interested in these internal links? Because you can give your entire site a boost to rank well when you correctly link your pages internally.

b) Using Internal Links Correctly

Although internal links do not give you quite the same PR juice as external links, the good news is that building internal links is easier and if you build them according to the 'Silo Structure' that I mentioned in the last part, this will give you ranking benefit. The job of these links is to tell your visitors and the search engine spiders which other pages are relevant to a certain page, and hence how your site or blog is structured. Since these internal links are not as important for your ranking as external links, many webmasters underestimate what you can achieve with them.

The first internal link on your site or blog is the most important link since it will tell Google what you want your site to get ranked for. This is where many get it wrong. Many sites have 'Navigation Links' such as 'Home Page', 'About Us' or 'Why Us' at the top of their pages and Google picks these links up as their first links. This means that Google and other search engines start ranking these sites for 'Home Page', 'About Us' or 'Why Us'. This may not be helpful to you as these pages are probably not the pages you want your new visitors to go to. You rather would like them to land on a page where you can show them a great review about the product they are interested in or a price comparisons etc. The point I am making here is that you don't want Google and the other search engines to pick up the links to your admin pages first because the links to these pages are at the top.

c) How Not to Dilute Links

To get a high page rank, you should also make sure that you don't dilute links: The general idea in link building is that you build links from other websites to your site to get your site ranked higher on the search engines and that you direct the incoming links to important pages of your site. You ideally want many good quality links pointing to these important pages. These incoming links direct PR value – I sometimes call it PR juice - to your sites. It's like water flowing into a bucket. The more links you can compile onto a certain page, or the more water flows into the bucket the higher the PR of that page.

Now, you want to make sure that you don't have a leaky bucket and that the water stays in the bucket or the PR stays on your page and doesn't flow out immediately to other pages, thus diluting the power of the links coming to your page. You therefore don't want many links pointing out from your important pages. When you have a link from your page to another, the search engines index that link and give the page that this link is pointing to a share of the PR you wanted to accumulate on your more important page. Many links going out from a certain page simply dilute this page's PR if the search engines index these links pointing out from the page.

Up to June 2009, you would have been able to put a so-called 'no follow' tag into these links going out from your important pages to seal the whole in the bucket. This 'no follow' tag simply is a message to the search engines, not to index any 'no-follow' links. So you essentially would turn all the links pointing from your important page to other pages into 'no-follow' links. These 'no-follow' links then would not take any PR value away from your page. All the PR value would stay on your important page and accumulate there.

Google has unfortunately just changed their policy on those 'no-follow' links. When Google now sees a 'no-follow' link it deletes the PR value from that link. This either means that you can't have any links pointing out from your important pages anymore or that you will have to use techniques to 'hide' outgoing links from your page.

Not having any links pointing out from your page in many cases is not practical so let's have a look at what else you could do to keep all your PR on your page, even when this page has indeed links pointing to other pages and sites. What you could do is for example:

- An embedded iFrame on your page containing links you don't want the engines to follow.
- Links that call a Javascript redirect script getting the access blocked for search engine robots.
- Embedding in Flash, Java or some other non-parseable plug-in that contains the links you want.

❍ Settings that turn off links for visitors that are not logged in or don't carry a cookie.

Just ask your IT staff or an external SEO consultant to set this up for you since this is not straightforward HTML.

The Value Of Your Page Rank

When you have a PR of 4, it simply means that you have more PR than your competitor who has a PR of 2.. However your competitor nevertheless can still surpass you in the rankings getting a better listing if he/she does a better job than you in optimizing his/her pages. Simply put: The sites in the highest positions on the search results pages will not always have the highest PR. You can easily test this by looking up the PR for the top ten listings of certain keywords you intend to target.

For example, below you can see a screenshot of the listing positions 7, 8, 9 and 10 on Google's first search results page. One would think that the lower a site is listed, the less PR it has, right? But as you can see this is not always the case:

Screenshot of the last four listings on a search results page in Google.

Opposite you can see the PRs highlighted. Listing 7 has no PR, listing 8 has a PR of 0. One slot down in position 9 there is a listing with a much higher PR 4, listing 10 PR has page rank of 3, a higher page rank than other sites which appear higher up on the results pages.

This means, PR is not the only factor to determine where your site gets listed, but it is a very important one. And although you can't always tell from the PR number in Google's toolbar whether or not you will be able to take a competitor's position in the listings, PR is still important as an estimate of how your site or blog will get listed on the search engines.

Understanding Your Competitor's Link and Page Rank (PR)

As we said in Part III, you can save yourself time and money by checking out what your main competitors on Google's first search results page have done to optimize their pages. This also applies to their linking strategies. Check which techniques the top five are using and how successful they are. Often, you can learn a great deal from what the best in a certain field do and apply it to your own site. I don't mean copy exactly but adjust what they do for your needs. Try to answer the following questions:

- How many links from high PR websites have they got?
- Have they put the keyword you want to target in their link descriptions, the Link Texts / Anchor Texts?
- Are their Anchor Text keywords matching the keywords on their pages?
- How many links from authority sites such as .edu/.gov sites are they getting?
- Are they getting high PR links from the top directories like DMOZ and Yahoo! Directories?
- How are they using 'Link Bait' techniques? (Link Bait will be explained just a few pages on)

Understanding what your top competitors are doing and what it took them to get to their position provides you with a major indication of what works in your sector. It can also give you ideas for what kind of content to put on your site, and how to promote it. Here are different ways of examining your competitor's site and the links he/she gets. These are the most effective ones:

1. Yahoo! lets you check the overall number of links to a site. Go to http://siteexplorer.search.yahoo.com and type in the URL.
2. BackLinkWatch – www.backlinkwatch.com, shows you backlinks to your competitor's pages with the Link Texts / Anchor Texts. See whether they are using the keywords in those links.
3. Google Webmaster Tools - www.google.com/webmasters/tools/, lets you check a much more complex list of links when you open a free Google Webmaster Tools account.

The Top 15 Link Building Techniques for SEO

You already have a pretty good grasp of how important links are and how to build them. But as there are so many things to know, and so much conflicting information out there, let us focus on information that has been agreed by a wide range of industry experts. To give you an overview, I have brought together the 15 most effective link building techniques, presented in order of importance - backed up by 72 SEO experts - to build links for your site. (From Rand Fishkin's study at SEOmoz). Immediately below you'll find a list of the 15 most important link techniques, followed by explanations of the different techniques lower down.

The 15 Top Link Building Techniques

Very High Value Link Building Techniques
1. Linkbait & Viral Content Creation

High Value Link Building Techniques
2. Blogging and Engagement With the Blogosphere
3. Classic 'Create Valuable Content' Strategies w/o Promotional Marketing
4. Public Relations (beyond just press release publication)

Moderate Value Link Building Techniques
5. Direct Link Purchases from Individual Sites/Webmasters
6. Widgets and Embeddable Content
7. Conferences, Events and In-Person Networking

8. User-Generated Content (which then incentivizes links to profiles/content/etc.)
9. High Trust/Authority Directories (DMOZ, Yahoo!, Lii, etc.)
10. Niche Social Media Communities
11. Local Link Building (via geographic lists, organizations, portals)
12. Social Voting Portals (Digg, Reddit, Mixx, etc.)
13. Quizzes + Results Badges
14. Social Bookmarking Services (StumbleUpon, Delicious, etc.)
15. Contributing to Charities, Non-Profits, Events, etc. to Earn Links

Now let's look at what these link building strategies mean and how you can use them:

Very High Value Link Building Techniques
Technique 1: Linkbait & Viral Content Creation

The most important link building technique is 'Linkbaiting' and has been for years. Linkbaiting includes a variety of practices to generate incoming links to your website or blog from other sites by providing unique and good quality content on your site. In other words, it means providing interesting content that other sites inevitably quote, link to, and refer to on their pages and in their articles.

Google's Matt Cutts defines linkbait as anything "interesting enough to catch people's attention." Linkbait can be a powerful form of marketing as it is usually viral, meaning if someone thinks you have a great article on your site, they are likely to tell others about your article, too. And when you assume that those who like your article will also put a link to your page onto their site, you can see the potential power of good Linkbaiting.

Aaron Wall of SEOBook.com explains how-to do Linkbaiting as follows: "The idea of Linkbaiting is to create a piece of content which is centered on a set demand from a specific audience. Who do you want to relate to? Why would they care? What would make them likely to spread your idea? For example, Salary.com sponsored research stating that work at home moms did $134,121 worth of work each year. Because it was packaged as research and a story people would want to spread, it spread far and wide".

Some common Linkbaiting techniques are…
- Talking about a specific community.
- Giving people a way to feel important about themselves, someone they care about, or something they feel should be important.
- Being provocative or controversial.
- Creating common link points. It is important not to waste your link equity. For example, some book authors do not create an official page about their book on their site, and thus just give away the link equity and top ranking to an online bookstore.
- Creating contests and polls to draw people in. Many people use Surveymonkey or some other 3rd party voting service when they create contests and polls. If you can include the voting script on your site you keep that link authority associated with your site even after the poll closes and people no longer talk about it.

Magnetic Headlines

You Linkbait content will be much more powerful if it has very informative and attractive headlines

- Be specific with your headlines. For example, Salary.com stating that work at home moms are worth $134,121 a year is probably going to spread further than if they had said they are worth $200,000.
- Write your headlines with the intent of spreading them. Focus more on writing something that evokes emotional responses rather than writing too rigidly for keywords and SEO.
- Given that many social news sites have a voting mechanism that does not even require people to read the article to vote, the title may be far more important than the actual content of your linkbait.
- Copy Blogger offers great free headline writing tips.

Formatting Linkbait

People want ease and convenience. If you make it hard to find and link to your link bait content, people simply will not do it. Here are some important suggestions:

- Make it easy to identify and connect with your content. Think about human emotions and tap the sense of empathy.
- You may want to focus your content quite tightly so that it especially appeals to one group and/or especially offends another. If other people are quarrelling over what you have said, you will get quality links.
- Make your Linkbait look comprehensive.
- Perception is more important than reality.
- Cite research, further reading, and link out to related resources from within your content. It makes your story look well researched and associates your work with other trusted names or brands in your field. You may even want to cite a few people or names that you are hoping to build links from.
- Dress up your Linkbait using quality design and/or relevant images from sites like Istockphoto.

Case Study: *How SEO and* **link building** *increased traffic to Spotty Gift Boxes*

As a new site, Spotty Gift Boxes is very-consciously building strong foundations for its link building strategy. On the homepage, it recently advertised a coloring-in competition for children. This came as a direct response to the increased traffic for child-related products. Spotty Gift Boxes founder, Caroline, says she has used the competition to attract not only parents, who are her key customers, but also schools, to whom she supplies children's cookery utensils and gardening equipment. "We were also trying to create linkbait and give schools a reason to give us a link that would allow parents to download the competition themselves. We have told them about the competition and even some local authorities have given us a link too." says Caroline.

Links from government sites can be powerful, either because Google trusts them more or because government sites get lots of quality links themselves and therefore have a lot of link power to pass on. As her website is product-based, Caroline says this has meant link building has been the most difficult part of the SEO process. "It's hard because you have to give people a reason to link to you, and I think this is much easier for an information site than for a site like us.

PART IV – Off-Page SEO

> It's been a challenge to get people to link to what is essentially a shop site, and that's why we have been looking at competitions and things that people can interact with, and that our customers will find useful." Caroline Blatchford of Spotty Gift Boxes shared her experience with Wordtracker's Rachelle Money.

The key 'take home' message from this case study is that Caroline created competitions especially to bait links from schools, not only to give her a better ranking with the search engines, but also to entice parents to interact with the site directly. This strategy also generated links from authority sites, which provided additional reputation and probably even more target market customers / parents using these links to get to the site.

High Value Link Building Techniques
Technique 2: Blogging and Engagement with the Blogosphere

Blogging is a good way of getting your new content indexed more quickly than other websites. Obviously, the earlier your new page has been indexed by Google and can be found online, the earlier you can profit from it. Plus, blogging and engaging with other bloggers can result in a good number of links to your site.

> *Case Study: iStylista combine **blogging** with keyword research to double sales in 4 months.*
>
> Blogging is not just an important way to connect with your audience, it's also a great way to include keyword-rich content on your site. Online personal stylist service iStylista.com found that their sales doubled in just a matter of months after they launched their blog. Hayden Allen-Vercoe, co-founder of iStylista.com, saw a gap in the market where people wanted to know more about personal stylists but felt self-conscious about actually hiring one or unsure about whether they could afford one.
>
> Allen-Vercoe says their success was bolstered by starting to write a keyword-rich blog just four months ago, a blog which has pushed their rankings and doubled their sales.
>
> Blogging success: Allen-Vercoe says the blog has led them to double their sales. "Since we launched the blog, it's taken two months for us to bed down

> in Google, but we have doubled our sales and we can track that through the blog. We find that people will type something like Babyliss hairdryer into Google and we'll come up - they read our blog, which may have reviewed that product, and then they have a closer look at our site and finally, make a purchase." Allen-Vercoe shared his experience with Wordtracker's Rachelle Money.

Technique 3: Classic 'Create Valuable Content' Strategies without Promotional Marketing

Content is king since good content will always attract links to it and the better the content is the less promotion it needs since other people will do the promotion for you.

Technique 4: Public Relations (Beyond Just Press Release Publication)

Public relations is the art of building goodwill and maintaining a positive image of a person, product or company. To achieve this, some companies donate a portion of their profits towards a worthy goal, while others spend heavily in other ways to keep their brand associated with the positive aspects of their business. In terms of press releases, first put your press release up on your site, then on to one of the Internet-based press release distribution services. The better quality services tend to charge anywhere between $40 and $500 per press release, although some are free. Here are a number of quality press release distribution services:

- 1888 Press Releases – www.1888pressrelease.com
- Click Press – www.clickpress.com
- Ecomm Wire – www.ecommwire.com
- PR.com – www.pr.com
- PR Log – www.prlog.org
- PR Newswire - www.prnewswire.com
- **PR Web – www.prweb.com**
- PR Zoom – www.przoom.com

Case Study: *In Good Company reaping the rewards of its media campaign*

Getting external sites to write about you, especially top news sites, can work wonders for your inbound links, and as a result improve your search engine rankings.

Here's how one company got top rate media coverage: In Good Company opened its doors in September 2007, offering women productive and flexible workspaces to hire. Within six months, their 'community' of female-only entrepreneurs grew to over 120 members. As the year came to a close, Fives and Abrams [the founders] made a list of goals for 2008; one of them was to feature in the New York Times, and [after writing to Marci Alboher, a journalist from the New York Times] in February they achieved that, despite never having had any experience in PR or marketing:

Over four days Alboher interviewed a number of the members of In Good Company, as well as investors and industry commentators for an article [in the New York Times]. The online publication [of the article] also carried a link to the women's websites. Fives says they were "ecstatic" with [Alboher's] finished New York Times article.

Just as Fives and Abrams sighed with relief that the article had been well received, the phone began ringing with inquiries from women wanting to become members, realtors asking to join their client list, and calls from people looking for advice on how to launch their own flexible workspace companies....They have since continued to reap the rewards of their coverage in the New York Times with more local media outlets covering their story. "I haven't stopped since the article was published so this is a really exciting and positive time for us," says Fives.

Adelaide's Five's top tips for getting good media coverage:

1. Decide what is newsworthy about your business. It's not enough to say you have a great service.
2. If you are a service provider sometimes it's easier to be quoted as an expert. Think about how you can pitch that.
3. Do your research. Identify appropriate and approachable local media first and then identify who within that newspaper would be the right person to speak to.
4. Reach out in a professional and open way and not in a 'salesy' way which can come across as too pushy.

> 5. Tell the journalist why you are interesting. You can't say 'here's a list of things about me - find out what's interesting', that's not going to work.
> 6. Stay on the journalists' radar but again, don't be pushy.
>
> Adelaide Fives shared her experience with Wordtracker's Rachelle Money

Moderate Value of Link Building Techniques

Technique 5: Direct Link Purchases from Individual Sites/Webmasters

While buying them will get you links, this might only be a short-term gain. Here is a word of warning: Google is attempting to stamp out the practice of buying links and doing so might lead to severe penalties in the future. My intuition is that Google will probably first penalize sites that buy links from known link brokers, but it might then proceed to also penalize sites that buy links from individuals.

The same also applies to selling links. Don't get tempted and sell links from your site. This might provide you with a short term financial gain, but it also will probably become a long-term ranking disadvantage for your site if you attract search engine penalties. The worst case scenario would be a complete site ban which could conceivably result in your site being removed from the search engines altogether.

Now, bear in mind that there is buying links and buying links. Google doesn't like especially those links that are exchanged directly for cash. However, there are a number of ways to buy links without getting penalized by Google. The most obvious link buying techniques are:

Google AdWords, Facebook Ads or Any Other Ads

You can safely buy ads in different places on the Internet today. Google Adwords and Facebook are two of the most effective, simply because of their share of traffic. However, if you go down the route of buying ads you need to make sure you have done your keyword research, the text of your ad and the landing page where your leads get sent to are well crafted (see the earlier sections of this book), otherwise you can lose money quickly.

PART IV – Off-Page SEO

Submitting to Web Directories

When you buy links from directories, make sure they send traffic to your site. You can test this for a period of time, and if you don't get traffic, close the account. If you would like to get ranking power through the links you buy from the directories make sure the directories themselves....

- get links from dir.Yahoo!, DMOZ, EDU or GOV sites
- don't link to bad neighborhoods
- exercise editorial control
- don't use 'NoFollow' links

When you are thinking about which directories to submit to, look at how relevant the directories are to your business sector and whether these directories themselves are appearing prominently enough in the search results. Here is a list of directories from a study in which Bob Mutch from SEOCompany rated web directories by inbound link quality:

No	ILQ	URL	$	Y!	ODP	EDU	GOV	Site	Age	PR
1	5.8mil	www.dmoz.org/	Free	78	0	128k	761	929k	1999	8
2	5.1mil	dir.yahoo.com/	$299/yr	0	8	111k	2060	2.2mil	1995	7
3	475k	www.lii.org/	Free	56	0	10000	110	350	1998	7
4	121k	www.stpt.com/directory/	$99/yr	0	0	2600	70	341	1995	4
5	113k	www.business.com/	$299/yr	36	4	2420	73	579k	1998	7
6	9397	www.cannylink.com/	$20	0	5	204	1	649	1997	3
7	5340	www.americasbest.com/	$20	14	0	99	13	177	1998	3
8	4911	www.joeant.com/	$40	14	2	106	1	128k	2000	6
9	4892	www.chiff.com/	$297	10	3	105	1	4310	1998	5
10	4814	www.jayde.com/	Free	14	1	106	0	139k	1996	4
11	4260	www.skaffe.com/	$45	14	5	9	0	37.3k	2003	5
12	3745	www.ezilon.com/	$69	10	0	83	0	155k	2002	6
13	3357	www.mavicanet.com/	Free	20	13	64	1	350	1999	4
14	2369	www.botw.org/	$250	22	1	50	1	159k	1996	7
15	2150	www.avivadirectory.com/	$75	13	0	46	1	11.2k	2005	3
16	1949	www.elib.org/	$97	14	0	43	0	15.4k	2003	5
17	1918	www.directory.v7n.com/	$50	13	2	41	0	5550	2004	5
18	1227	www.rlrouse.com/	$50	12	0	27	0	3120	2002	5
19	1169	www.gimpsy.com/	$49	14	4	23	0	51.9k	2001	5
20	1110	www.goguides.org/	$40	0	4	22	0	89.4k	2001	8

Top 20 web directories, Source: Bob Mutch, SEOCompany

Below are 12 creative ways to buy links without getting penalized:

- **Testimonials:** Testimonials help increase sales because they are a sign of social trust. Many content management systems, web designers, programmers, and web hosts offer links to featured clients. Some keep full directories of sites using their services, while other sites, such as Pligg, also allow people using their software the opportunity to buy an ad on the official software site.
- **Conferences:** If you attend conferences and use them as a good networking and/or credibility-building opportunity, organizers, speakers or attendees may reference you on their blogs. Some conferences also list speakers, post official lists of attendees, and highlight sponsors with direct links.
- **Freebies:** Giving away t shirts or coming up with viral games (such as drinkbait) can get you links, too.
- **Association memberships:** Trade organizations tend to have significant global authority and topical authority. In order to push the agenda of the organization, many list their members and link to their sites in order to show proof of social value.
- **Donations:** Support causes you believe in even if the link equity you might get of it is also a motivating factor for you. Better yet, you might be able to donate software or services to a charity at little or no expense to you. Imagine the SEO value of a link on a PR8 charity site worth in terms of branding and distribution!
- **Free samples of your products:** This acts in a similar way to freebies and donations. And, if people like what you offer, they may review it on their sites.
- **Widgets:** Many embeddable tools provide static links back to the original source site. Some companies also provide emblems that their site is hosted on a green host. Most of them carry links back to their site when you use them on your website.
- **Sponsorship [Offers]:** Many email newsletters are archived online. If you target a compelling offer to the right audience this may lead to additional links, even after the initial publication date. Services like 'ReviewMe' also allow you to put targeted offers in front of audiences who may help spread the word.
- **Affiliate programs:** Even if affiliate links do not provide direct link juice, good affiliates still send a relevant stream of traffic to your site. **Social media:** Partner with someone who enjoys writing for sites like Digg, etc..

PART IV – Off-Page SEO

- **Link Out to bloggers:** This is a way of buying links by paying with your attention and distribution. People like getting mentioned, and are more likely to link to people who agree with them.
- **Press releases:** Some mainstream media outlets like CNN syndicate press releases, while others may chose to interview you based on your press release." (Source: Aaron Wall, SEOBook)

Now we have had a look at how to buy links for your sites without getting penalized, let's return to the Top 15 Link Building Techniques for SEO. What other methods can you use to build links?

Technique 6: Widgets and Embeddable Content

To build links to your site, you can offer widgets and other embeddable content that people put on their site and which link back to your site. The more people like it, the more people will install it on their sites and possibly send it on to their friends. Examples are Twitter badgets which link back to your Twitter profile, or embeddable videos that link back to your site.

www.twitter.com/karlortenburg

Other examples of embeddable content are videos from content sharing sites such as Youtube.com or Vimeo.com.

Technique 7: Conferences, Events and In-Person Networking

Conference-organising bodies sometimes list speakers, show the list of attending companies, and highlight their sponsors with direct links. In-person networking can also generate links but it is limited by your time and the benefits depend on the level of online authority possessed by your networking contacts.

Technique 8: User Generated Content (which then incentivizes links to profiles/ content/ etc.)

> *"We see social media, such as blogs, as a great way to build your business and tap into the ideas and input of people using your products."*
> Carlos Dominguez, senior vice president in Cisco's Office of the Chairman of the Board and CE, Cisco, about sites consisting of user generated content.

With the arrival of Web 2.0 and social media sites, user generated content has gained importance. Many more people now use content sharing and video sharing sites to build links to their own sites or blogs. When you place an article or video on these sites, your backlink can benefit from the site's authority provided that the link hasn't been restricted with a 'no-follow' tag.

(Above I explained that 'no-follow' doesn't work anymore which means a site cannot stop ranking juice flowing to your site through a link. That should be to your advantage when you are building links. But these sites have simply started using some of the other methods I have mentioned above to make sure they don't lose PR from their pages through outgoing links. The simple rule is that if a site is using techniques to prevent PR from flowing out of its site, this site then won't be useful in getting you PR.)

Technique 9: High Trust/Authority Directories (DMOZ, Yahoo!, Lii, etc.)

When you submit your site to web directories and they accept your submission, you will get a link back to your site. See 'Submitting to Web Directories' above for the value of links from different directories.

Techniques 10: Niche Social Media Communities

Many social media sites, such as Facebook, LinkedIn and others, offer entry into various groups and communities. Participating in these group and communities can produce links to your site and blog.

> *"I tend to think of ROI in this case as "Risk of Ignoring." If you are a high tech company that prides itself on innovation, being responsive to customers and providing its employees the freedom of a start up with the brand strength of an industry leader, are you supporting that identity by avoiding social media? I believe the real measure will be in opportunity lost."*
> Polly Pearson, vice president of employment brand and strategy, EMC.

PART IV – Off-Page SEO

Here are 20 useful sites to build links, leverage web 2.0 & social media sites by marketing your brand & controlling your message:

1. Digg
2. Del.icio.us
3. Reddit
4. Technorati
5. Squidoo
6. Netscape
7. LinkedIn
8. Newsvine
9. Wikipedia
10. Ma.gnolia
11. StumbleUpon
12. Shoutwire
13. Facebook
14. 43 Things
15. YourElevatorPitch
16. Flickr
17. WikiHow
18. BlueDot
19. StyleHive
20. JotSpot

N.B. I also run a niche community for web 2.0 experts and people interested in Social Media (www.InternetExperts-Live.com).

At first, these networks might seem a bit odd or geeky to you and you might think they have a short shelf life and/or are not worth your effort. Not so. With numbers of members approaching 1 billion, and younger generations using them enthusiastically, they will be around for quite some time and, more importantly, contain large numbers of your prospective customers. You just need to learn to tap into those markets in an appropriate way since old style marketing doesn't work here.

Ideally, you want to spread your message as wide as possible and to as many web 2.0 networks and communities as possible that connect people within your target audience. If you don't do any of this, you will be leaving a lot of business to your competitors. Starting your presence, maintaining it and connecting with people in those communities can take a lot of your time, especially if you are new to it. However, from my experience, you will maximise your efforts and build a good foundation if you start with these key networks. Then learn how web 2.0 (business) communication works from there and expand once you have built a decent number of friends and followers:

- **LinkedIn (**www.LinkedIn.com): Even with over 30 million members (at the time of writing) LinkedIn is not the biggest network. However, it is the most professional one. How can you use it? In many ways. Possible business partners and employers check your 'social' records here and they see what kind of network you have. LinkedIn lets you search by company name or industry to find key players and decision makers. If you want to get connected to someone, see who in your network is connected to them, and ask them to make a connection. Market your expertise by answering questions that others post in LinkedIn and ask questions you might have which you can also use for marketing purposes. Observe how others are using the site and start with an approach that you are comfortable with. Set up your own group and build it. Recruit high-profile people for events, find investors and so on. (If you have more questions about LinkedIn, find me at www.linkedin.com/pub/karl-ortenburg/3/87b/421)

- **Facebook** (www.Facebook.com): Facebook is huge and has evolved from students chatting, to a forum where large numbers of people from all walks of life are joining every day. Facebook is solid and is not going to go away anytime soon. However, it is a more general social network, so it's harder to get business-focused on it. Here are some Facebook statistics (at the time of writing). Have a look to see whether any of them appeal to you:

    - **General Growth**
      More than 300 million active users
      50% of active users log on to Facebook in any given day
      Fastest growing demographic is 35 years old and older
    - **Applications**
      More than 3 million events created each month
      More than 45 million active user groups on the site

- ❏ **International Growth**
    More than 65 translations of the site
    About 70% of Facebook users are outside the United States
- ❏ **Mobile**
    Over 65 million active users currently accessing Facebook through their mobile devices.
    Over 180 mobile operators in 60 countries working to deploy and promote Facebook mobile products.

Facebook is a big network, and some of its groups might connect with some of your target customers. Set-up your account today and have a look. (If you have questions about Facebook, find me at www.facebook.com/people/Karl-Ortenburg/1081637210).

○ **Twitter** (www.Twitter.com). Twitter is a free online service that allows its users to send and read messages known as '140 character Tweets'. It attracts more than 54 million visitors a month and was recently given a nominal value of 1 billion dollars by its investors. Not bad for a company that started in 2006! A lot of famous people use Twitter in one way or another these days. Some examples of how Twitter is currently being used, which illustrate its huge potential are; Barak Obama's Twitter campaign during the US election, images of the plane that crashed on Hudson River going around the world on Twitter before TV could send them out, the sounding board that Twitter provided during the Iranian election and the life saving value of Twitter during the California bush fires. How might you use Twitter? Simply by letting people know what you are up to, you gain access to an additional audience. Just think of being able to send people e-mails in a short format possibly several times a day instead of just once per week.

There are several websites with tips for using Twitter as a business tool and I listed a few here:

- ❏ Twitip (www.twitip.com) - 13 Twitter tips and tutorials for Beginners
- ❏ Twittertips (www.twittertips.org) - Tips and tricks for Twitter users who want to get more out of Twitter and improve their tweeting experience.

❏ Problogger (www.problogger.net) - Tips for bloggers, 35 Twitter tips from 35 Twitter users

(If you have questions about Twitter, find me at http://twitter.com/KarlOrtenburg).

❍ **MySpace** (www.MySpace.com) With its chaotic interface design, MySpace caters foremost to the young and tends to focus on music, media, arts, etc. If this is your target audience, it could be worth your while to build your profile and collect 'friends'. Otherwise, it might be a waste of time.

Remember, when you are using social networks for business purposes, your profile, communications and friends become part of your appearance, your product and your service presence. Always bear in mind that you primarily want to focus on prospective customers and business or joint venture partners. In the main, therefore, you want to separate personal and business usage although it's worth bearing in mind that on Twitter, the mix of personal (but not too personal) and business 'tweets' is what really works.

The alternative to the more general networks mentioned above are platforms and communities that are very specific to your industry, whatever that may be. You can find them via Google when you type in search terms such as 'network' or 'community' together with your industry sector or terms from your industry.

Note: You can use social networks for link building only when these networks are not behind a 'sign-up' wall, meaning that you have to sign up to get in. Search engines won't be able to index your page behind such a sign-up wall and therefore they won't be able to see and evaluate the quality of the page the link is coming from.

Having looked at social media communities and their value in building links, let's now see a few more link building techniques.

Technique 11: Local Link Building (via Geographic Lists, Organizations, Portals)

Links from local listings gain in importance since Google is placing a lot of effort in developing relevant local listings. For information on how to find places to get links to your local listing see Part I: 'Think Global – But Act Local'

Technique 12: Social Voting Portals (Digg, Reddit, Mixx, etc.)

These sites are a subset of social media sites in the sense that they all use a reader / user 'voting' system to rank their pages on their site. Links from these sites can help with your rankings only if your site does not get social media links alone.

Technique 13: Quizzes + Results Badges

Similar to other embeddable content, if you provide badges for quizzes and their results in these software badges you can include a link to your site or blog.

Technique 14: Social Bookmarking Services (StumbleUpon, Delicious, etc.)

Social bookmarking has developed into a mainstream tool for SEO. It involves linking your site from forums, blogs and message boards on social networking websites and blogs and it can increase the number of links from relevant, quality sites if done correctly. See more on using Social Bookmarking later on in : 'Being Social with Your Bookmarks Will Help You'.

Technique 15: Contributing to Charities, Non-Profits Events, etc. to Earn Links

Contributing to charities and non-profits events etc. to earn links can work if the non-profit organisations or events are related to the content on your site.

That's it – now you have the 15 most effective link building techniques at your fingertips. Use them and you will see your rankings and traffic go up. Once we have looked at how to build links, let's see now how you can use these links to achieve higher rankings, more clicks and more visitors to your site.

When Links Do the Most for You – Keyword Matching

A link is substantially more effective for your site when the keywords in its Link Text or Anchor Texts match the keywords on your site. Basically, the Link Text / Anchor Text is the part of text that shows up in a link. When you set up links, always make sure you include relevant keywords you want your page to rank for.

Keywords in Links Should Match Keyword on Target Site

So-called '**Keyword-Matching**' is what some experts call **the** most important way to tell Google that your site or blog is relevant for a certain search term. Link texts are, therefore, considered by many SEO consultants to be one of the most important overall ranking factors.

> *"There are many different ranking factors to consider when building a website, but Theme Matching [on-page keywords matching off-page keyword] is by far the most important."*
> Russell Wright, Themezoom.com

Search engines use any text to learn more about the content of a specific page. In particular, they read the text within a link that points to that particular site. For Google, the Link Text is like a description which plays a major role in determining the rankings of your page. That's the reason why the Link Text should contain the keywords you want to target. This is important because you can increase the competitiveness of any of your pages if you match the keywords on your page with keywords in the Link Text / Anchor Text of the links leading to your page. When the keyword Link Text used in your links matches the keywords on your site, you have helped Google to determine what your site is about.

Keywords in Link Should Match Keyword on Source Page

It is important to choose relevant pages (the 'Source Page') from which to create these links. This means that your page will get the most ranking juice from a 3rd party page which is relevant to yours. The main way the search engines determine relevance is through keywords and it has become important that not only the keywords between the target page and the Link Text match, but that the keywords on the source page match the keywords in the Link Text and the keywords on the target page (your page) as well.

Google's thinking here is that if a lot of respected, relevant other sites and pages point links to a specific page on your site or blog with the same keywords as you use on your page, your page indeed must be relevant for that keyword term or phrase and, therefore, should be ranked in the top search results. Getting listed in the top ten on Google immediately gives you credit and a one-in-ten chance that you get the click, the prospective customer to your site and the opportunity to start communicating with him or her to create a new, loyal, lifelong customer.

What Kind of Links to Acquire

The most valuable links are so-called **'non-reciprocal' or 'one-way' links** pointing from another website to your site or blog. These links should come from sites that are **relevant** to your industry as explained earlier, and these pages should not have restricted the link with a 'no-follow' tag since Google made it clear that hyperlinks with rel="nofollow" attribute would not count towards your site's PR.

Reciprocal or two-way links have less value than one-way links (if they come without a no-follow restriction) and so called FFA (free-for-all) links and link farms have almost no value at all.

Links from High PR Sites

We have already explained that Google uses PR to categorize sites for their importance or relevance. To achieve a high PR, you really need inbound links from high PR websites like, for example, popular Web 2.0 sites. Simply put, the higher the PR of the site your link comes from, the better. The watershed is around PR 5. Links from lower PR sites provide much less ranking power.

Such higher PR links help you gain **importance** for your web pages in the eyes of Google. This means you are also seen as an expert in your field when other expertly (highly ranked) sites refer to you and consider your website/blog 'link-worthy'.

However these links can be difficult or costly to get – we'll talk about how to get them later on – and you should, therefore, also consider getting links from carefully-selected, lower PR websites on the basis that the link value of these sites could improve in the future.

Links from Low PR Sites

As I just said, links from low PR websites don't immediately help the PR of the sites they link to. But as long as they have your keywords in the Link Text / Anchor Text, lower PR links still help you gain **relevance** for your website/blog and for the keyword terms you are positioning yourself around.

Although these links don't give you much ranking power, they show that other websites consider your site to be relevant and worth consulting. So, this goes some way towards affecting your position on the search engines as well. Certainly, it is better to have some low PR links than no links at all, because otherwise Google might not find and index your site for a long time, even if your site is fairly frequently updated with fresh content. And, of course, low PR links are easier to get and cheaper to buy. Thus, they enable you to achieve the objective of improving the relevance of your website more cost effectively.

Bear in mind, too, that lower PR link pages often increase in PR over time, more rapidly as compared to higher PR link pages. For example, a PR1 page is likely to jump to PR3 much faster than a PR4 page would jump to a PR6 page. Should you decide to buy some links, you might get some PR3 or PR4 links for which you pay a lower cost, and those links may turn into PR4 or PR5 links in just three to six months time.

Building Long-Lasting Quality Links Over Time

Link building is a task undertaken over the course of several weeks and months. Search engines will simply disregard a large number of links built in a day or two. Worse than that, if you try to move too quickly, your credibility could be damaged and it could result in your site being penalized for so-called 'search engine spamming'. I, therefore, recommend to all clients to build quality incoming links over time from a mix of websites that will lend your site/blog a higher Google PR for many years to come.

Also, don't use the same keywords in the Link Texts of all of the links pointing to your site. Make sure you rotate primary and secondary keywords using different keywords which are part of your theme. Otherwise, again, there could be a danger that you might be penalized for spamming. Here are some of the quality guidelines we use, to ensure that our clients get the maximum benefits from their links:

- ❍ Only use links from trusted sources, since links from trustworthy websites count more than links from low traffic, rarely used, and rarely cited websites.

PART IV – Off-Page SEO

- Focus on links from established sites that have been on the Internet for some time. New sites rarely get link value immediately.
- Links from pages that point to competing sites, too, will give you more relevance to help you rank in your chosen sector.
- Links from topic-related websites and pages will count more than links from sites that are unrelated to your topic.
- Links with Link Texts matching not only the keywords on your page but also the link source page. Make sure that the Link Texts do not match exactly but very closely.
- Use unidirectional, inbound or incoming (non-reciprocal) links.
- Only use links from indexed pages.
- Don't use links from
    - "framed" pages
    - Link Farms
    - FFA (Free-For-All) link networks
- Don't use "flash" embedded links.
- No linking with redirected pages.
- No links from adult sites, racially-prejudiced sites and other sites containing offensive content or coming from other so-called 'bad neighborhoods'.

Do-It-Yourself or Get-It-Done

Link building provides great value for your website or blog, since it can help you greatly in reaching prospective customers online. At the same time, link building is time-consuming if you do it yourself.

Even if you intend to build links yourself, it would still be good to discuss your linking strategy with an expert link builder who can warn you of some of the perils in link building so you don't get your site banned by the search engines by, for example, simply building links too quickly.

SEO Consulting

At this point, let me make a brief general comment on outsourcing SEO work and the possible costs of doing so. SEO consultants, on average, charge between $5,000 a month and $60,000+ a month, depending on the intensity of the campaign. This might seem like a lot of money to some but whether it's value for money comes down to the simple question of how much value gets generated for your company.

To Sum Up:

Building good quality links to your site remains one of the most if not **the** most important part of SEO. At the same time, link building needs to be handled with great care, as building links to your site too quickly could also negatively affect its performance. Link building is a very effective long-term strategy and will give you long lasting results. Before moving on, take GROW Step 7:

GROW Step 7:

Create **quality links that point to your website**, ideally with the keywords in the Link Text matching the keywords on your page and the pages where the links are coming from. Create these links from relevant websites, where in a perfect world the keywords on the site match those in the link.

GROW Step 8:
Promote Your Site Further with 'Social Bookmarking'

Technically speaking, Social Bookmarking is very similar to the way you bookmark something on your computer so you can find it again later. It is called 'Social Bookmarking' though because it allows other people to see the bookmarks you use on the Internet, which is regarded as being 'social'. It is also an effective way of building links and promoting your content.

Why Being Social with Your Bookmarks Will Help You Build Links

When you bookmark something on the Internet you use so-called 'Bookmarking Sites'. A social bookmark site is an online community of web users who store and share their bookmarks. Instead of only bookmarking pages on their own computers, people who social bookmark on the Internet use keywords to 'tag' these pages and create entries in the social bookmarking sites, thus making them public for everyone to see. 'Bookmarkers' categorize their bookmarks with these tags so others can find content that interests them more easily.

Many of these sites allow users to 'discuss' tagged articles by posting comments about them. The most popular tags appear higher in the respective categories, the articles associated with these tags get read more widely, and the links included drive more traffic to the bookmarked site.

This video explains how social bookmarking works. Just copy and paste the link into your browser window:

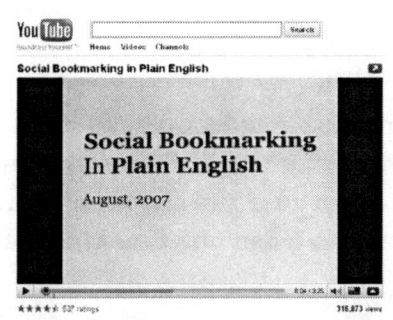

Social Bookmarking Video on YouTube.com

You can find this video at www.youtube.com/watch?v=x66lV7GOcNU&fm=18
[**Note**: Do not change the code, since it will give you higher quality on YouTube.com than you usually get.]

When you social bookmark, you include links to the bookmarked web pages from these Social Bookmark websites. Therefore, whenever you social bookmark your own content, you build links to your content.

However, be aware that these Social Bookmarking sites were built to provide value for everyone and if you are only bookmarking your own content, the Social Bookmarking site owners won't consider that as being very social and might close down your account on their sites. This will also delete the links to your content and website. Remain social and bookmark content that you think might be interesting for others too, and from time to time, sprinkle some bookmarks to your own content in there as well. I would suggest that for one link to your own content you should bookmark at least six to ten other pages that are not your content.

What You Can Achieve with Social Bookmarking

More Targeted Traffic to Your Site
Since your bookmarks are categorized with different tags, you will get targeted traffic from people searching within a particular tag. They will click on your bookmark link and visit your site.

Faster Search Engine Indexing
Most of these Social Bookmarking sites have high PR. Remember, PR (PageRank) is Google's way to rank your site - ranging from 5PR to even 8PR. Therefore, search engine spiders visit these sites often and your new links and your new content will be crawled fast and indexed quicker than if you had not bookmarked them.

Higher Search Engine Ranking
Getting top quality one-way incoming links is key to higher search engine rankings. With Social Bookmarks, you can get unlimited links to your site. Having more bookmark links that are relevant to your site can result in a higher search engine ranking for your site. Even more so when you find bookmarking sites that allow for 'follow' links.

How to Do 'Social Bookmarking'

Social Bookmarking is relatively straightforward to do. Once you have set-up the Social Bookmark link from the Social Bookmarking site to your page, you just need to write a short description of your page content and put the keywords you use into the 'tags' section. That's it. There is not much more to it. But Social Bookmarking can be time-consuming since it requires you to create your accounts at Social Bookmarking sites and you will have to log into your account at each of these Social Bookmarking sites to add your page's URL, keywords and descriptions, one by one.

Social Bookmarking Software to Save You Time

If you want to cut down the time you are using for Social Bookmarking, here are two tools to help you with it. I won't go into detail about how these work, since their sites explain that pretty well. The first one, Social Marker, is a free tool that you find online at the following URL:

Social Marker

http://socialmarker.com

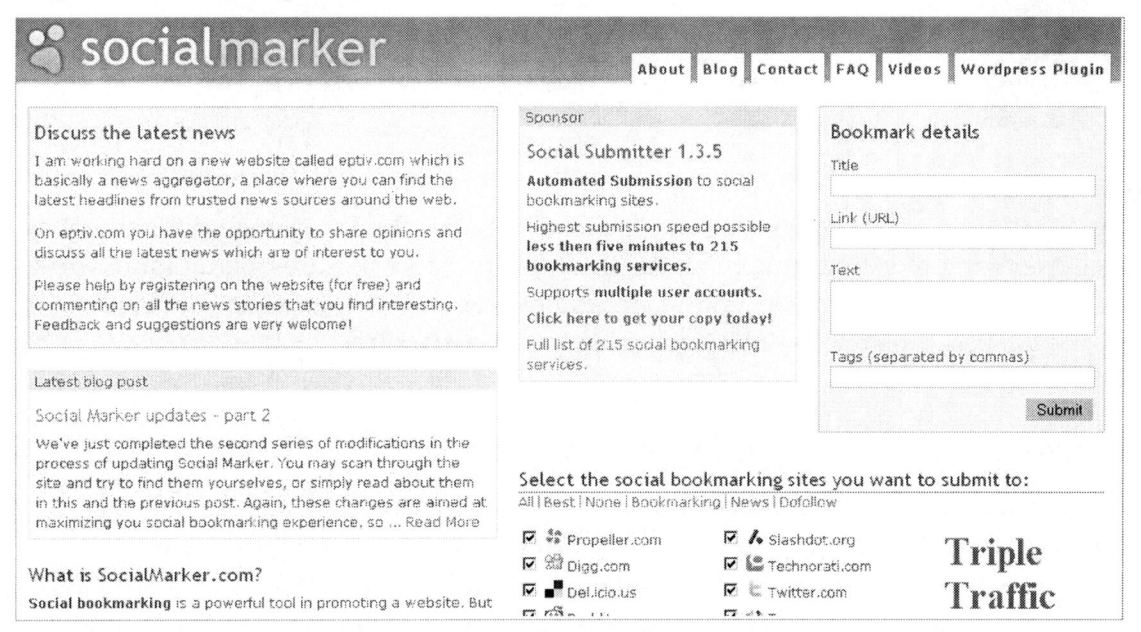

Socialmarker.com

PART IV – Off-Page SEO

Just follow the straightforward instructions on the site to start Social Bookmarking your content, as well as other interesting content on the Internet.

The second bookmarking tool is called Bookmarking Demon and provides greater automation, which can save you even more time:

Bookmarking Demon

http://bookmarkingdemon.com/

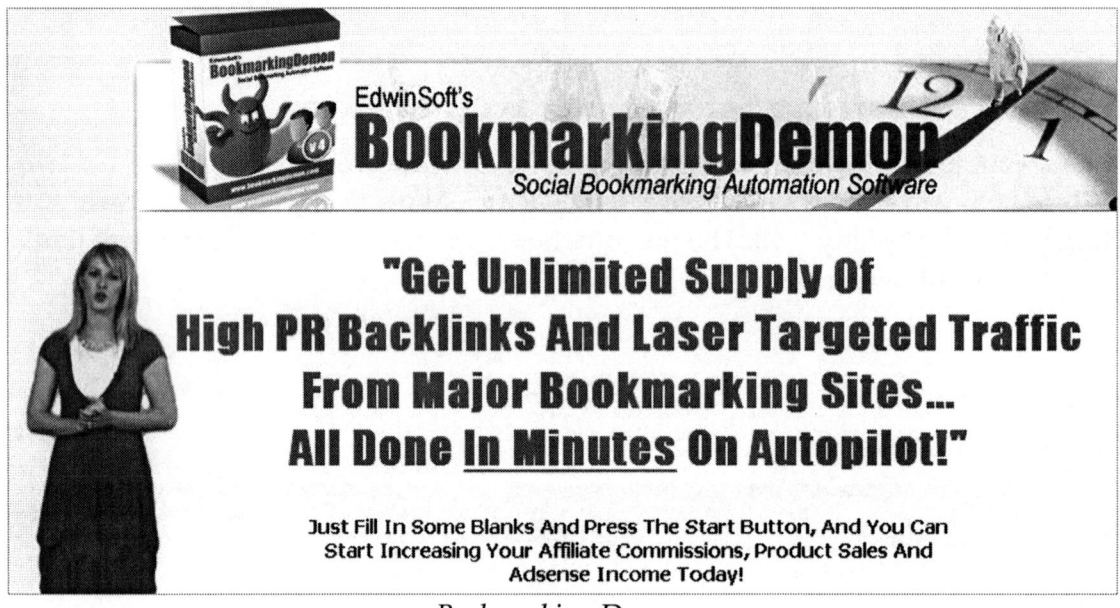

Bookmarking Demon

Again, follow the instructions on the site to start Social Bookmarking your content as well as other interesting content on the Internet. This tool requires a little more work initially, but provides greater time saving thereafter. In my opinion, it is currently one of the best tools for Social Bookmarking on the market.

Outsourcing Your Social Bookmarking

As I explained earlier, there is a certain amount of risk involved with Social Bookmarking. It is important to be aware of this, even if you are thinking of outsourcing. If you overdo Social Bookmarking and bookmark only your own pages, your account could be deleted, or even worse, your site could get banned from that Social Bookmarking site.

Here is what you can do to reduce the risk: When you bookmark your sites, you must be careful not to bookmark with the same content title, tags and description across multiple bookmarking sites since this creates a so called 'footprint' on the Internet. Search engines will understand that all these bookmarking links were set up by the same person and thus will be discounted as being 'artificial'. On top, your site might receive a penalty from the search engines for building all these artificial links. This would not be good for your search engine rankings, visitor traffic to your site, etc.

However, if you pay attention and bookmark professionally - using varying titles, keyword tags and descriptions. Plus you frequently book mark other pages too, you should have no problem. Here are 7 top Social Bookmarking sites that can bring an astonishing amount of traffic to your site when you use them well:

> www.stumbleupon.com
> http://digg.com
> http://technorati.com
> http://delicious.com
> www.reddit.com
> http://buzz.Yahoo!.com
> www.mixx.com

To Sum Up:

Social Bookmarking is a web 2.0 technique to tell others that you value a certain page. Furthermore bookmarking is used to build links to the content on your site.

GROW Step 8:

Social Bookmark your pages to promote your content by creating links with keyword tags. Bookmark professionally by not only bookmarking your own content but by socially bookmarking pages of other web content too. Make use of bookmarking tools to help you save time and enlist the help of high traffic Social Bookmarking sites.

GROW Step 9:
Use Articles as Your 24/7 Sales Agents

Article marketing is another powerful method of building links to your site that bring targeted traffic to your website or blog. Good, original, high-quality articles can bring an avalanche of interested traffic to your site or blog and, this way, your words can have real power.

> *Case Study:* John Pye & Sons [were] getting their highest ever web traffic, which rose by more than 50%, leading to a record level of registered bidders through article marketing.
>
> John Pye & Sons Auction House, based in Nottingham, England had a good relationship with local media throughout its forty years of business, but they didn't hit the big time until an opportune moment and a dose of good luck propelled them onto the front pages of the money supplement of the Guardian's Saturday paper.
>
> John Pye & Sons' [first name] Miller, said the article provided the company with "marketing gold" when it was published online, complete with a link to their site. The impact of the coverage was felt by the auction house almost immediately. They recorded their highest ever web traffic, which rose by more than 50%, leading to a record level of registered bidders in the auction house.
>
> Miller said the Guardian was the second highest referral domain with Google coming top. "So, we know that people are coming to our site directly because of the article. "For a morning's work writing an email and then helping the journalist when he was here, that's pretty good going," says Miller. Sheldon Miller shared his experience with Wordtracker's Rachelle Money.

The above is a pretty straightforward example of how articles can bring your site a lot of good quality traffic for much longer than if you had put an ad into the same newspaper on the day. Just remember, the link from the newspaper site to your site will be there for much longer than the ad on a particular day.

Yes, there was a bit of luck involved in getting the article into the newspaper, but there are ways to reduce the element of luck and increase the chances of getting your articles published. Let's look at some of them now:

When you use article marketing well, prospective customers with intelligent, relevant inquiries essentially come to you, free of charge. The only cost you have is the time involved in writing and submitting the articles which may include the time you spent learning how to do this effectively.

When you're writing an article that includes great information that is of interest to your target market, readers will come to your site wanting more. That's when you can encourage them to download free reports from your site and subscribe to your newsletter.

When you get the opportunity to publish an article on a high profile website, it's the equivalent of a referral from another highly-regarded site owner saying "look; this person has written such a great article that I've put it on my site. Read it (and go to their site) …"

When other site owners download your article, you get more direct traffic to your site and links back to you, the author. The more links from other websites you get, the better your site/blog ranking becomes, the higher your articles get ranked, the more traffic you get, …- you get the idea. This makes article marketing a great way to build your brand and expand your business.

Direct Traffic through Article Marketing

Great articles are useful to your prospective customers and they increase the likelihood that these individuals will take action – returning to your site frequently, signing up for your newsletter, buying your products/services etc.

Here are some effective ways to maximise the potential of articles to generate **direct traffic to your website:**

1. **Links:** Articles can be found almost anywhere on the Internet from social networking sites to blogs, and each one can contain at least one, possibly two **links** to your site/blog or a specific page, like an opt-in page on your site/blog. The more articles you publish, the more links you can get to your website. By building these links to your website, you not only get more traffic to your website but also increase your search engine rankings.

2. **Ranking Power:** The more articles you publish, the more links you will get and the higher your website's search engine ranking can go.

3. **Customers**: Articles can increase the number of potential customers who not only visit your website, but return again and again to see what you're up to. Article marketing can also improve the quality of customers coming to your site, since they already know what you are doing from your article.

4. **Expert status** in your field: When you regularly submit original, high-quality articles to the Internet, you can quickly establish yourself as a respected expert in your field and others will come and seek your help, advice, products and services.

How to Write Great Articles

People are always drawn to good, meaningful text copy, whether spoken, written or watched.

> *"Words have power. They can make you laugh. Or cry. Build a cathedral or skyscraper. Fight for your country. Who can ever forget the speeches of Winston Churchill, which stirred a nation. March for peace. Back your ideas with a million dollars. Or flock to buy your product!"*
> Ted Nicholas

Here are some brief guidelines to bear in mind when you write your articles:

Using Keywords

As we have seen in the first half of this book, the keywords you use in your text are extremely important. When you know what your prospective customers are looking for, and you are using the words they are using, they will find you and you get the chance to start communicating with them – offering them your products and services.

A prerequisite for using keywords effectively, however, is being able to write good text that incorporates the keywords as a natural part of the text. Your aim is to generate strong sales as a direct result of the combination of good copy writing and the use of wisely-chosen keywords in your text. This can make you stand out and attract a stream of customers.

Writing can be somewhat time-consuming, so, when starting your article, keep these article marketing cornerstones in mind:

- Choose your primary and secondary **keywords** that you want your article to rank well for.
- Write a compelling **title** for the article which includes the primary keyword as well as the title tag (if you are allowed such tag).
- Write the **Description Tag** using your primary and secondary keywords. (Again, if you are allowed a Description Tag.)
- Write the first paragraph as a **summary** of the whole article, and the last paragraph as a **conclusion**. Include both primary and secondary keywords.
- Lay out the **structure** of the article, writing headings and subheadings that each contain secondary, long tail and related keywords.
- Make sure links to the article contain keywords in the Link Texts that **match** your chosen **keywords** on your website or blog page.
- Finally, fill out the structure with high quality **informative** content, giving unbiased **advice**.

The Copywriting Roadmap

Copywriting is a personal matter and everyone has his/her own personal style and approach. Expert copywriter Paul Gorman says that there is no single copyright formula. So, how can anyone master good article copywriting?

The most important is to keep in mind that writing sales copy won't help here. Remember, over 80% of your readers are looking for **information** or a solution to their problems, not someone trying to sell to them. In one of my reports, called '**The Copywriting and Article Writing Roadmap**', I have put together a step-by-step guide, equipped with expert copywriting tips and techniques, to help you organize your work. Here is a summary of the elements for good article copywriting to get you started.

I advise you to think of the writing process in terms of three essential elements:

Element 1: **Headlines** - How to grab the attention of almost every single one of your potential customers, instantly.

Element 2: **Emotional Writing** - free passionate writing about the product or service and its benefits. The aim here is to demand attention, arouse curiosity, create sympathy, appeal to their needs and possibly induce pain thus creating a 'want' in their minds and hearts.

Element 3: **Rational writing**, consisting of facts, figures, testimonials, possibly endorsements, case history etc. This is how you provide the foundation for believability, credibility and meaningfulness.

Let's look at these three elements in a bit more detail.

Element 1: Headlines - How to Grab the Attention ...

… of almost every single customer. The world's best copywriters agree that the headline is the most important element of your copy.

> *"Good Headlines can outperform bad Headlines by 1950%."* John Caples

> *"One average, five times as many people read the headline as read the body copy. It follows that unless your headline sells your product, you have wasted 90 percent of your money."* David Ogilvy

> *"I have re-written the headline for one of my Books over 200 times."*
> Ted Nicholas

The most important part of ANY communication - video, audio, phone, text - is the headline. It is the one reason why you should stop doing what you are doing and take notice of what the author is saying. Copywriting masters spend 80-90% of the time writing the headline. If you do not have the right headline, you won't get high numbers of readership.

You need to capture tightly and quickly what is different, immediate, truthful and what makes your audience want to read on. That's what makes a good headline. To do this, imagine yourself in front of a huge crowd of people with big budgets to spend. You are on stage with 50 other competitors, and you get only 30 seconds to gain as many customers as possible.

You get one shot, and one shot only, whether it is on that stage or on the Internet. You may be the best in your field, but if you cannot lift yourself above the other professionals in your field – with headlines grabbing the immediate attention of your market place - then most of your efforts are wasted. Your website visitor or article reader will have gone elsewhere.

Element 2: An 'Emotional' Style of Writing

> *"Don't worry about grammar for now, or punctuation, don't wordsmith every sentence, make it human"*
> Ray W. Intkins

Emotional writing means you just sit down and let your emotions flow. You spill out onto paper what you want to communicate. You don't stop for facts, figures or proof; you simply write what you feel is important for the reader in order to solve their problems. Some people like doing this first, before getting bogged down with the detail.

In order to write copy that compels, a good copywriter has to have a passion for what he/she is doing and a genuine love for people. Write quickly and stay focussed. Don't allow interruptions. Don't bother correcting anything right now; you are just spilling out the essence of your copy without thinking about it. Write what you 'feel' you need to say and let it flow – however jumbled or repetitive it might be when it first emerges. Leave the fine tuning until later. A less formal style of writing also allows the less experienced writer to overcome writers block. When you write like this, keep in mind that you should …

a) show that you genuinely want to solve your reader's problem
b) generate excitement
c) show enthusiasm for your product or service
d) make your product or service as appealing as possible.

Element 3 – The Rational Copy

You have now poured out on paper – without much order, restraint or discipline - the value you are presenting and your passion for your product or service. You have emphasized the benefits to your reader and have addressed their needs. Now you can fill your copy with some hard facts, figures and evidence about your product or service, the market it is in and also something about yourself. Once your article is done, you can start thinking of where to send it to.

Where to Send Your 24/7 Sales Agents

Here are five important places to which you can submit your articles:

1. Your own site/blog
2. Web 2.0 sites
3. Relevant, high profile / high PR / high readership sites
4. Other blogs
5. Article directories

It is now time to submit your article, sit back and watch the traffic arriving. A case of "Build It and They Will Come". If you write great article content delivering unbiased information and advice and you promote your article professionally, then visitors will indeed come to you. Naturally, the best version should always go on your own website, so you can build your expert status for your chosen field. Your readers discover the content you have written and your site can benefit from your articles becoming indexed and ranked on the search engines. However, don't just put your articles on your website as they might not get indexed by the search engines as quickly. And if you have a relatively new site, your article might not appear on the search engines for some time if you do not have links from other websites.

So, upload variations of your article to a number of top web 2.0 sites and article directories. When a site gets updated regularly and has a lot of fresh content, then Google and the other search engines believe the content is relevant and therefore ranks the content quickly and highly. You don't have the same advantage with your own website as these user generated web 2.0 websites do. It's just too much work to update your own site with fresh, good content as regularly as they do. This is why you want to 'stand on the shoulders' of those web 2.0 giants and benefit from their ranking power and indexing speed.

Web 2.0 Sites: 'Standing on the Shoulders of Giants'

Web 2.0 or 'Content Sharing Sites' sites, such as Hubpages.com, StumbleUpon.com, Propeller.com and others, grow quickly because users create content for them every day, and on some of the bigger sites, almost every hour. Millions of visitors arrive at these sites every month. Some sites are more specialized and offer mainly document uploads, while others include video, audio and pictures in their various formats. Many of the top content sharing sites allow almost every imaginable type of digital upload including PDFs, spreadsheets, JPG, GIF, word documents as well as video and audio.

Putting your article onto Web 2.0 sites has three main benefits:

1. **Your content gets found and recognized fast by the search engines**:
   When you link from an article on such a web 2.0 site back to content on your own site, this content will get found and indexed faster and therefore can appear faster in Google.

2. **You increase the page rank of your site through links**:
   The links from these web 2.0 sites also spill over 'ranking juice' to your own site. The more web 2.0 links you get, the more 'ranking juice' your site will receive if these links are 'follow' links.

3. **Your site gets more direct Traffic**:
   These web 2.0 sites are one of the best places to upload unique variations of your articles, since when your articles become popular, countless searchers pick them up, click through to your website and you get large amounts of direct and interested traffic to your site or blog.

A Word of Warning

Be aware that Google gets suspicious if you have a lot of links from web 2.0 sites but no links from other sites. According to Michelle McPhearson and others, Google is starting to discount social media links if you have links from social media sites only. Google deems this unnatural link building. Therefore, you need links from different sites, not only web 2.0 sites and you will see below how you can do that.

Getting Presence on non-Web 2.0 Sites that Matter

Another powerful way to create links from high PR sites and thus get direct traffic from them is to get your articles on other websites with high profiles and high readerships. When you begin to submit your articles to third party websites, focus first on sites and blogs with a high traffic volume. This makes it much more likely that your article will get read more often. When you offer well established sites **exclusive** content, written especially for their site and their target market readers, you will have a far greater chance of getting your articles accepted. Since most webmasters simply don't have enough spare time to fiddle around with your article, a good way of making the whole process really convenient for them is to put together an 'Article Package' that enables them to publish your article on their site in a single click.

When you have succeeded in submitting your article to a good quality site, don't just sit back - start promoting this article on their site by bookmarking it on sites like StumbleUpon.com, Digg.com and Delicious.com and others to maximize the traffic potential of the article and the link to your site.

Getting Offline Readership

When you research top sites with high profile and high readership, remember, if the site has an offline publication, it may also publish your article in their offline edition, i.e. trade magazines etc. Sites like The Wall Street Journal, The Financial Times, Businessweek, The Economist, and other high profile publications can do wonders for your brand, when they choose to include your articles.

You can either submit your article using their submission service and guidelines, or compose an email to the appropriate person at each company. Make sure you include information about your company, products and services and why you are requesting that they consider your article for inclusion in their site and off-line publication. Send your e-mail and request a confirmation or a reply. Better still, call them and request to speak to the editor. Remember, these sites can provide high leverage for your site. If you consider the amount of traffic and brand value you could get from high profile, high readership sites and offline publications, it might make sense to create a unique variation of your article for each site.

Submit Your Article to Blogs

Also, submit your article to high quality blogs, too, since blogs tend to get indexed more quickly than static websites. As with web 2.0 sites, blogs usually get updated more frequently than websites. This makes Google believe that blog content is, in general, more up-to-date and, therefore, more relevant than content on the average, static website. As a result, the Google robots index blogs faster, which means your new content gets ranked faster and your traffic and sales start earlier. Today, blogs can look like websites, complete with designated sales pages, and you can get design structures, called 'blog themes' that are already SEO optimized.

A Word about Duplicate Content

We have talked about duplicate content on sites being one of the most common on-page SEO problems. To recap, sites that have the same content on various internal

pages are limiting their ability to rank highly. Reasons for this duplicate content are that old or back-up versions get saved on the same server directory or because a webmaster mistakenly believes it will be of ranking benefit.
(You can find other more technical reasons in the Glossary)

Writing and Publishing Regularly

What most people find challenging is to write and submit articles on a regular basis. There was a time when you could create new content constantly and automatically submit it using RSS feeds, for example. Again, most of the search engines now understand this tactic and disregard such automatically created content as 'duplicate content'. Therefore, it is now important to create unique, informative articles on a regular basis if you want the customers and profits.

When you consistently submit articles to directories online, you will build your brand as an expert in your field. Equally as importantly – you have heard it before – 'people buy on average on the 7th contact online'. What I mean by that is that your prospective customers will probably read some of your articles, or at least see the list of your articles, or see your name come up again and then again, before they are familiar with you enough to give you some credit. Only then will they start trusting you and get intrigued enough to come to your site and see what you are offering. It is a bit like what they might have told you at school about when you put a dollar or a pound/euro etc. into your bank account every day, "…the effect of compound interest is what can make you rich." There is no shortcut to wealth and success. As Stephen Pierce says, "the intangibles to winning are focus, consistency and patience". It is the consistent delivery of good value articles which do not anticipate an immediate return that will bring you your greatest success.

To Sum Up

Article marketing does take a bit of time and thought to get right. But the long-term benefits are significant and will last. Therefore, I recommend that you start this technique to generate traffic, links and customers for your site or blog as soon as possible.

GROW Step 9:

Place articles with unique content firstly on your own website or blog, then on other sites or blogs that are highly relevant to your business or profession. Include a link back to your website or blog with matching keywords in the Link Text / Anchor Text. This increases your link power and direct traffic to your site.

SUMMARY:

Off-Page SEO

Promoting your website by uploading relevant content in the form of articles, videos etc to high ranking sites across the Internet, can give your site a massive boost on the search engine listing. It's not difficult, but it takes a little more time than some of the techniques discussed earlier. Mastering this milestone by taking some or all of the steps will give your business a solid foundation for long term growth and success.

So, let me recap on the steps you need to take to use other sites on the internet in order to promote your own site very effectively:

GROW Step 7: Build Quality Links and Get Listed Highly on Google

Create **quality links that point to your website**, ideally with the keywords in the Link Text matching the keywords on your site. Create these links from relevant websites, where in a perfect world the keywords on the site match those in the link.

GROW Step 8: Promote Your Site Further with 'Social Bookmarking'

Social Bookmark your pages to promote your content by creating further links to them.

GROW Step 9: Use Articles as Your 24/7 Sales Agents

Place articles with unique content firstly on your own website or blog, then on other sites or blogs that are highly relevant to your business or profession. Include a link back to your website or blog with matching keywords in the Link Text / Anchor Text. This increases your link power and direct traffic to your site.

The more present you are across the web, and the more links with matching keywords you have from relevant quality sites, the higher Google values you and ranks your site. This leads to more traffic and customers finding your site.

PART V:

How to Turn Visitors into Customers

Converting Browsers into Customers

Getting more and more prospective customers to your site is the foundation of all success, online. However, converting these new visitors into buying customers is where the rewards are. There are many enticements to get a person who has come to your site for the first time to stay to purchase once, twice, or again and again: The choice of products on offer, your pricing, site presentation, website style, service guarantee, sales copy etc all have an influence on how well your customers convert at the end of the day.

I won't be able to cover all of these in this book. However, I will introduce you to two of the most effective conversion techniques around, which have a significant bottom line effect on whether a visitor ends up becoming a buying customer. These are a) using video online, and b) offering free value.

GROW Step 10:

Gain Customers' Trust Fast Using Video

Video on the Internet has massive potential, and it is experiencing sensational growth. eMarketer predicted that spending on online video ads is projected to more than triple by 2011. YouTube has already become the 2nd biggest search engine, overtaking Yahoo!, and it now charges $ 175,000 per day for putting a video on its front page.

I believe that in five years time, even the most resistant company will have to do video marketing to keep up with their competitors. But you can be ahead of the game. You see, videos are huge on the Internet already but video marketing somehow still has a 'novelty' factor to it, which makes it even more effective and more of opportunity for you if you start using it now. Video is useful in two fundamental ways:

a) It can bring substantially more traffic to your website.

b) Once the traffic is on your site, video can help converting these new visitors into buying customers.

Videos Bring More Traffic to Your Site

A strategically-produced video can increase your website's presence on the Internet quite quickly and significantly. The reason is this: Video is picked up much more quickly by search engines than text ads and can get indexed and listed on the search engines within hours; not days or months. Viral video tools can put your brand in places you never thought possible. Plus, once a video appears on Google, visitors are far more likely to click on a listing with a video attached to it.

Videos Increase Conversion

Videos have great power to turn your visitors into customers. Users select video over other forms of content by a ratio of 4 to 1, and 78% of visitors believe that video is more compelling than text! Tests have proven that a video attracts attention when people are visiting your site. For example, Dynamic Logic's MarketNorms has proved that brand awareness doubles with online video. A marketing study undertaken by Marketing Sherpa even revealed that adding video can increase an ad's responsiveness by up to 49.5%.

How can video produce such remarkable results? It does so simply by making your site's products and services far more real and easy to understand, even when visitors hear about you for the very first time. A video featuring one of the individuals behind a business, for example, makes the business more personal, and much more quickly instills trust in the company. Strangers can immediately see that you are for real and can connect with you.

Before too long, most companies will have video ads, and all a prospective customer has to do is click "play" to see your business in action. Plus, viewers can easily forward your video to their friends, giving you free advertising! When video marketing is implemented professionally, its effect of reaching new customers, converting them into customers and triggering repeat business can be significant. Making a video can also be quicker, cheaper and more effective than you might expect.

How to Produce and Optimize Your Videos So They Convert Well

Everybody can produce a video these days – the technology is easily accessible and affordable. Easy-to-use editing packages like Windows Movie Maker, which comes free with Windows, or, for better quality, Sony Vegas have sparked a revolution in DIY video production. If you want to go more upmarket and commission professional packages, you'll find that even they are increasingly affordable. But remember, it's not that important that your video is slick, glossy and professionally produced. It is important, however, that your video is easy to find online, that the viewer can relate to it, and that it provides him or her with valuable information. Here's a shortlist of 12 critical video optimization features you should keep in mind when producing a video, or having it produced for you:

1. Video content

Since content is still king, compelling content is where all optimization starts.

2. Video to personalize your company

Video plays an important role to demystify and personalize your company in the perception of the visitor. Often, a simply-shot piece to camera, for example featuring a friendly executive speaking a few words, or another employee explaining an aspect of your company's philosophy, can leave a lasting impression and make it much easier for a visitor to relate to you. It can ensure that your company stands out and that browsers remember your site and company better.

3. Format

Videos don't have to go on and on. Short and sharp is often much more effective then a long rambling, informational mini film. People have a short attention span and, although the standard length of an online video tends to be 1-2 min, yours could be substantially shorter and still do the trick.

4. Video script

With its new audio indexing technology (GAUDI), Google can now read a spoken script and decide whether a video is relevant for a particular search, based on what's said in the script. Therefore, you should start video optimization at the script stage, making sure that those all-important targeted keywords and semantically-related words are in the script, in order to get indexed quickly and correctly by Google.

5. Keywords and competition

Advertisers need to make absolutely sure that the keywords they use to optimize their videos get enough searches and click-throughs, enjoy a manageable level of competition, plus - most importantly - convert visitors to customers. Websites that don't optimize properly might get high numbers of visiting browsers who are looking for information but those visitors, most probably, will not buy. The same applies to videos. This is a key distinction to bear in mind in working towards higher conversion rates.

6. Share

Videos need to be share-able with so-called 'embed codes', such as those used on video sharing sites such as YouTube. And they need to be easily distributed by email and via RSS. Don't worry, you can protect your video from it being downloaded and used in a way you don't want by watermarking it. Your videos should, of course, be uploaded to top video sharing sites.

7. Call-to-action

Video viewers now expect appealing call-to-actions, almost like a reward worth their interest. Videos, combined with a compelling call-to-action are 400% more likely to convert!

8. Trackable

Video advertisements on an online directory site can and should be interactive and trackable. It is important for you to see how many more new customers are streaming in as a direct result of your video advertising campaign.

9. Video player

Superior, interactive video players transform passive video ads into active, revenue-generating leads, by allowing potential customers to interact with videos and to connect directly with you via phone, sms, fax and email. (Graphic: Art Technology Group, Inc.) They can also go to your website and save the video as a document, contact or bookmark.

Add Interactive Value To Your Customer's Video Advertising

'Call Us Now' lets Viewers call Advertisers directly from the Video.

'SAVE/SEND' lets Viewers
- GO directly to the Advertiser's Website
- SEND the Advertiser's Listing, by SMS, E-Mail, Fax
- SAVE to File, Contacts, Bookmarks

Video Viewers can access Advertiser Connect Features and go back to the Video at any Time.

It is important, though, that video viewers must be able to access all interactive features and the viewer must be able to easily go back to the video at any time.

Five Effective Ways to Publish Your Video on the Internet

Once your optimized video is ready, you can do far more with it than just upload it to your own website. Here are five important ways in which you can use it to boost your ranking and drive additional prospective customers to your site:

1. Keyword Placement

To ensure this has the desired effect, make sure you put the right keywords into your video title, into the **video description** and into the tags of the video. This way, you ensure that the search engines find your video for the keywords you want to target.

2. Online Exposure

Post your video on as many high ranking sites as possible to give it maximum exposure. Your videos can be easily uploaded with video submission services and/or multi-media widgets. Their long-term effect will be substantially enhanced if these videos are professionally marketed on social media sites like YouTube and many others, because this way, you benefit from the enormous ranking power that social media provides today.

3. Link Building

When you upload videos to video sharing sites such as YouTube.com and other web 2.0 sites, you can create links back to your website. You can usually include your URL / website address in the text of the video description. When you do this, you are showing readers how to find your site via a link, and you increase your ranking with the search engines.

4. Social Marketing

Provided you include links, participating in social networks such as Facebook or LinkedIn, commenting in blogs related to your products and services and blogging (including micro-blogging on sites like Twitter) are new and powerful ways to build ranking power for your video.

5. Social Bookmarking

This is another way to tell potential customers and the search engines about your website. There are a number of bookmarking sites where a direct link to your video can be placed. This gives the video ad significantly higher exposure and your website higher search engine authority.

PART V – Turning Visitors into Customers - Introduction

To Sum Up

Applying the techniques above will allow you, the business owner, to tap into the new and explosive growth of online video advertising.

GROW Step 10:

Boost your ranking, instil your visitors with trust, and turn them into subscribers and customers using effective **video optimization and marketing** techniques.

GROW Step 11:
Turn Searchers into Customers by Providing 'Free Value'

In a previous part, we saw that, according to Google Analytics expert Avinash Kaushik, 80% of all searches on the Internet are people looking for information rather than buying anything. If you want these people as prospective customers, your best chance is to draw them in by offering them free products, services or quality information. 'Free Value' also works a treat on a potential buyer who is hesitant to take the final step, or is busy shopping around. Providing a freebie could make him choose to buy from you rather than from your competitors. Have a think about how you could apply this principle to the products and services you offer, and take Step 11:

The Freebie Product

On the Internet, it is increasingly common for companies to provide unbiased, free advice with the hope that prospective customers come to their site and 'opt in' by giving you their details. This method of using a 'bribe' has been around for years. It is not as effective anymore as it was when first started, but still works when you offer the right kind of value.

The better targeted your free report is to the needs of your prospective customers, the higher your chance of seducing them to opt in, in exchange for what you offer them for free. Once they have agreed to receive your freebies, you can send them another bonus, another free report, and slip in a special offer. You continue to provide great value, get your company name and brand recognised, all of which makes it more likely that they will eventually buy from you rather than from your competitors. The bottom line is that **if** you give away something of great value, free to your prospective customers, you have a chance of catching the 80% of your target market that is, initially, just surfing for information.

It has also become quite common for service providers to offer their basic product package for free, and to charge for the premium version. Yanik Silver puts it succinctly:

"Think about all the different pieces of software you might have on your computer that cost you zero to download but have some annoying advertising or some features disabled.

Then you need to pay for the premium version to get the whole enchilada. Enough people [actually] do this to make that model work.

Or how about services that start off at no-charge like Jott.com and then because enough eyeballs and people have tested it out, improved it, made adjustments, etc - they move to a paid model. (And of course they probably got 10x as many initial users because the barrier to get started was zero.)

Or now with Twitter being such a huge hit - there are tons of services like Tweeteffect.com that are just completely and totally gratis… "

Chris Andersen, the editor at WIRED magazine, (www.wired.com/techbiz/it/magazine/16-03/ff_free), describes this aspect of the Web as "the freaky land of the Free". He reminds us that in 2007 the New York Times went free, with the Wall Street Journal soon following suit. Radiohead, Trent Reznor of Nine Inch Nails, and many other bands have built on their success very effective by offering free music. A Brazilian band became a very successful performing band on the back of allowing street sellers in Sao Paulo to bootleg their CDs and put the profits in their own pockets. The up-and-coming gaming industry is largely free to the player and financed through advertisements, and most of Google's services are free to consumers, such as Gmail, Picasa and GOOG-411.

Chris Andersen describes what has made the 'free' business model possible:

"Over the past decade …. a different sort of free has emerged. The new model is based …. on the fact that the cost of products themselves is falling fast. It's as if the price of steel had dropped so close to zero that King Gillette could give away both razor and blade, and make his money on something else entirely."

The Freebie Event

There are other ways to make your products and services highly noticed in a crowded marketplace. Yanik Silver mentions the 'Freebie Event', a teleseminar or webinar or another free event, with the main purpose of making a product attract a lot of attention with a lot of people. The free drinks launch party to promote a newly-opened restaurant or bar is a classic, off-line example. A competition, raffle draw, an online seminar or other informational event that your potential customers can log in for free are classic Internet-based freebie events.

Why the Free Models Works: Scale

Chris Andersen explains this phenomenon like this: "The Web is all about Scale, finding ways to attract the most users for centralized resources, **spreading those costs over larger and larger audiences** as the technology gets more and more capable…".

As an example, Andersen demonstrated what happened to the revenues of Google and Yahoo! when they radically dropped their prices for email storage in 2004. The results speak for themselves. Google was the first to drop its prices, to include 1 gigabyte free to every user, to get more customers. Yahoo! went further and offered infinite storage for free. As a result, the number of subscribers for both email providers increased rapidly, and as each webmail page comes with advertisements, revenues grew exponentially.

Andersen explains: "Basic economics tells us that in a competitive market, prices fall to the marginal cost. There's never been a more competitive market than the Internet, and every day the marginal cost of digital information comes closer to nothing …There's nothing new about technology's deflationary force, but what is new is the speed at which industries of all sorts are becoming digital businesses, and thus able to exploit those economics. The moment a company's primary expenses become things based in silicon, free becomes not just an option but the inevitable destination."

'Freemium' and the 1 Percent Rule

For an online subscription site or software this principle goes a step further. Often, there is a range of tiers on offer, from free trial or basic service to the more expensive pro version (like FlickR.com and the $25-a-year FlickR Pro). For Chris Anderson, this goes way beyond the traditional free sample being the promotional candy bar handout, or the diapers mailed to a new mother:

> "..Since these samples have real costs, the manufacturer gives away only a tiny quantity — hoping to hook consumers and stimulate demand for many more…

But for digital products, this ratio of free to paid is reversed. A typical online site follows the 1 Percent Rule — 1 percent of users support all the rest.

In the freemium model, that means for every user who pays for the premium version of the site, 99 others get the basic free version. The reason this works is that the cost of serving the 99 percent is close enough to zero to call it nothing"

What Does All This Mean for You and Your Business?

The bottom line is this: The more freebies, free trials, free basic service, unbiased valuable and relevant information you are able to provide to your prospective customers, the more customers you are likely to attract to your enterprise. Ideally, you'd have a free video on your site offering a free product and some information about it as a bonus to the interested visitor.

Think about which of the business models above might apply to the product or service you sell in order to establish how, by providing free value, you could get any more customers interested in your products and services in a way which would lead to substantially larger back-end profits. Once visitors have opted into your site, continue to provide highly targeted, valuable, free information, products and services to your rapidly growing list, since it is the quality and responsiveness of your list that will turn your subscribers into customers.

Once in a while, slip in a highly-targeted and compelling offer that makes your subscribers want to become your customers. To do it better than your competitors, find out in what ways they already use this tactic and how successful they are. To do this you can use the competition analysis tool mentioned in Part VI, the section about SEO Tools. Then, do what they do a little better. Offer better products, better prices, better quality, better service – you get the picture.

SUMMARY:

Customer Conversion

The big part of your website visitors are only of benefit to you if they eventually buy from your site. To persuade visitors to become loyal, lifetime customers, use these two highly-effective conversion techniques: Video marketing and offering free value. As we have seen FREE is already one of the most powerful words on the Internet and it will gain increasing importance as a business model in various industry sectors. Video marketing has proven to attract site visitors and video viewers in astonishing numbers and corporate videos have demonstrated to be able to convert visitors into subscribers and buyers at rates hardly ever achieved with text before. Let me recap these two remaining steps:

GROW Step 10: Gain Customers' Trust Fast Using Video

Boost your ranking and instil your customers with trust, using effective **video optimization and marketing** techniques.

GROW Step 11: Turn Searchers into Customers with 'Free Value'

Always create **great value content** on your site and other sites linking to you, to persuade your visitors to opt in. Provide free products and services, where possible.

Continue to provide great value to people on your growing list and offer your products and services on a commercial basis once you have formed a trusting relationship with your subscribers.

PART VI:

SEO Tools

SEO Tools For Your Keyword Research and Competition Analysis

By now you probably have a good idea which SEO steps to take to optimize your website to get targeted traffic to your site or blog. In this part let's look at the tools that can save you time and money in carrying out these steps:

On the following pages you will find quite a number of SEO tools that I have listed for you. I am using most of these tools myself or my team is using them, and we are using them for our clients. Additionally I have listed one or two other tools since you and your IT staff will have their own style of carrying out SEO tasks, and different tools suit different users.

Therefore please be aware that the list I have put together in this part is a biased list and does not show all of the high end corporate tools on the market. Therefore you will find a list of personal or company preferences here, not a review over the entire market of SEO tools. But, in my opinion, you can get most of the data nowadays with the tools listed in this part.

The tools listed here are very helpful in saving you time to gain insights which could otherwise take you hours and hours of work. But clearly my team and I have not tried and tested every tool in the market. Whenever a highly acclaimed new tool comes onto the market, we will have a look at it if our time schedule allows.

Now, I am not suggesting you should make it your favorite past time to try all SEO and keyword tools on the market. That would probably not be the best use of your time. Leave the majority of the tools to your IT / SEO people and concentrate on what you do best. Most businesses can achieve 80% of the results with 20% of the techniques, in this case, 20% of the SEO tools available (not all of them). If you want to start with a small selection of powerful and easy-to-use tools to check demand and competition, these are the three tools I would suggest:

1. If you want to check the possible **demand** for your products and services in terms of how many people search for it online and how much would someone be willing to spend on advertising. use Google's free Adwords Keyword Tool at https://adwords.google.com/select/KeywordToolExternal.

2. If you would like to get a quick overview of what the **overall competition** is like for a certain product or service keyword you want to target, install the free SEO for Firefox tool from http://tools.seobook.com/firefox/seo-for-firefox.html.

PART VI - SEO Tools

3. Once you need a more in depth competiton analysis to find out how well specific competitors have optimized their pages, get a free 12 days trial from Market Samurai at www.marketsamurai.com/. This is an 'all in' tool that has various functions and modules but still is straightforward to use and affordable for most businesses. (P.S. There has been a new release of the Keyword Elite tool, Keyword Elite 2.0 which puts it on par with Market Samurai and in some areas above Samurai.)

Additionally Google offers some of the best free tools on the Internet:

1. **Google Webmaster Tools** (www.google.com/webmasters/tools) - Just open an account and Google Webmaster Tools provides you with detailed reports about your pages' visibility on Google. To get started, simply add and verify your site and you'll start to see information right away.

2. **Google Analytics** (www.google.com/analytics) – "is the enterprise-class web analytics solution that gives you rich insights into your website traffic and marketing effectiveness. Powerful, flexible and easy-to-use features now let you see and analyze your traffic data in an entirely new way. With Google Analytics, you're more prepared to write better-targeted ads, strengthen your marketing initiatives and create higher converting websites." [Google] Indeed, Google Analytics is so powerful that, according to one expert, you can "cancel the contract with your favorite expensive analytics vendor. Use that $40,000, or $80,000 or $160,000 to hire a smart analyst and put the rest in your pocket. Your smart analyst will be able to extract just as much value from Google Analytics as from your old tool. In fact, it is quite likely that a smart analyst will be able to extract a lot more value from Google Analytics compared to the part-time report writer you might have had in the past." [Analytics Expert Avinash Kaushik]

Tools to Maximize Your Business Profit Potential

There are a lot of specialized tools out there and, on the following pages, I have listed some of the top resources available within the Internet Marketing, SEO and Social Media Marketing fields. These are tools to help you maximize the profit potential of your business, and I have categorized them as follows:

1. Keyword Suggestion, Selection and Traffic Tools
2. Competition Analysis Tools
3. Trend Analysis Keyword Tools, Keyword Popularity Tools
4. SEO Toolbars

1. Keyword Tools – What Do You Use Them For?

You can use these Keyword tools to get new keyword ideas and to see related word searches. Keyword tools can help your website rank higher on the search engines and save you a lot of time, when used properly. They will help you to see which keywords you should be targeting to increase your website rankings, traffic, and profit. Find out how often particular keyword phrases are searched for, and choose relevant and popular terms related to your primary keyword term.

As we discussed in the beginning of the book, keyword research is crucial for your successful search engine website site optimization, managing PPC keywords and achieving top search engine rankings. And there are a number of competitive intelligence tools that provide in-depth research and tracking for PPC , SEO and affiliate campaigns to find the keywords that your competitors are using.

Which Keyword Tools Will Deliver the Results - For You?

There are excellent keyword research tools on the market that can save you a lot of time and money when you do your keyword research, or when you are researching your successful competitors. There are free tools out there, which will help to keep your costs down and a number of the best commercial keyword tools offer free trial periods. Bear in mind that the commercial tools will give you information that the free tools do not provide. Do not rely on only one source for your keyword research data. Checking different sources, such as search engines, keyword databases and PPC engines, through a variety of tools will give you a broader perspective.

Google offers some of the best free **Google's Keyword Tools** Trend. Although Google says that some of its tools are designed for Google Adwords users, you can use these tools for SEO, natural searches and organic listings. All these tools have different features, and you will quickly find out which tools match your business model and research style. For example, some tools provide the keyword lists your competitors are using. This can save you a lot of time, since your competitors probably have done some of the keyword research for you already. This allows you

PART VI - SEO Tools

to simply download their keyword list, legally. Many of the keyword tools have short-term trials that allow you to use all the features for a limited time period, and if one of the tools suits your research style and helps you to save time and make more profits, you can subscribe to the chargeable version. As with all tools, master the most essential ones first before you move on to the more advanced tools.

Keyword Suggestion Tools and Keyword Selection Tools

These are tools that you would be using when you do keyword research. These tools help you to brainstorm and build an initial list of keywords from which you then select your primary keywords – your main and most important keywords as well as your secondary keywords, such as related, synonymous and log-tail keywords.

These tools are important because by extending your keyword list you will get options to choose from which probably make your online campaigns, based on those keywords, much more cost effective and give you a higher return on your investment (ROI). One of the best tools you can use for brainstorming and selecting your keywords is the following:

Google AdWords: Keyword Tool
https://adwords.google.com/select/KeywordToolExternal

Google's free Adwords Keyword Tool is probably your best starting point for any keyword research, since you can do 80% of your keyword research with it. It shows you synonyms and related keywords based on the keyword you have entered, all with Monthly Search Volumes, Advertiser Competition, and Average CPC numbers. Instead of a certain keyword, you can also put your own URL or a competitor's URL into the keyword tool, too, and it will give you keyword suggestions based on that site. This is helpful for competition analysis.

Google Search-Based Keyword Tool
www.google.com/sktool

Google explains the difference between its two main keyword tools as follows: "The main difference between the Search-Based Keyword Tool and the Keyword Tool currently in AdWords is that the former generates keyword ideas based on your website, and identifies those currently not being used in your AdWords account." One of the main reasons I use Google's Search-based Tool is that it allows you to find out quickly which keywords a certain domain ranks for, according to Google. It is easier to rank a site higher for keywords for which it already has an initial ranking.

SEO Tools

Wordtracker Free Keywords

http://freekeywords.wordtracker.com

WordTracker is a classic, and was one of the first keyword tools that dominated the keyword research landscape before Google. Its tool is easy to use and allows users to quickly find relevant keywords for both SEO and PPC campaigns. Wordtracker's best use probably lies in finding secondary keywords, such as modified and long tail keywords. There is a free limited version and a chargeable version, and a new version with more up-to-date features is on its way (www.wordtracker.com/blog/new-wordtracker-keyword-tool-is-coming/).

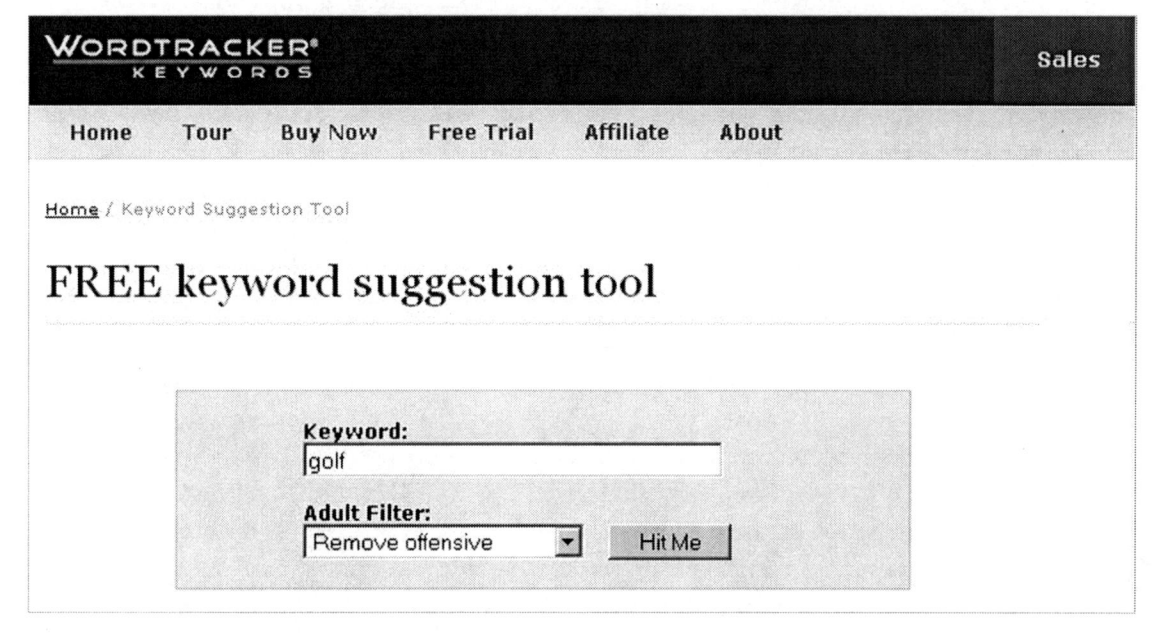

Keyword Suggestion Tool Wordtracker.com

PART VI - SEO Tools

Case Study: *How Travel Intelligence Turned its 8000 Website Pages into Assets*
"Travel Intelligence (TI) has over 8000 pages of extremely rich and completely unoptimized content. When fully optimized it will be a force to be reckoned with, and taking on the big guys will be of particular satisfaction" beamed David Deutsch of Travel Intelligence [at the time].

So, TI went [at one point had to go] back to basics and rebuilt their marketing plan [because they weren't satisfied with the results they had achieved so far].

"The first step is simple meta-tagging, followed by building link popularity with properly managed SEO marketing." Deutsch adds. Deutsch uses Wordtracker as his keyword research tool. "On analyzing the site we saw which keywords we should be using. 'Hotel review' for example, is a popular keyword but it doesn't bring in sales and we want to optimize for keywords that focus on booking." Having identified the major changes on which to focus, Deutsch's next step for TI was to work out why they weren't at the top of the search engines when a user, for example, typed in 'Paris Hotel'.

"TI has several hundred pages of subject matter but they weren't optimized - all similar pages should focus on one general keyword like 'Paris Hotel' as well as on more specific individual/niche words such as Hotel Crillon Paris" explains Deutsch… "Wordtracker's keyword research tool is so useful. If I want to focus on Paris in order to attract all the relevant traffic from those looking in that sector I need to know that people are searching with both 'luxury hotels Paris' and 'five star hotel Paris'.

I can also use keyword research for reverse SEO - finding out which keywords were used to visit my site. Web analytics gives me 50,000 keywords. I can look at each keyword and they can be removed if all they are producing is bouncing traffic. Or I can take them and type them into Wordtracker and it will show which other terms someone who used that particular word also uses. I can add those terms to target more keywords and attract more traffic."……..

Once the site has been SEO'd, extra strands of content added, and the navigation sorted - then the fun starts. The focus is now on keywords which will drive sales. "The end result when using keyword research for PPC is a keyword list of several hundred thousand words, attracting the correct type of visitor to your site, together with proper website usability to produce a 2% or more sales conversion rate", concludes Deutsch. David Deutsch shared his experience with Karen Durham-Diggins (kdd PR) an independent PR Consultant for Wordtracker.

This case study shows you why it is important to use keyword tools such as Wordtracker to find out which keywords really make you money and therefore should be your focus.

Wordtracker Keyword Questions

http://labs.wordtracker.com/keyword-questions

This is another tool from Wordtracker which shows you the questions containing your keyword that people have searched for. Naturally, it is important to get an idea of what searchers actually are looking for, for example, when they have a product or service related questions. And this tool can give you a pretty good idea of the searcher's objectives.

When you are thinking of writing new content for your site or blog, it can be helpful to see either that most of the searchers have more or less the same questions about your subject, or that their questions are very different. If the questions are more or less the same, you can concentrate on answering those, if the questions are very different, you need to find out the most important one for you. For example, if you were selling 'golf bags' this tool could tell you some of the questions people have asked on the Internet regarding 'golf bags' and below is a screenshot for a 'golf bag' query in Wordtracker's Keyword Questions tool:

Find the questions that people are asking in your market

Enter a single or short keyword: `golf bag` [Search]

Results for: *golf bag*   Download

#	Question	Times asked (?)
1	what type of golf clubs should men have in their golf bag	8
2	what is the best travel golf bag to buy?	7
3	what clubs are in a legal golf bag	6
4	what is the best golf bag	6
5	what is a hybrid golf bag	4
6	how to organize a golf bag	4
7	how to set up a golf bag	4
8	what clubs should i carry in my golf bag	3
9	what clubs should be in your golf bag	3
10	chocolate molds who makes them golf bag	3
11	what is a hybrid golf travel bag	3
12	how many clubs in pga golf bag	3
13	what is the proper way to pu golf clubs in a golf bag	3
14	what kind of beer does the tap in al's golf bag dispense?	3
15	what is in greg norman golf bag	3

Questions people have asked about 'golf bags'

The "times asked" figure is the number of times that the question has been asked on Wordtracker's partner search engines in the US, over the last year. You can see here, therefore, that there is a wide variety of questions being asked about golf bags. This is useful, in that you need to identify the underlying themes of the different questions so you can group them into subjects or themes. You then know, how many different pages that are themed to answer specific questions you will need, in order to capture the types of searchers that ask these questions online.

Search Funnels
Microsoft adCenter Labs
http://adlab.msn.com/Search-Funnels

This tool tells you which sites people were on before coming to your site or blog and where they went afterwards. Why is this important? Because it tells you something about the intent of the searcher. Was he/she interested only in information, or in actually buying something? After all, you don't want to target a keyword with a mainly-informational bias in your product ad. Also, you don't want to show an informational ad to someone who actually wants to buy your product right now.

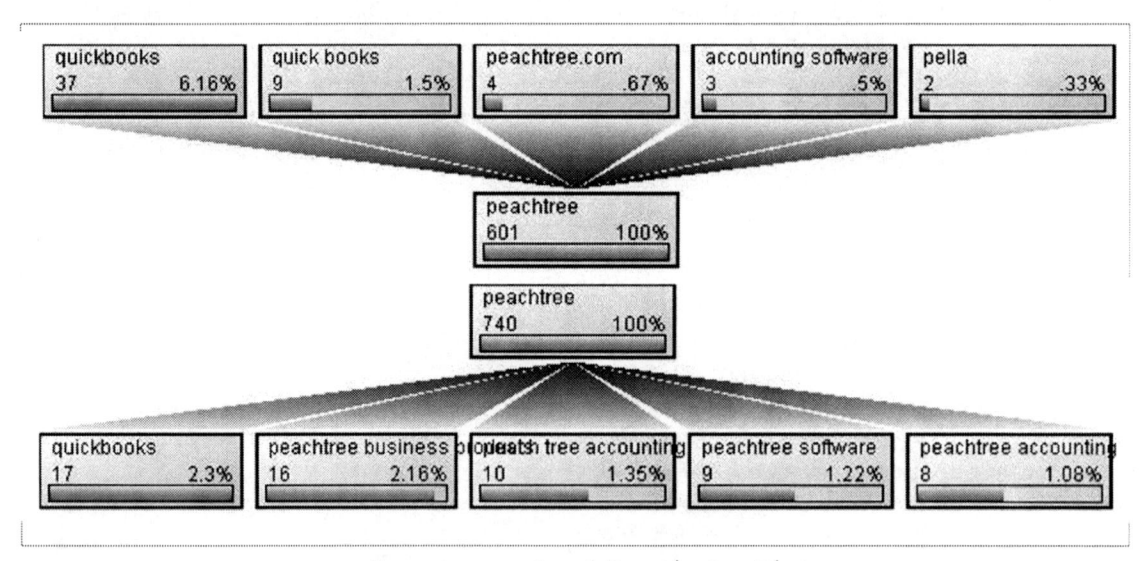

Source: www.kaushik.net/avinash/

This screenshot from Avinash Kaushik (www.kaushik.net/avinash/) shows the sites that searchers visited before and after coming to 'peachtree.com'.

Market Samurai

www.marketsamurai.com

This tool aims to be an all-in solution. It can save you a lot of time because you don't have to switch between various tools.

Keyword Suggestion Tool Market Samurai

Below is a list of Market Samurai's different modules: A Keyword Research module to find additional relevant keywords - then analyze the total traffic, visitor values, competition and likely buying intentions around these keywords. A SEO competition module to analyze the competition on the top 10 web-pages in your current keyword market. A module to find content for your website. A promotional tool that will help you to 'boost your search engine rankings, pump-up your site traffic, to build high quality back links'. It even helps you with publishing content monetizing your site, and your Adwords campaigns.

To see an example of how I use this comprehensive tool, go back to Part II, where I have used Market Samurai in one of the examples of how to analyze the competition.

KeywordElite.com

www.keywordelite.com

Keyword Elite is a well known tool and also pretty comprehensive. It combines five tools in one and has advanced features for analyzing and spying on Adwords competition.

PART VI - SEO Tools

Keyword Suggestion Tool KeywordElite.com

The new release, Keyword Elite 2.0 will give you 8 different modules:
1. Keyword Surge
2. Market Research Sleuth
3. AdWords time Machine
4. Search Engine Dominator
5. AdWords Competition Sniper
6. Advanced Google Site Targeter
7. JV Diamond Miner
8. CPA Magnet

If you haven't used an all-in-one keyword tool yet, Keyword Elite 2.0 is a good choice to start with.

Which of these 'all-in' tools is best to use will depend on the specific task at hand and your own personal style of 'doing keyword respectively SEO research'. You will quickly learn what works for you once you get started.

Keyword Discovery
www.keyworddiscovery.com/search.html

KeywordDiscovery is a free keyword tool from Trellian, who also offer a paid version. One of its big advantages over Wordtracker.com is that it contains seasonal searches e.g. for the Christmas Season for longer periods than Wordtracker. (That is at the time of writing, Wordtracker is about to release a major update, too.)

Keyword Discovery claims to collect search term data from over 200 search engines world wide. It also offers many language specific keyword databases, sourced from regional search engines and users from those regions.

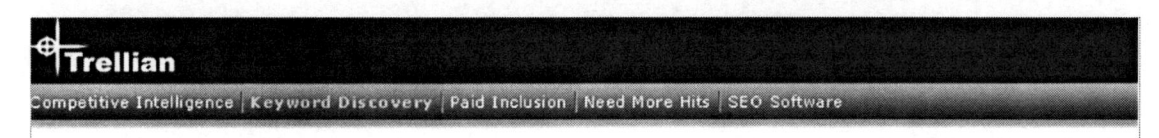

Trellian
Competitive Intelligence | Keyword Discovery | Paid Inclusion | Need More Hits | SEO Software

Free Trial | Features | Related | Spell

Free Search Term Suggestion Tool

For many years the Overture Keyword Suggestion was the only free, publicly available keyword research tool. Now, due to its recent outages we are pleased to offer an alternative.

Our keyword data is compiled and collected from a number of search engines to provide a far more accurate cross section of searches performed world wide.

Simply type a seed keyword in the below field and have KeywordDiscovery generate the top 100 keywords for you.

Keyword Suggestion Tool in Trellian

2. Competition Analysis Tools

SEO for Firefox
http://tools.seobook.com/firefox/seo-for-firefox.html

The SEO for Firefox tool is one of the most useful free tools around. For a description of how to install it in your Firefox browser and how to set it up, go to the URL above. For an example of how to use the tool in your competition analysis, see 'A Fast Way to Check your Competition' in GROW Step 3 of this book.

Compete
www.compete.com

- Compete has a free service that lets you:
- compare different sites;
- see who you are competing with on specific keywords and phrases;
- investigate how your competitors are getting traffic;
- compare your traffic acquisition strategy to that used by competing sites;
- identify rival search marketing strategies; and
- discovers how to improve your own SEM and SEO campaigns.

Compete offers a upgraded professional service for which it charges.

PART VI - SEO Tools

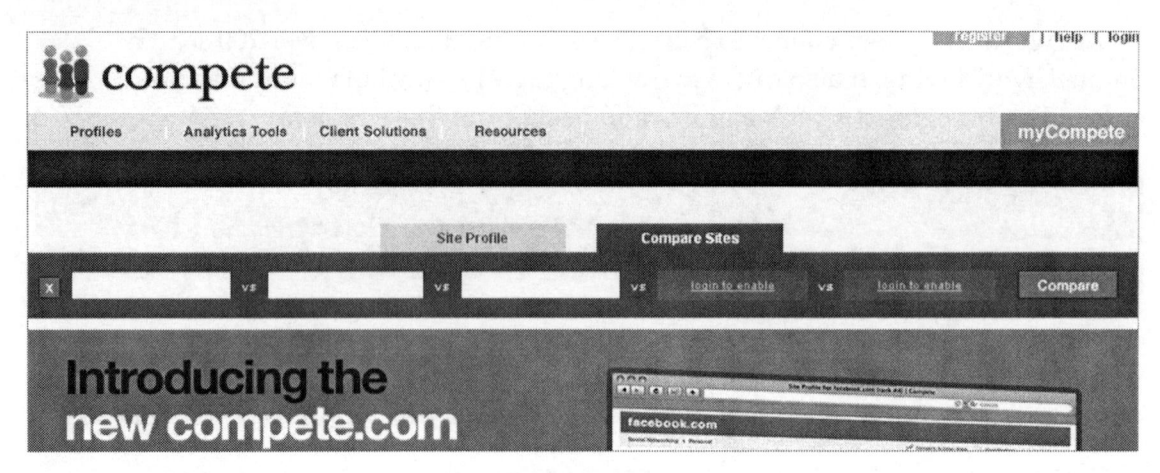

Compete.com

You can use Compete.com's competitive research tools, for example, to estimate click distribution, meaning which site gets how many clicks, since Compete's search analytics allows you to view the top five destinations for the exact match version of a keyword for free, and offers further data if you subscribe to their paid service.

Volume Rank	Destination Website	% Total Keyword Volume	% of Site's Search Traffic	Average Monthly Search Referrals
1	golfsmith.com	18.36%	2.72%	276,713
2	tgw.com	10.42%	1.63%	287,550
3	worldwidegolfshops.com	6.46%	14.04%	18,568
4	globalgolf.com	5.52%	2.86%	82,983
5	golfoutletsusa.com	5.12%	6.13%	37,164

Compete.com showing the top five results for 'Golf Clubs'

PPC WebSpy
www.ppcwebspy.com

This is one of the latest keyword tools. It contains features such as:
- the CPC, or amount your competitors are paying for each keyword they're paying for;
- the actual Adwords ads your competitors are using for each keyword;

- your competitor's Adwords rank, to determine how much you should be spending to get to a similar PR;
- the landing page (i.e. destination URL) that the Adwords advertiser is sending visitors to;
- your competitor's targeted keyword list, which you can use to build an even larger, more targeted keyword list; and
- the identity of Adwords advertisers that are promoting Clickbank.com, Paydotcom.com, or Amazon.com products.

Keyword Research Tool PPCWebspy.com

GoRank (Free)

www.gorank.com/analyze.php

GoRank is an SEO tool that helps you determine the relevance of your competitor's web pages based on certain keywords. Simply type your competitor's URL and the respective keyword into the GoRank search fields to see how well your competitor has optimized their pages.

PART VI - SEO Tools

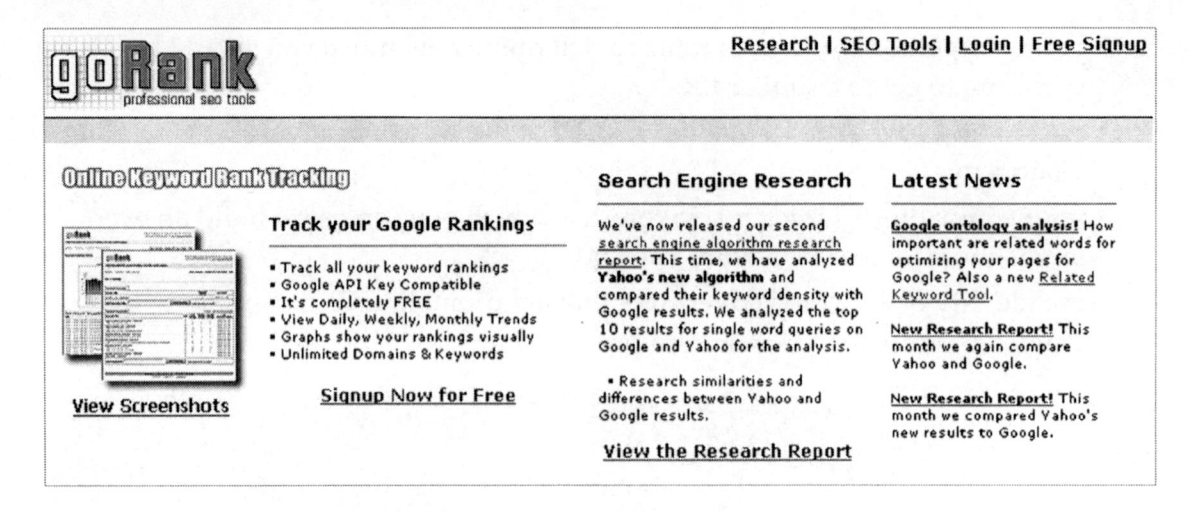

GoRank.com

KeywordSpy
www.keywordspy.com

Keyword Spy is an advanced keyword & competition research tool, mainly for results on PPC campaigns.

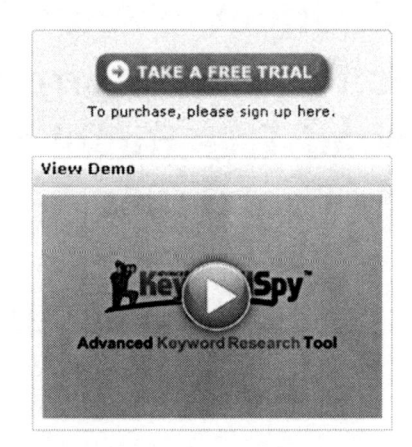

Keyword Search Tool KeywordSpy.com

3. Trend Analysis Keyword Tools and Keyword Popularity Tools

Keywords Tools that Analyze Trends

There are many ways to track trends and news online. For example, news sources such as the New York Times (www.nytimes.com) the Wall Street Journal (http://europe.wsj.com/home-page) and others provide email updates of key stories. Google also has several tools that give insight into global and regional search trends, past and present, and I have listed them below:

Google Trends
www.google.com/trends/

Google Trends allows you to get a broad look at search query data, by entering up to five search terms. This shows the relative popularity of those terms, over time.

Google Hot Trends
www.google.com/trends/hottrends

Google Hot Trends shows you the US's top 100 fastest-rising search queries right now, with updates throughout the day. It also gives you estimates of seasonal search volumes (e.g. Christmas Season), which allows you to filter by geographic regions in the US.

Google Trends for Websites
http://trends.google.com/websites

Type a website address into Google Trends to see visitors by region and related sites visited.

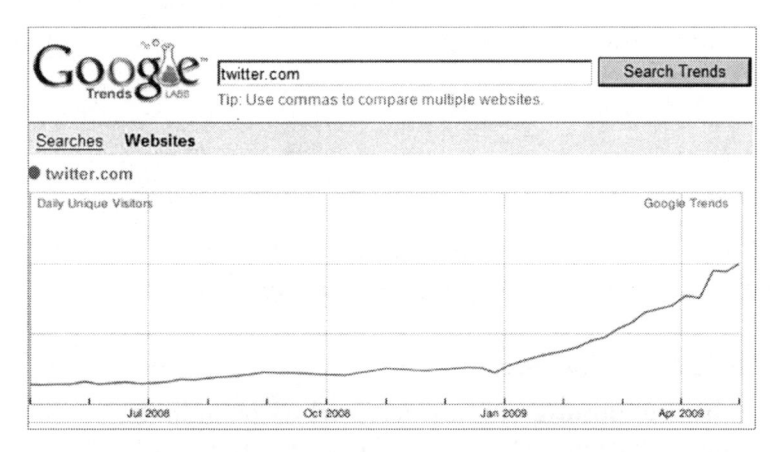

Google trend numbers for Twitter.com Jul 2008 – Apr 2009

PART VI - SEO Tools

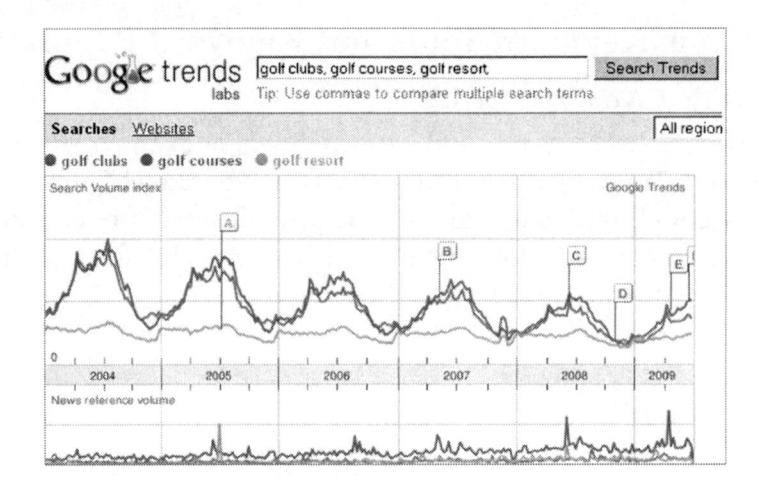

Google trend numbers for 'Golf Clubs', 'Golf Courses', 'Golf Resort', 2004 - 2009

Google Insights for Search
www.google.com/insights/search

Google calls it "a deeper dive into search query data for marketers and power users". Create your own lists of "most popular" and "fastest rising" queries for different geographic regions over time and by topic.

Google Zeitgeist
www.google.com/intl/en/press/zeitgeist/index.html

"Zeitgeist" means "the spirit of the times", and Google reveals this spirit, which is a German word for trend through the aggregation of millions of the search queries they receive every day.

Google Alerts
www.google.com/alerts

Google Alerts allows you to receive e-mail alerts for whatever keyword you choose, i.e. your personal or company name, your products or services, competitors, etc.

Some uses of Google Alerts include:
- monitoring the mentioning of your personal name online;
- monitoring the mentioning of your products/services;
- getting a developing news story as soon as it is published;

SEO Tools

  ○ keeping up-to-date on a competitor or industry;
  ○ getting the latest on a celebrity or event;
  ○ keeping tabs on your favorite organizations, teams etc.

Yahoo! Buzz - Top Overall Searches
http://buzz.Yahoo.com

Yahoo! also has a trend tool, Yahoo! Buzz, that can give you information about breaking stories on major news or viral videos on personal blogs and much more. Stories get submitted by anyone and the best ones get "buzzed up" by the community.

Key Phrase Forecast
Microsoft adCenter Labs
http://adlab.msn.com/ForecastV2/KeywordTrendsWeb.aspx

This is another tool I hear good things about, but as I have only just started using it myself, I will let analytics expert **Avinash Kaushik (www.kaushik.net/avinash/)** explain how to use it:

> *"What this wonderful tool allows you to do is get an outsider's opinion of what the next few months look like for your Top 10 keywords, and compare it to your competitors ..."*

He gives this example:

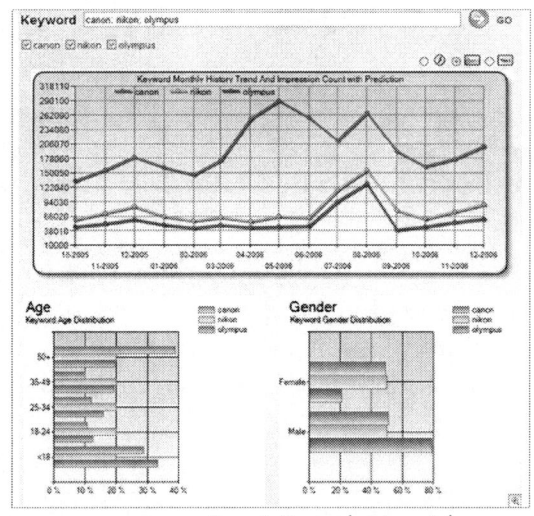

Source: www.kaushik.net/avinash/

203

PART VI - SEO Tools

"... It is to be expected that during holiday season sales of digital cameras will pick up. But I wonder if the folks running the web strategy for Nikon and Olympus know what Canon is doing so much better than them, and is predicted to do much better (slope of the line in the yellow area of the graph) than them during the holiday season. Could they use this data to adapt their strategy to do better against Canon? Maybe come up with a more robust strategy around non-branded keywords to counter this strong brand keyword trend?"
(Source: Avinash Kausik)

The Microsoft adCenter Labs invest heavily into search, keyword and information technology and provide a range of tools that are getting more interesting every day.

SEOMoz Popular Searches

www.seomoz.org/popular-searches

Updated once daily, this is an aggregation of popular search queries, gathered from various sources like Technorati, Flickr, Del.icio.us, Yahoo! Buzz, Google Hot Trends, Ebay, AOL, Lycos and Amazon.

Keyword Popularity Tool SEOmoz

Social Media and Social Bookmark Sites That Tell You about Trends

The new breed of Social Media and Social Bookmarking sites like Digg, Del.icio.us, Flickr, Technorati, Topix and others give you good insights into current trends within their communities through their ratings systems. Some of them use so called 'cloud tags' which show you the most popular tags / keywords on their sites.

Delicious

http://delicious.com

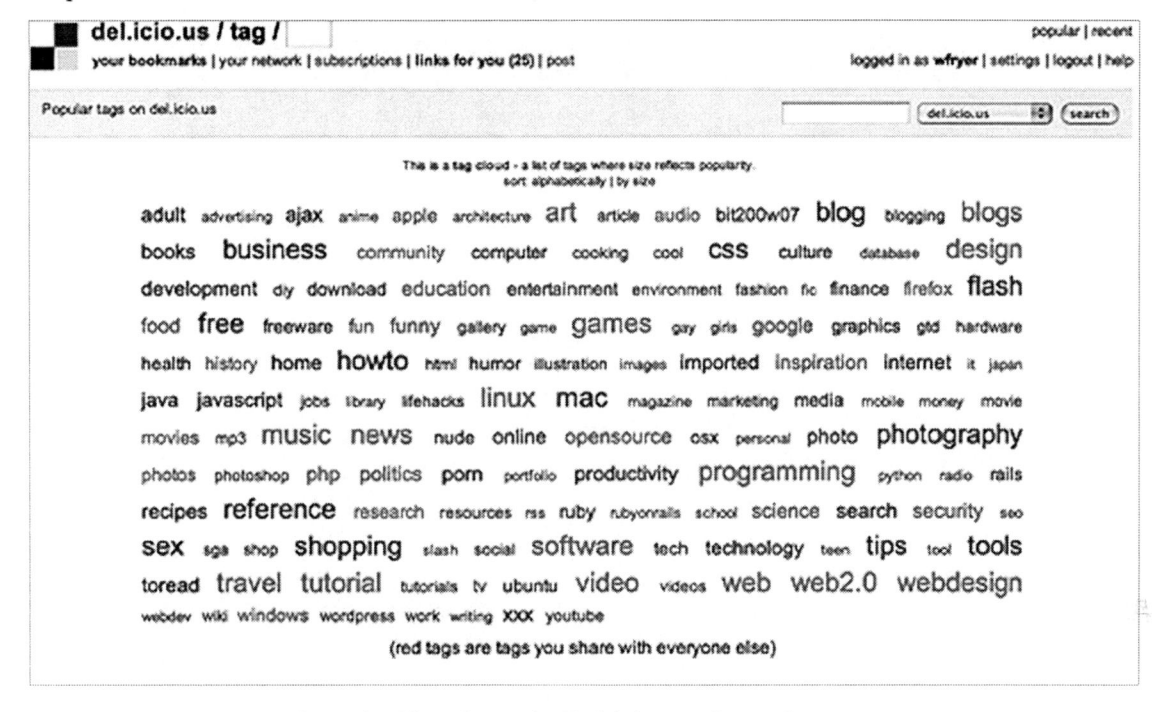

*Sample **Cloud Tag** in Del.icio.us of popular tags.*

Digg

http://digg.com

This screenshot shows you the top articles in Digg over the last 365 days. The more 'diggs' you get, the more popular your article becomes, the longer it will stay on the front pages of Digg and the more traffic Digg and your article can send to your site or blog.

As Gary Vaynerchuk of Wine Library TV recently said:

> *"I would rather be on Digg.com's page one than on the front of the New York Times."*

PART VI - SEO Tools

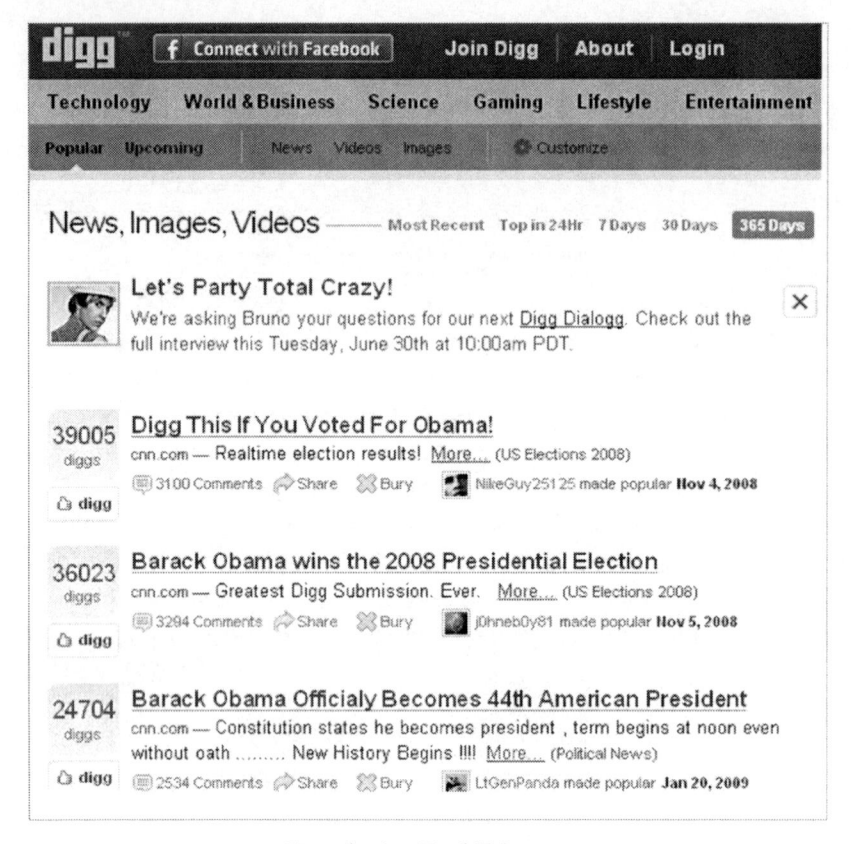

Popularity Tool Digg

Topix

http://topix.com

Topix aggregates news and trends from different sources and makes them searchable by location, source, and keyword.

Keyword Tracking Tool Topix

Trendy Commercial Keywords

Amazon
www.amazon.com

Amazon provides market information about best sellers, new releases, and movers & shakers. Due to the size of the Amazon site and the items selling on it, this can give you good insight into what currently sells, at what rates, and which items are 'trending up' (ie. become more interesting).

EBay Pulse
http://pulse.ebay.com

Ebay Pulse is a free tool with daily snapshots of current trends and hot picks. EBay is probably the single largest marketplace of buyers and sellers on the Internet. This is a good way to see what is currently trending up or down. When you go to http://pulse.ebay.com, you will see what the most popular search terms are.

EBay offers a marketplace research service, which allows you to see what items are frequently searched for on eBay. EBay's research partner Terapeak (http://pages.terapeak.com/us/learn_more/) also offers a paid tool with more detailed information on what items are selling on eBay and for how much.

4. SEO Toolbars

Google Toolbar
http://toolbar.Google.com

Google's PageRank rating has become the industry standard. In order for you to see your own website's PR or your competitor's PR you can download Google's free toolbar at http://toolbar.Google.com. Once you have installed this browser plug-in, it will produce a PR score for every page you visit.

If you want to take this a step further and not only see the PR of your competitors but also information about their linking structure, you can install another useful browser plug-in:

PART VI - SEO Tools

SEOBook Toolbar
http://tools.seobook.com/seo-toolbar.

Keyword Popularity Tool SEOToolbar

This toolbar provides a lot of information about your competitors. Aaron Wall, the owner of the site and the tool says about it: "The idea of this toolbar was to put the best competitive research data and the best SEO research tools at your fingertips - free of charge. The SEO Toolbar was designed to make it easier to evaluate how strong a competing website is. It pulls in useful marketing data to make it easy to get a more holistic view of the competitive landscape of a market right from your browser."

Take it With a Grain of Salt ...

Using keyword and competition analysis tools, you can find out a lot about your competitors, legally, on the Internet. It is the most transparent business environment I know of, as long as you understand how to find the figures that count. However, it is important to take the information you'll discover with a grain of salt.

Although you will be able to assemble a lot of information, in some cases you should take the results not as an absolute number but as a trend figure. Yes, this is powerful information, but the way you should apply it requires you to think in a slightly different way to the way you might be used to.

... Where My Website Appears on Google

For example, when you look at who is listed **in what position** on Google and you want to share this with someone who might be across the ocean, what he sees as the top ten listings on his PC screen might differ from what you are seeing at your end. This makes it less easy to pin down who the competition really is that you have to beat.

One of the reasons why you see these different listings is that Google stores its search results in various local datacenters around the world, and it doesn't update these datacenters at the same time. When you and your business colleague see different search results, it simply means that you get the results from different datacenters that were not upgraded 'in parallel'. Don't let this worry you too much. It just means that you have to check more often who is in the listing position that you ideally want to occupy yourself.

... How Much Traffic a Site Gets

When you are trying to figure out exactly how much traffic your competitors are getting, you also have to take these results with a grain of salt. Most tools won't give you a reliable number for traffic volumes of other websites, and you will need a number of 'traffic indicators' to get close to an actual traffic figure.

For example, the Alexa Rank (Alexa.com), an indicator that is almost as well known as the Google Page Rank (Google.com/toolbar), tells you whether one website gets more traffic than another one. But be aware that Alexa numbers will always rank companies better when its webmasters use the Alexa Toolbar themselves and do Internet Marketing with companies that also use the Alexa Toolbar.

So, how reliable is the Alexa Rank and other similar tools to predict traffic? The short answer is that, currently, you just can't get highly reliable numbers in this SEO area. In a recent study, Rand Fishkin compared a number of what he calls 'traffic predictors', to see which tool best indicates actual traffic numbers. Here is what he found: (www.seomoz.org/article/search-blog-stats). The better the tool or service can predict traffic volumes, the higher on the list it appears (at the time of writing):

1. Number of Technorati Links - http://technorati.com/
2. SEOmoz Page Strength - www.seomoz.org/
3. Number of Links to the blog via Yahoo! Site Explorer - https://siteexplorer.search.com/
4. Number of Links to the Domain via Yahoo! Site Explorer - https://siteexplorer.search.com/
5. Bloglines Subscriptions - www.bloglines.com/
6. Technorati Rank - http://technorati.com/
7. Alexa Rank - http://alexa.com/
8. Netcraft Rank - http://news.netcraft.com/
9. Newsgator Subscribers - www.newsgator.com/
10. Compete Rank - http://compete.com/
11. Ranking Rank - www.ranking.com/
12. Google PageRank – http://google.com

Since the publication of Rand Fishkin's study, some tool providers have made considerable efforts to improve the quality of their results, so the order might have changed slightly. However, even if these tools don't predict traffic numbers of other websites well, you should not dismiss traffic indication tools – far from it. They do provide you with some very useful figures. For example, how much your traffic is growing or falling in response to a campaign, and at what speed and whether your competitors are gaining ground or not. These tools will provide you with good information. Just be mindful of how you apply what you find.

Now it's over to you. Start using these tools with the steps I showed you in this book and optimize your website or blog to attract new customers to your business today.

PART VII:
Conclusion

The Long-term Benefits of Professional SEO

SEO cannot be done overnight or produce sensational results within a day. But it can work faster and more effectively than other conventional marketing and advertising campaigns. It is a long term and long lasting investment in your business and, if done correctly, it will significantly grow your business for many months and years to come.

In this book, you have seen a method to put all necessary SEO steps in place to grow your customer base significantly. Remember, you don't have to do it all at once, since even using just some of the techniques will make a difference to the presence of your website on the search engines, and the amount of prospects finding and clicking on your site. However, using all the steps together in one coherent method will increase the chances of growing your business even further. The method we use is the **GROW Method** and it can achieve a steady stream of targeted life-long customers to your site or blog - when implemented correctly – by listing you in the top ten on the search engines for your chosen keywords.

To achieve a search engine friendly site, let's revisit the most important building blocks of the **GROW Method**:

1. Keywords: Remember, in the beginning is the keyword! Keywords are the foundation of your online success. You leave hundreds of thousands, possibly hundreds of millions of Dollars, Pounds or Euros to your competitors, if you don't do your keyword research properly. After all, you want to get massive, targeted traffic from the search engines, and from anything you place online. Simply put, your prospective customers won't find your site or blog if you don't use the keywords **they** are using. That would mean minimum sales instead of maximum sales.

2. Links: Links pointing to your site or blog from other websites that are highly relevant to your industry, are one of the most important factors for Google to evaluate whether your site / blog is important. Link building is the most important 'off-page' SEO factor. Links are most effective when coming from unique content pages on other high PR websites, or blogs that are relevant to your industry sector.

You build links by placing unique articles, videos, images etc on third party websites, such as sector relevant sites and blogs, web 2.0 sites, video, image and slide-content sharing websites, press release and announcement sites and many others, which all have a link back to the 'landing page' on your site or blog. Your site / blog's internal linking structure is, to a lesser extent, also important, but your first link on any page is the most important one for Google.

3. Keyword Matching: Matching the keywords on your pages with the keywords in the links pointing to it, plus matching them also with the keywords on the page from where your links are coming, is imperative. This can make a significant difference to the number of customers you get, the amount of sales you make each week, and to your bottom line, namely the amount of profit you make.

4. Themes: Theming is just a word for a group of keywords on a page that is focused on one subject only. Combine your primary and secondary keywords, such as modified / long tail and related keywords into one theme per page, so the search engines know what the page is about, find it relevant to the search and rank it highly on their search results pages.

5. Silo Structure: Building your pages as 'silos' is a good way of telling your visitors and Google what your website is about. What you do is categorize your products and services into separate 'silos' of content and then link from one silo to the top page of the other. This way, you keep clear distinctions between your various products and services, for both Google and searching customers.

6. Free Value and Video: Turn strangers into loyal, lifetime customers using effective techniques such as search engine optimized and - more importantly - optimized videos portraying you and your business. Plus, provide amazing free value and you will win over skeptic Internet searchers more easily and quickly than your competitors.

These are the cornerstones of the 'GROW Method'. To put it in place is straightforward: Just take the steps outlined in this book - one at a time – and you will climb to the top of this steep mountain called the Google SERPs (search engine results pages) in no time. You have probably taken some of these steps already anyway.

Always remember, there is a big difference in how much traffic you will be getting from a listing on Google's Page 1: The company in the 1st position gets on average about 42% of clicks, the 2nd position, 12% and the 3rd position, 8.5%. Your position on that list will therefore have a direct effect on your profits. Here are the steps again which I urge you to take, one by one:

GROW Step 1: Choose the Best Keywords for Your Target Customers

Decide on your single, primary keyword by brainstorming your initial keyword list and evaluating it with the Google Keyword Tool. Check your keywords for search volume, competition, CPC and keyword value. Powerful keywords allow you to target prospective customers, head on, so that they find you quickly and easily, despite other competitors trying to gain their interest.

GROW Step 2: Focus Your Campaign with 'Long-Tail Keywords'

Find secondary keywords and keyword phrases, modified/long tail keywords and related keywords that are relevant to your primary keyword, by again using the Google Keyword Tool. These secondary keywords will broaden your business's presence in the market place and strengthen your search engine ranking when you combine your keywords on themed pages.

GROW Step 3: Know Your Competition to Fast Track to the Top

When **analyzing your competition**, start with the first listing on search engine results Page 1 – the place where you would ideally like to have your page listed - and then work your way down the nine consecutive listings on Page 1. Use competition analysis tools to check up on competitors so that you focus your campaign at the places where you to achieve the greatest advantage.

GROW Step 4: Place Your Keywords Where They Give You Most Power

Place your primary and secondary keywords in the most essential places on your website – URL, title tag, meta tag, headline, sub-headline etc. to help your online text achieve a high search engine ranking. Do this carefully to avoid search engine spamming.

GROW Step 5: 'Theme' Your Content and Get Found by the Search Engines

'Theme' the content of your site using primary, secondary, long tail, related keywords and place separate themes on separate pages. This way your site becomes highly relevant to what the searcher is looking for.

GROW Step 6: Create a 'Silo Structure', Turning Your Store into a Goldmine

Organize your site well using a 'Silo Structure'. This simply means you keep the 'themed' pages separate in single categories. Interlink them only from one sub-page to the top page of another silo category, not horizontally. This makes your pages very specific to what prospective customers are looking for. As a result, your site becomes very user friendly, searchers will like you, and search engines will rank you highly.

GROW Step 7: Build Quality Links and Get Listed Highly on Google

Create quality links that point to your website, with keywords in the Link Text matching the keywords on your site. Create these links from relevant websites, where ideally the keywords on the source page match those in the link and on your page. This will give you a higher page rank and bring significantly more visitors to your site. The more present you are across the Web, and the more links with matching keywords you have from relevant quality sites, the higher Google values you and ranks your site. This leads to more traffic and customers finding your site.

GROW Step 8: Promote Your Site Further with 'Social Bookmarking'

Social bookmark your pages to promote your content by creating further links to them.

GROW Step 9: Use Articles as Your 24/7 Sales Agents

Place articles with unique content firstly on your own website or blog, then on other sites or blogs that are highly relevant to your business or profession. Include a link back to your website or blog, with matching keywords in the Link Text. This increases your link power and direct traffic to your site.

GROW Step 10: Gain Customers' Trust Fast Using Video

Instil your visitors with trust and turn them into buying customers **using effective video optimization and marketing techniques.**

GROW Step 11: Turn Searchers into Customers with 'Free Value'

Always create great value content on your site and other sites linking to you, to persuade your visitors to opt in. Provide free products and services where possible. Continue to provide great value to people on your growing list and offer your products and services once you have formed a trusting relationship with your subscribers.

You now have a complete set of techniques and tools available to give your business a significant advantage over your competition and to get a top spot on the search engines. Even just using two or three of these techniques can give you a massive increase in the number of new customers arriving at your site or blog. Start right now. Do not postpone it until later, since 'later' usually means never.

Add one of the techniques to your marketing today or at least commit to a plan putting the necessary steps in place to boost your site's revenues and profits.

PART VII - Conclusion

What to Do Next

Every Journey Starts With a First Step

Reading this far will **propel your business forward and give you a big advantage over your competition, no matter how fierce,** *if* **you apply the steps suggested in this book.** Otherwise, all the opportunities you now have at hand will fade away. You will have increased your knowledge, but without putting at least some of the Steps into place, you won't have made a difference to your bank account, your lifestyle and dreams.

> *When you hear something, you will forget it.*
> *When you see something, you will remember it.*
> *But not until you do something, will you understand it.*
> *Old Chinese proverb*

I want to help you to get all that you find in this book into practice. This is why I am offering you **free access to the GROW Membership Site** for some time.

In the membership site you will find the GROW Course which supplements the contents of this book. You can use it in parallel or after reading this book to apply to your business everything that was laid out to you in here.

In the course I illustrate the techniques outlined in the book with easy-to-follow weekly steps and I give practical examples of how to:

- make potential new customers choose you
- take advantage of the campaigns of your competitors
- get the click and get prospective customers to your site
- get search engines to love your site
- create effective links to promote your site
- get new customers wanting to see your offers
- make online marketing even more effective
- ... and much more.

Please be aware that the GROW Course is not available **free** without a code!

Therefore, to claim free access to the GROW Course for a limited time, go to **www.Internet-Experts-Live.com/members/growcourse/** and please use this **code:**

GROWCode0910.

SEO GROW Course

What you will discover is a step-by-step guide that reflects the material of this book but also goes beyond it. The guide is a good companion to this book and will help you to put the techniques provided in here into good practice.

After all the reason why you picked up this book is probably because you want to massively increase the numbers of customers you get from the Internet. The GROW Course will help you to achieve this. The different parts build on each other, step by step, and progressively add value and return to your site.

Enjoy!

I wish you the very best of success.

Karl zu Ortenburg

P.S. If you enjoyed reading this book, I would be most grateful if you could send me your feedback to **PAKarlOrtenburg@Internet-Experts-Live.co.uk.** This will help me to understand where I can improve the content of the book and the way I have provided it for you.

P.P.S. If you have any questions or constructive critics at all, let me know as well. All this will help to understand how we can do an even better job in helping you to put what we explain into practice, apply the techniques shown, find new customers, and increase your profits.

APPENDICES

1. 11 GROW Steps To Get New Customers Rapidly on the Web
2. USP Template
3. Keyword Template
4. Search Engine Friendliness Template
5. Page and Competition Assessment Templates
    a) Positive Search Engine Ranking Factors
    b) Negative Search Engine Ranking Factors
    c) Local Search Engine Ranking Factors
6. Ways to Build External Links
7. 31 Most Effective Link Building Tactics
8. 18 Guidelines for Getting Quality Links
9. 11 Steps to Set Up a Well Themed Site

Appendices

Appendix 1: 11 GROW Steps To Get New Customers Rapidly on the Web

GROW Step 1: Choose the Best Keywords for Your Target Customers.

GROW Step 2: Focus Your Campaign with 'Long Tail' Keywords.

GROW Step 3: Know Your Competition to Fast Track to the Top.

GROW Step 4: Place Your Keywords Where They Give You Most Power.

GROW Step 5: 'Theme' Your Content and Get Found by the Search Engines.

GROW Step 6: Create a 'Silo Structure', Turning Your Store into a Goldmine.

GROW Step 7: Build Quality Links and Get Listed Highly on Google.

GROW Step 8: Promote Your Site Further with 'Social Bookmarking'.

GROW Step 9: Use Articles as Your 24/7 Sales Agents.

GROW Step 10: Gain Customers' Trust Fast, Using Video.

GROW Step 11: Turn Searchers into Customers by Providing 'Free Value'.

Appendix 2: USP (Unique Selling Proposition) Template

Your SEO Plan starts with your business goals and your USP. Looking at your products and services and those of your competitors, what makes your company unique? What unique proposition can you make to a potential customer to convince him or her to switch brands and buy from you?

Your message to your prospect needs to say: "Buy this product or service, and you will get this specific benefit." Examples of unique propositions that were pioneers when they were introduced are:

- Domino's Pizza: "You get fresh, hot pizza delivered to your door in 30 minutes or less - or it's free."

- FedEx: "When your package absolutely, positively has to get there overnight"

- M&M's: "The milk chocolate melts in your mouth, not in your hand"

- Wonder Bread: "Wonder Bread Helps Build Strong Bodies 12 Ways"

Your USP answers this question: "What makes you and your products and / or services special, even unique?"

Your USP ...

- is not only the starting point of your online marketing campaign, it is the where all marketing begins. Any company and business has an image in the world, whether they put it out deliberately or not.

- is your chance to put out into the world how you want to be seen.

- has to fill a gap, a need in the market. If there is no need for what you promise (with your USP), obviously you then have no business.

- should be 'unique', it distinguishes and differentiates you, and your products and services from your competition.

○ must appeal to someone and that someone can't be everyone!

○ has to speak real benefits for your customers.

ideally is a two or three sentence explaining who you are and what your business does. Use it to explain to a potential customer the benefits you can take to them. How their lives will be improved by what you do, and why you are obviously the best choice to provide them with this product or service.

Doug Hall says:

> "Writing your USP is more than describing your company, or what type of person you are, or even what type of job you do. Your USP must define the overt benefit and dramatic difference you bring to your client. It must be written greatly … Figure out how to articulate it so it is a mind-stopping thought."
>
> This might sound like a tough call to some but let it inspire you. You don't have to get it right from the beginning. Even successful companies change their USP message and so can you. Your USP will not address everything you do, or all the products or services you offer. It should serve only to begin a conversation and encourage the reader or listener to think or say: "Tell me more."
>
> So when you 'test' this on potential new customers, you will see whether your USP produces this kind of reaction. You can tell whether they turn their listening off, whether they get confused, excited etc. if you really watch their reaction. This tells you whether you are heading in the right direction or not. Try your USP out on as many people as you can since as someone (can't remember who it was) said, fail quickly and then improve.

Here is an example of an USP:
"At [company name] we view marketing in an entirely different way – we believe that you already have a variety of true marketing assets. What we really do is help you identify theses assets – optimize and leverage them to grow your business exponentially – in three ways, not just one."

An example of a marketing hook:

"We provide catalyst and strategy to small and emerging businesses bringing them more clients and more profits – more often.

An example Metaphor:

"Do you know how a doctor helps you solve your health issue? … We do the exact same thing for your business – we go in – assess the situation and work with you to implement prescribed solutions."

USP (Unique Selling Proposition)

Here are some questions about your USP, use the space and time right now to fill in the blanks.

Nine Questions and one answer to develop and improve your USP:

1. What business are we in?
   > ....

2. What is it that we really do well?
   > ....

3. What the three most important results our potential customers are looking for?
   > ....

4. What are the three most important reasons prospective customers should do business with providers like us?
   > ....

5. What are three reasons prospects should do business with us rather than our competition?
   > ....

6. What is the main problem our target market is experiencing? How do they hurt?
   > ....

7. What is the unique solution we provide for this problem?

| USP | Goals | Keywords | SE Friendliness | Positive Ranking Factors | Negative Ranking Factors | Local Listing Factors |

Download the USP worksheet from: www.Internet-Experts-Live.com/members/templates to help you to develop your USP further and to include a marketing hook that can be integrated in all your online marketing campaigns.

Appendices

Appendix 3: Keyword Template

You can use this template to brainstorm an initial keyword list, re-order the list according to the keyword's search volume, competition, Cost-Per-Click (CPC) etc. Feel free to adjust the keywords to your particular needs.

Keyword Template

Download the Keyword Template from: www.Internet-Experts-Live.com/members/templates and click on the '**Keywords'** tab at the bottom of the page.

Appendix 4: Search Engine Friendliness

Use this worksheet to assess your site for its search engine friendliness. Check the factors listed to see whether your site makes it easy for the search engines to index the pages of your site. Remember if the search engines can't read and index your site, you won't get much search engine ranking power, not a good listing, less traffic and subsequently less sales.

Site Assessment Sheet - Search Engine Friendlin

(With this worksheet you can assess your site for its search engine friendliness. Check the different factors to see whether your site makes it easy for the seach engines to index the pages of your site. Remember if the search engines can't read and index your site, you won't get much search engine ranking power, not a good listing, less traffic and subsequently less sales.)

Search Engine Friendliness	Your Site yes / no / not sure	How to check	Tool
Is my site indexed in Google, Bing etc.?		Put 'site:yourdomain.com' in e.g. Google to see how many pages Google shows.	Google - 'site:yourdomian.com'
Are some of my landing pages invisible to the search engines?		Check one-by-one whether landing pages have been indexed by putting the page URL into the browser window.	Firefox or Internet Explorer
Is my site using 'Frames'?		Check Source Code for 'Frames'	Source Code for 'Frames'
Do my major pages have optimized Titles (Title Tags)?		Check Google search results page or source code for 'Title Tag'	Source Code for Meta Tag 'Title Tag'
Do my major pages have Descriptions optimized for the readers Description Tags)?		Check Google search results page or source code for 'Description Code'	Source Code for Meta Tag 'Description'
Is my site navigation visible for the search engines?		Check source code for JavaScript e.g. 'menu.js'	Source Code for 'menu.js'
Do I show Flash animation on my home page, landing pages?		Check whether you have 'Intro' sequences other than video on your pages.	Firefox or Internet Explorer
Does my site / blog use real text or is the text embedded into images?		Can text be changed or does image need to be redesigned for text changes?	Page file
Am I using my keywords grouped into 'Themes' on my pages?		Check with Google Keyword Tool for 'relatedness' of keywords.	https://adwords.google.com/select/KeywordToolExternal
Do I have links pointing to my important pages?		Check with Link Tools such as Yahoo! Site Explorer	http://siteexplorer.search.yahoo.com

Goals / Keywords / SE Friendliness / Positive Ranking Factors / Negative Ranking Factors / Local Listing Factors /

Sheet to assess whether your site can easily be indexed by the search engines.

Download the Assessment Worksheet from: www.Internet-Experts-Live.com/members/templates and click on the '**SE Friendliness**' tab at the bottom of the page.

Appendix 5: Page and Competition Assessment

6a) Positive Search Engine Ranking Factors

This is an Excel Worksheet to assess your own pages against the pages of your competition. When you download the worksheet you will find space to compare your own page against the top five listings on Google for a particular keyword. Once you have assessed your competition on Google you can do the same on Bing etc.

Why have I included only the top five listings? Ideally you want to get listed in the top three listings on the first page of e.g. Google since the top three listings get the most amounts of clicks / traffic. However the top three also have the toughest competition and listings change. The page ranked on number five yesterday, might get ranked on number 3 today.

Search Engine Ranking Factors	Your Page	Competitor Rank 1	Competitor Rank 2	Competitor Rank 3	Competitor Rank 4	Competitor Rank 5	What to improve	By When

Downloadable Assessment Sheet

Whom should you assess first, your own site or your competition? This is up to you but here is how we do it most often: We look at the business and SEO goals first, and then see what the competition is like for the top five search engine ranking factors. Then we look at our client's page with the top ranking factors to get a feel of how close our client is to its competitors for that particular keyword.

We get an overall picture first to see how competitive a certain keyword (phrase) is before we commit more time to evaluate the competition in detail. In general you will have to go into more detail, assessing your page and the competition on more ranking factors if your competition has used more optimizing techniques. If you find the competition being really tough for the first five listings, extend it to the top ten listings for that keyword

Templates

Assessment Sheet – Positive Search

(With this worksheet you can assess your own page and the competition for a keyword you want to ta[rget] down to see how well your competition has optimized their pages for that particular keyword. If your [page ranks higher, then you can focus on] the additional ranking factors listed below.)

Top 10 Search Engine Ranking Factors	Your Page	Competitor Rank 1	Competitor Rank 2	Con[petitor] R[ank 3]
1. Keyword-Focused **Anchor Text** from External Links,				
2. External **Link Popularity** (quantity/quality of external links),				
3. Diversity of **Link Sources** (links from many unique root domains),				
4. Trustworthiness of the **Domain** Based on Link Distance from Trusted Domains (e.g. TrustRank, Domain mozTrust, etc.),				
5. Keyword Use Anywhere in the **Title Tag**,				
6. Existence of Substantive, **Unique Content** on the Page,				
7. **Page-Specific TrustRank** (whether the individual page has earned links from trusted sources),				
8. Keyword Use as the First Word(s) of the **Title Tag**,				
9. Iterative Algorithm-Based Global Link				

▶ ▶|\ Goals / Keywords / SE Friendliness \ **Positive Ranking Factors** / Negative Ranking Factors / Local Li[nks]

Assessment Sheet with Top 10 Search Engine Ranking Factors

Download the Assessment Worksheet from: www.Internet-Experts-Live.com/members/templates and click on the '**Positive Ranking Factors**' tab at the bottom of the page.

6b) Negative Search Engine Ranking Factors
This Assessment Worksheet allows you to check whether your competitors have used any 'gray or black hat' SEO techniques that could get their page (and site)

Appendices

penalized by the search engines. Gray/Black Hat SEO techniques are for example 'Cloaking with Malicious Intent' which means a site is giving wrong information about what its content is about. It could say 'Free iPod' in an ad and lead to an online pharmacy selling Viagra and the likes. 'Link Acquisition from Link Brokers' is another Gray/Black Hat SEO technique that can get your site in trouble. Many so called Link Brokers are nowadays known to the search engines and when you buy links for your site from them Google etc. might just not give you any ranking power for the links acquired.

Page Assessment – Negative Factors

(With this worksheet you can assess your own page and the competition for a keyword you want to target. Start wit competition has optimized their pages for that particular keyword. If your niche is really competitive, you might war

Top 5 Negative Ranking Factors	Your Page	Competitor Rank 1	Competitor Rank 2	Competitor Rank 3
1. Cloaking with Malicious Intent 2. Link Acquisition from Link Brokers 3. Cloaking by User Agent 4. Frequent Server Downtime 5. Linking Out to Spam				
Very High Importance				
Cloaking with Malicious/Manipulative Intent				
High Importance				
Link Acquisition from Known Link Brokers/Sellers				
Moderate Importance				
Links from the Page to Web Spam Sites/Pages				
Cloaking by User Agent				
Frequent Server Downtime & Site Inaccessibility				

Tabs: Goals / Keywords / SE Friendliness / Positive Ranking Factors / **Negative Ranking Factors** / Local Listing Factors

Negative Search Engine Ranking Factors Assessment Sheet

Templates

Why is checking for these negative ranking factors important?

Firstly, you want to make sure that your page and site is **not** using such Gray/Black hat techniques, so your site doesn't get penalized or even banned. Secondly if your competitors are indeed using these techniques to boost their rankings, it might be only temporarily to their advantage.

Let's say the competitor that got his page ranked in the second search results listing is using Gray/Black hat techniques. This gives him a short term advantage but he might be gone tomorrow and he probably won't come back for a long time. So you have a chance to take his spot.

As with all SEO and rankings in specific you need to keep checking. How often? The more competitive your niche - the more often. In general, since it is advisable to check your SEO campaign every 3 months (at least 6 months), include checking the rankings too.

Download the Assessment Worksheet from: www.Internet-Experts-Live.com/members/templates and click on the **'Negative Ranking Factors'** tab at the bottom of the page.

Appendices

6c) Local Search Engine Ranking Factors

This Assessment Worksheet lets you assess your competition and your own site for the local search ranking factors.

The worksheet shows the top as well as an extended list of local listings ranking factors. Start with the most important factors first, assess your top five competitors for your intended keyword first. Once you have found attractive keywords with competition you might be able to overcome, go into more detail.

Site Assessment Sheet for Local Listings

Download the Assessment Worksheet from: www.Internet-Experts-Live.com/members/templates and click on the **'Local Listings Factors'** tab at the bottom of the page.

Appendix 6: The 9 Ways to Build External Links

1. Submit your website to **directories** with a link pointing back to your site/blog.

2. Write and submit unique articles to **article** directories sites such as EzineArticles.com with links back to your site/blog included.

3. **Web 2.0** Sites: Create content on so-called 'content sharing sites' with text, video, images etc. like Hubpages.com, Squidoo.com or Propellor.com and include text links to your site/blog. Some of them provide excellent PageRank (PR) value, others no value due to their 'nofollow' tag in place. You will have to check the sites you intend to build links from.

4. Write comments on relevant **blogs** with highly searched discussions, including a back-link in the comments you make.

5. Upload **videos** with search engine optimized descriptions including your URL to video sharing sites like YouTube and others, and therefore get at least one link to your site or blog.

6. Upload images to **image** sharing sites like FlickR.com with a link to your site/blog. You can also add keywords to the ALT attributes of your images, but search engines don't weigh ALT text as highly as link text.

7. Put together packages for webmasters at relevant **websites** which makes it easy for them to link to your site. Then ask other **relevant websites** whether they are willing to give you a link, by offering them content like writing an article exclusively to their site, or you ask to exchange links with them.

8. Ask other relevant websites whether they are willing to give you a link, by offering them content, such as writing an article exclusively to their site".

9. **Buy links** from well ranked sites only if you get real value for your money and don't overdo it.

Appendix 7: The 31 Most Effective Link Building Tactics

Below find the 31 most effective link building tactics as agreed on by 72 SEO experts participating in Rand Fishkin's Search Engine Ranking Factors Study 2009.

Very High Value

1. Linkbait + Viral Content Creation

High Value

2. Blogging and Engagement with the Blogosphere
3. Classic "Create Valuable Content" Strategies w/o Promotional Marketing
4. Public Relations (beyond just press release publication)

Moderate Value

5. Direct Link Purchases from Individual Sites/Webmasters
6. Widgets and Embeddable Content
7. Conferences, Events and In-Person Networking
8. User Generated Content (which then incentivizes links to profiles/content/etc.)
9. High Trust/Authority Directories (DMOZ, Yahoo!, Lii, etc.)
10. Niche Social Media Communities
11. Local Link Building (via geographic lists, organizations, portals)
12. Social Voting Portals (Digg, Reddit, Mixx, etc.)
13. Quizzes + Results Badges
14. Social Bookmarking Services (StumbleUpon, Delicious, etc.)
15. Contributing to Charities, Non-profits, Events, etc. to Earn Links

Low Value

16. Leveraging Twitter for Link Building
17. Generic Directory Links (BOTW, JoeAnt, Business.com, etc.)
18. Contacting Webmasters or Sites with (Non-Paid) Direct Link Requests
19. Offline Advertising Branding and Media
20. Press Releases
21. Long Tail Directory Links (niche directories, small generic directories, etc.)

22. Social Networking Services (Facebook, MySpace, LinkedIn)
23. Purchasing Links from Link Brokers
24. Launching & Later, Redirecting Microsites via 301s
25. Buying Old Domains & Placing Links on Them

Minimal Value
26. Buying Old Domains & 301'ing Them
27. Reciprocal Linking (trading links with other sites)
28. DoFollow Blog Comments
29. Web Advertising (Banners, PPC, etc.)

Very Minimal Value
30. Forum Link Building (Signatures, Link Drops, etc.)
31. Automated Blog, Guestbook and Open Form Comment Spam

To see explanations of these Link Building Methods see Part IV of this book. For information how to use them, download the Site and Competition Assessment Worksheet from: www.Internet-Experts-Live.com/members/templates
and click on the **'Link Building Strategies'** tab at the bottom of the page.

Appendix 8: 18 Guidelines for Getting Quality Links

1. Secure "unidirectional" or incoming (non-reciprocal) links.
2. Develop relevant keyword Link Text / Anchor Texts with Matching Keywords.
3. Get links from industry-relevant pages or so-called authority sites with Matching Keywords to the Link Text.
4. Links from indexed pages only.
5. No links from "framed" pages.
6. No "flash" embedded links.
7. No links from Link Farms.
8. No links from FFA (Free-For-All) link networks.
9. No linking with redirected pages.
10. No links from adult sites, racially prejudiced sites and other sites containing offensive content.
11. The site you get your links from must be **relevant** to your site or blog otherwise the link value will be little.
12. The page you are buying your link from should have a good Page Rank (PR).
13. Make sure that the page you are getting your link from doesn't have too many other links going out.
14. Make sure the keywords in the Link Text / Anchor Text are matching the keywords on the page the link is pointing to.
15. Also, keywords on the source page where the link comes from should match the keywords in the link text and the keywords in your own page.
16. Make sure Google is actually spidering that page by checking the page's last cache date. If the page hasn't been spidered for more than three weeks, this is a concern, if it has not been spidered for a couple of months, move on to another site.
17. Check in Google whether the site has been attacked by spammers with this command: 'site:thesiteinquestion.com [spam words like sex, porn, Viagra etc.]. You can tell whether they have been hacked when you find a good number of links with spam words in them.
18. Do not buy links from 'bad neighborhood' sites as this can easily reflect badly on you.

Appendix 9: 11 Steps to Set Up a Well Themed Site

1. Choose the subject of your theme from your market research.
2. As with initial keyword research, put your primary, most important keyword into Google's free keyword tool to find modified / long tail and related keywords, and combine these into one group per page.
3. For each keyword phrase find a handful of variations that go into the themes page. Variations are usually plurals, single, or add-ons such as "ing", "ed", etc. In many cases you can change the order of words in keyword phrases, too.
4. Use the top 10 listed websites or blogs in Google (Yahoo! and Bing) to extract the most common keywords used within that theme.
5. Go to an article site like Ezinearticles.com and select the top 10/20 articles written by experts on your chosen theme. Go through articles and extract words and phrases commonly used in the articles.
6. Cross reference your selection of themed keywords with keywords on web 2.0 authority sites like Hubpages.com and Squidoo.com etc.
7. Select titles for your theme and text sub titles with a good volume of search traffic and moderate competition.
8. Write a 500 -1000 word piece of text on your chosen topic for your page theme or get someone to write it for you. (Ideally create two unique themed pages for a certain theme at a time to allow for 'double listings' on Google's Search Results Pages.)
9. Finally, integrate the top most commonly used modified / long tail and related keyword search phrases into your text and put it onto your site, in your blog or on a web 2.0 authority site.
10. Promote your own piece of text with Social Bookmarking and other link building techniques.
11. Monitor how your page is moving upwards in the rankings with tools such as Marketing Samurai, and improve the performance as you see fit.

Glossary

Today the English language has five times as many words as it had during Shakespeare's times, and almost every day new words get created, especially in the technology arena.

Here are explanations for a number of terms that are used in the industry and within this book:

Above the Fold
In the old days, 'Above the Fold' used to describe the top half of the front page of a folded newspaper. So when the folded newspaper was lying on a pile, this was the part you could see. In email or web marketing the part of the page you see first when you open a website is called the top fold.

Ad Words
This is Google's PPC based text advertising. AdWords takes click-through rates (CR) into consideration in addition to the advertiser's bid to determine the ad's relative position within the different ads. Google applies this to feature paid search results that are more popular and thus probably more relevant and useful. Google has also started taking into account the quality of the landing page and applying a quality score to the landing pages.

Affiliate Programs
In an affiliate program the affiliate promotes a business and is rewarded for every visitor, subscriber, customer, and/or sale made through his/her efforts.

Age of Site, Age of Page etc.
Search engines such as Google and Bing take site age, page age, user account age, domain age and related historical data into account when determining how much one can trust a website, blog or document. However, fresh content can sometimes override age of site and will temporarily rank better, because many of the other websites will initially quote this content on their high ranking homepages which gives your page a boost. But in the days and weeks that follow, those quotes will move lower down and eventually into the archive pages where the linking juice to your site is much lower. This is when Age of Site or Age Of Page becomes more important again.

Glossary

Aggregation of Content

Aggregation is the process of combining and remixing content from blogs and other websites that provide RSS feeds. The resulting content can be displayed in a so called aggregator website such as Bloglines (www.bloglines.com/) or Google Reader, (www.google.com/reader/view/) or on your desktop using software programs called 'newsreaders'.

Alerts - Google Alerts

Search engines such as Google (www.google.com/alerts) let you specify words (e.g. your name, company), phrases or tags that you want to keep an eye on. The alerts usually arrive in your mailbox by e-mail and some can be read by RSS feed. Alerts allow you to see whether you, your business or other terms that you regard as newsworthy have been mentioned online.

Algorithm – Search Engine Algorithm

A set of rules that search engines use to rank listings. Search engines do not disclose the algorithms they use, as they are the unique formulas used to determine a website's or blogs relevancy. A bit like the formula for Coca Cola, everyone drinks it but no-one really knows what's in it.

Alt Text – Image Alt Text

A description of an image, which usually isn't displayed to the user, unless the image can't be shown. The alt text is the description of the images for the search engines since they can't distinguish one picture from another.

Anchor Text - Link Text

Anchor or Link Text is the part of a link that contains text (usually underlined) and is used by the search engines as an important ranking factor. Google in particular pays attention to the text used in a link. If the Anchor Text contains the keywords which can be found on the page it links to the page will get good 'ranking power' from the search engines. If this Link or Anchor text contains keywords that match not only the keywords on the page it links to, but also the keywords on the page it links from, the ranking benefit for the page it links to will even be greater.

B2B

Means 'Business to Business' and describes a business that markets its services or products primarily to other businesses.

Glossary

B2C
Means "Business to Consumer" and describes a business that markets its services or products primarily to consumers.

Back links
Back links are inbound links pointing from another website to your page or blog post.

Ban – Banned - Delisting
Websites and blogs get usually banned or delisted from search engines for using so- called 'Black(-)?Hat', spamming or other malicious techniques.

Blog – Blogs
Blogs, also known as a 'weblogs' - are online diaries with entries, called 'blog posts' made on a regular, preferably daily basis. Posts are dated in reverse chronological order and may have keyword tags associated with them. They are usually available as RSS feeds, and often allow commenting. Blogs are websites where the content (e.g. text, photos, video, audio) can also be identified by tags. These tags can act as keywords and can be searched individually. Blog posts can be made available in an RSS feed subscription (usually free). You then can subscribe to a blog RSS news feed and read it via a newsreader or aggregator. That means you don't have to visit a blog site to read it - you can pull the content to your desktop.

Body Copy
This is the text content of a web page that is not part of the site's navigation.

Bookmarks – Social Bookmarking
Most browsers today come with the ability to bookmark your favorite pages. Bookmarking is saving the address of a website or item of content in your browser. Social bookmarking means sharing your bookmarks with others on 'tagging' sites like del.icio.us.com. The popularity of a document as measured by the number of bookmarks is a signal for the quality of the content. Some search engines may use bookmarks to help their search relevancy.

Brand and Branding
"A brand is a customer experience represented by a collection of images and ideas; often, it refers to a symbol such as a name, logo, slogan, and design scheme. Brand recognition and other reactions are created by the accumulation of experiences with the specific product or service, both directly relating to its use, and through the

Glossary

influence of advertising, design, and media commentary. A brand often includes an explicit logo, fonts, color schemes, symbols, sound which may be developed to represent implicit values, ideas, and even personality." (Source: Wikipedia)

Broad Match
Broad Match is a form of keyword matching and refers to the matching of a search listing or advertisement to selected keywords in any order. "Description: With broad match, [for example] the Google AdWords system automatically runs your ads on relevant variations of your keywords, even if these terms aren't in your keyword lists. Keyword variations can include synonyms, singular/plural forms, relevant variants of your keywords, and phrases containing your keywords. For example, if you're currently running ads on the broad-matched keyword 'web hosting', your ads may show for the search queries 'web hosting company' or 'webhost'. The keyword variations that are allowed to trigger your ads will change over time, as the AdWords system continually monitors your keyword quality and performance factors. Your ads will only continue showing on the highest-performing and most relevant keyword variations. Benefits: One of the primary benefits of broad match is that it helps you attract more traffic to your website. In addition, broad match saves you time when constructing your campaigns, lets you take advantage of global search trends, and is cost-effective." (Source: Google Adwords)

Call To Action (CTA)
A call to action is copy used in advertising to encourage a person to complete an action as defined by the advertiser. Call to action words are 'action words' such as 'Click here', 'Buy Now', 'Enter Now', 'Go to' or 'Click to download'.

Categories
Categories are ways to organize content - for example, a set of keywords. Dividing your content into distinct categories helps your website visitors to find what they are looking for and categories have nowadays become more important to search engine optimization. Categories that separate your different products and services from one another are the basis to build a proper silo structure on your site or blog. You can use Google's Search Keyword Tool (www.google.com/sktool) to get ideas for relevant categories, to categorize Keywords and find Google categorized Long-Tail keywords. (See this video on how to find categories: www.noblesamurai.com/blog/keyword-research/google-debunks-lsi-then-shows-you-how-to-do-it-532)

Competitive Analysis

Competitive Analysis (within SEO) is the assessment and analysis of strengths and weaknesses of competing web sites, including identifying traffic patterns, major traffic sources, keyword use and selection, advertising success, etc.

Conversion – Conversion Funnel - Conversion Rate (CR)
A conversion in marketing happens when a prospective customer takes the marketer's intended action, for example:

- a product sale
- completing a lead form
- a phone call
- capturing an email
- filling out a survey
- getting a person to pay attention to you
- getting feedback
- having a site visitor share your website with a friend
- having a site visitor link at your site

The Conversion Funnel, in Internet marketing, is the process of tracking website visitor's conversions across a series of process steps.

The Conversion Rate (CR), in Internet marketing, indicates the percentage of visitors who take a desired action on a website, in a blog, in a newsletter etc. A conversion is reached when a desired step is completed. In general online conversions are easier to track than offline conversions. Online Bid management, affiliate tracking, and analytics programs make it easy to track conversion sources. See Google Conversion University (www.google.com/analytics/conversionuniversity.html) for free conversion tracking information and Google Website Optimizer (http://services.google.com/websiteoptimizer/) for a free multi variable testing software.

"Conversion rates are measurements that determine how many of your prospects perform the prescribed or desired action step. If your prescribed response is for a visitor to sign up for a newsletter, and you had 100 visitors and 1 newsletter signup, then your conversion rate would be 1%. Typically, micro-conversions (for instance, reading different pages on your site) lead to your main conversion step (making a purchase, or signing up for a service).
The number of visitors who convert (take a desired action at your site) after clicking

Glossary

through on your ad, divided by the total number of click-throughs to your site for that ad. (Expressed as: Conversion Rate = total click-throughs that convert divided by total click-throughs for that ad.) For example, if an ad brings in 150 click-throughs and 6 of the 150 clicks result in a desired conversion, then the conversion rate is 4% (6 / 150 = 0.04). Higher conversion rates generally translate into more successful PPC campaigns with a better ROI." (Source: www.Sempo.org)

Cost Per Action (CPA) – Cost Per Acquisition
"Cost Per Action or CPA (sometimes known as Pay Per Action or PPA) is an online advertising pricing model, where the advertiser pays for each specified action (a purchase, a form submission, and so on) linked to the advertisement.
Direct response advertisers consider CPA the optimal way to buy online advertising, as an advertiser only pays for the ad when the desired action has occurred. An action can be a product being purchased, a form being filled, etc. The desired action to be performed is determined by the advertiser. [For example, if a campaign cost $100 and resulted in 5 conversions, the CPA is $20 ($100 / 5). It cost $20 to generate one conversion.]

"CPA is sometimes referred to as "Cost Per Acquisition", which has to do with the fact that most CPA offers by advertisers are about acquiring something (typically new customers by making sales). Using the term "Cost Per Acquisition" instead of "Cost Per Action" is more specific. "Cost Per Acquisition" is included in "Cost Per Action", but not all "Cost Per Action" offers can be referred to as "Cost Per Acquisition"." (Source: Wikipedia)

Cost-Per-Click (CPC)
Cost Per Click is the amount search engines charge advertisers for every click that sends a searcher to the advertiser's web site.

CPM – Short for Cost Per Thousand Impressions (ad serves or potential viewers). Compare to CPC pricing (defined above). CPM is a standard monetization model for offline display ad space, as well as for some context-based networks serving online search ads to, for example, web publishers and sites. CPM or "Cost Per Thousand" – A unit of measure typically assigned to the cost of displaying an ad. If an ad appears on a web page 1,000 times and costs $5, then the CPM would be $5. In this instance, every 1,000 times an ad appeared, it would incur a charge of $5.

Cost Per Lead (CPL)

"The Difference between CPA and CPL Advertising - In CPL campaigns, advertisers pay for an interested lead (hence, Cost Per Lead) — i.e. the contact information of a person interested in the advertiser's product or service. CPL campaigns are suitable for brand marketers and direct response marketers looking to engage consumers at multiple touchpoints — by building a newsletter list, community site, reward program or member acquisition program. In CPA campaigns, the advertiser typically pays for a completed sale involving a credit card transaction. CPA is all about 'now' — it focuses on driving consumers to buy at that exact moment. If a visitor to the website doesn't buy anything, there's no easy way to remarket to them.

There are other important differentiators:

1. CPL campaigns are advertiser-centric. The advertiser remains in control of their brand, selecting trusted and contextually relevant publishers to run their offers. On the other hand, CPA and affiliate marketing campaigns are publisher-centric. Advertisers cede control over where their brand will appear, as publishers browse offers and pick which to run on their websites. Advertisers generally do not know where their offer is running.
 2. CPL campaigns are usually high volume and light-weight. In CPL campaigns, consumers submit only basic contact information. The transaction can be as simple as an email address. On the other hand, CPA campaigns are usually low volume and complex. Typically, consumer has to submit credit card and other detailed information." (Source: Wikipedia)

Click-Through-Rate (CTR)
Click-through rate or CTR is a way of measuring the success of an online advertising campaign. A CTR is obtained by dividing the number of users who clicked on an ad on a web page by the number of times the ad was delivered (impressions). For example, if a banner ad was delivered 100 times (impressions delivered) and one person clicked on it (clicks recorded), then the resulting CTR would be 1 percent.
   Banner ad click-through rates have fallen over time, currently averaging much less than 1 percent. In most cases, a 2% click-through rate would be considered very successful. By selecting an appropriate advertising site with high affinity (e.g. a movie magazine for a movie advertisement), the same banner can achieve a substantially higher CTR. Personalized ads, unusual formats, and more obtrusive ads typically have higher click-through rates than standard banner ads.

CTR is most commonly defined as number of clicks divided by number of impressions and generally not in terms of the number of persons who clicked divided by the number of impressions. As a person clicks a single advertisement multiple times, the CTR increases using the latter definition, whereas the CTR doesn't change using the former definition." (Source: Wikipedia) For example, if an ad has 1000 impressions and 60 clicks, the CTR is 6%.

Deep Linking - Deep Links Ratio
Guiding a searcher or a search engine crawler to a specific internal web page other than the homepage or other top level (landing) pages.
The Deep Links Ration is the ratio of links pointing to internal pages compared to links pointing to a website homepage. A high deep links ratio is often a sign of a good natural link profile.

Description Tag
The Description Tag refers to the information contained in the description Meta Tag. This tag carries the brief description of the web page content it is on. The information contained in this tag is generally the text displayed beneath the link on many search engine result pages.

Directory
A Directory is a categorized catalog of websites, typically manually organized by topical editorial experts. Some directories focus on specific niche topics, while others are more general. Major search engines place significant weight on links from DMOZ.org and the Yahoo! directory. Smaller general directories carry less ranking weight. The search engines will probably not trust links from a directory if it does not exercise editorial control over its listings.

DMOZ
The Open Directory Project is the largest human edited directory of websites. DMOZ is owned by AOL, and is primarily run by volunteer editors.

Duplicate Content
Content that appears more than once on your own site or on your and other sites. Search engines have no interest in indexing multiple versions of similar content and if you have duplicate content on your pages search engines might give you less ranking power.

"For example, printer friendly pages may be search engine unfriendly duplicates. Also, many automated content generation techniques rely on recycling content, so some search engines are somewhat strict in filtering out content they deem to be similar or nearly duplicate in nature.

See also: Duplicate Content Detection (http://video.google.com/videoplay?docid=-9028425054136856586#1m18s) - video where Matt Cutts talks about the process of duplicate content detection. Identifying and filtering near-duplicate documents (www.nevelos.com/seo/andre-aka-andrei-broder.html), Stuntdubl: How to Remedy Duplicate Content. (www.stuntdubl.com/2006/06/12/dupe-content/)" (Source: SEOBook.com)

External Link – Incoming (Inbound) Links – Outgoing Links
An External Link is a link that comes from or goes to another domain. Incoming links ('Inbound' Links) from other relevant quality sites provide search engine ranking power for your site. Links from low quality sites or reciprocal links may not provide any ranking power. Links from your site (Outgoing Links) to other websites or blogs can help the search engines to understand what your site is about. It is therefore important to choose quality sites to link to and to avoid 'bad neighborhoods'. Most search engines allow you to see a sample of links pointing to a document by searching using the link: function. Google typically shows a much smaller sample of links, even when you log into your Google Webmasters account, than for example Yahoo! (http://siteexplorer.search.yahoo.com).

Forums – Discussion Forums
Forums, also known as discussion forums have primarily been used to ask questions / exchange information. Users can typically post their messages either to a group or to specific users.

Geo-Targeting – Local Listings
Geo-Targeting with Local Listings uses marketing and advertising based on your specific geographic location. Online advertising nowadays allows for specific targeting of countries, states, cities etc.

Google
Google was created by Stanford students Larry Page and Sergey Brin and pioneered search by analyzing link data via PR (www.google.com/corporate/tech.html). Despite the recent rise of Bing, Google is still the world's leading search engine in

Google Analytics

Google Analytics is a free web analytics tool offering detailed visitor statistics. The tool can be used to track all the usual site activities: visits, page views, pages per visit, bounce rates and average time on site etc. But it can also be used to specifically track Adsense traffic – therefore helping webmasters to optimize Adwords adverts based on where visitors come from, time on site, click path and geographic location.

Google OneBox

The part of the search results page above the organic search results which Google sometimes uses to display vertical search results from Google News, Google Base.

Headings - Heading Tag

The heading element describes the subject of the section it introduces. Heading elements go from H1 to H6 with the lower numbered headings being more important. Only use one H1 element on each page, and you may want to use multiple other heading elements to structure a document. An H1 element source code would like this: <h1>Your Heading</h1> Search engines often pay attention to text that is marked with a heading tag.

Hits

A Hit is a download of a file from a web server and does not correlate with web page visits since every image on a web page counts as a hit. Thus, a single access of a web page with 10 unique images on it register as 11 hits - 10 for the graphics and 1 for the HTML page.

Inbound Link (IBL)

see 'External Link'

Information Architecture

Designing, categorizing, organizing, and structuring content in a useful and meaningful way. Good information architecture considers both how humans and search spiders access a website. Information architecture suggestions:
- focus each page on a specific topic
- use descriptive page titles and meta descriptions which describe the content of the page

- use clean (few or no variables) descriptive file names and folder names
- use headings to help break up text and semantically structure a document
- use breadcrumb navigation to show page relationships
- use descriptive link Anchor Text
- link to related information from within the content area of your web pages
- improve conversion rates by making it easy for people to take desired actions
- avoid feeding search engines duplicate or near-duplicate content.

(Source: SEOmoz.org)

Internal Link
An Internal Link is a link from one of your pages to another page on your site. Descriptive internal linking can be used to make it easier for search engines to understand what your website is about and therefore can help you in achieving higher search engine rankings. How internal links are structured on your site will influence the way in which search engines spider and index your pages.

Key Performance Indicators (KPIs)
Key Performance Indicators help organizations to evaluate the progress towards their vision and long-term goals. Key performance indicators usually are long-term considerations for an organization and differ depending on the nature of the organization and the organization's strategy.
For example: "Increase Average Revenue per Customer from $1.000 to $1.500 by EOY 2009". In this case, 'Average Revenue Per Customer' is the KPI.

Keyword - Keyword Phrase - Keyphrase
A specific word or combination of words that a searcher might type into a search field. Includes generic, category keywords; industry-specific terms; product brands; common misspellings and expanded variations (called Keyword Stemming), or multiple words (called Modified or Long Tail keywords). All might be entered as a search query. For example, someone looking to buy coffee mugs might use the keyword phrase "ceramic coffee mugs." (Source: A-Z of Social Media)

Keyword Density
Keyword Density gets used in different ways. For some time it was claimed to be an exact formula of how many keywords per text words should be on a page. SEO professionals today mostly agree that there is no exact formula and the term

keyword density nowadays just gets used as a shorter form of saying: "the quantity of keywords on a specific page".

Keyword Funnel
The relationship between various related keywords that searchers search for.

Keyword Matching
Keyword matching describes a) the process of selecting and providing advertising or information that match the user's search query and b) the matching of keywords in Link or Anchor Texts and the keywords on the link target page as well as the source page.

Keyword Popularity
Keyword popularity describes the search volume for a keyword during a specific time period, typically over the last month or the last 12 months as in Google's Keyword tool.

Keyword Prominence
Keyword Prominence describes the location of a keyword in a specific location. This can be a web page or a Title Tag etc. On a web page keyword prominence would describe how high up on the page or how early in the text the keyword appears. In a Title Tag whether the keyword appears as the first, second, third etc. word in the tag.

Keyword Tag
The Keyword Tag is a meta tag within a webpage and can hold a number of keywords. If you use this tag, do not include your top keywords since the keyword meta tag is also an easy way for your competition to see what you are focusing on. Due to people stuffing many keywords into the keyword meta tag, sometimes using the same keyword several times, Google does not give any weight anymore to the keywords stated here.

Link
Text or graphics that, when clicked on, take the Internet user to another web page, blog etc.

Link Bait
A concept that webmasters use to compel others to link to them.

Link Building
Means requesting links from other sites to increase your 'Link Popularity' and/or 'PR.'

Link Equity
Link Equity measures how strong a site or page is based on its number of inbound links and the authority of the sites providing those links.

Link Hoarding
A method of trying to keep all your link popularity by not linking out to other sites, or linking out using JavaScript or through redirects. Generally link hoarding is a bad idea for the following reasons:

many authoritative sites were at one point hub sites that freely linked out to other relevant resources

if you are unwilling to link out to other sites then people are going to be less likely to link to your site

outbound links to relevant resources may improve your credibility and boost your overall relevancy scores (Source: sempo.org)

Link Popularity
Your Link Popularity is the total number of links pointing to your domain. Link Popularity gets measured for internal and external links. Internal link popularity refers to the number of links or pages within your web site that link to a specific URL. External link popularity refers to the number of Inbound Links from external web sites that are pointing to your site.

Link Reputation
Link Reputation is the combined score of your link equity and Link Text / Anchor Text.

Link Rot
Link Rot is a measure of how many website links are broken. Broken links may be an indication of a site that has not been properly maintained for some time and therefore might be seen as less relevant in the eyes of the search engines, resulting in lower rankings. See Xenu Link Sleuth (free) or WebAnalyzer for programs to find broken links.

Log File Analysis
The analysis of records stored in your server's log file. In its raw format, the data in the log files can be difficult to read but log file analyzers can help to convert log file data into user-friendly charts and graphs.

Long Tail
"The Long Tail" as a term was coined by Chris Anderson in an Wired magazine article (Oct 2004) which described the niche strategy of businesses, such as Amazon.com or Netflix, to sell a large number of unique items, each in relatively small quantities.
Long Tail keywords are keyword phrases with at least three, sometimes four or five, words. These long tail keywords are usually specific and draw lower traffic than shorter, more competitive keyword phrases, which is why they are also cheaper. However often long tail keywords, in aggregate, have good conversion ratios for the low number of click-throughs they generate. See:
The official Long Tail blog (www.thelongtail.com/) and the Long Tail book (www.amazon.com/Long-Tail-Future-Business-Selling).

Meta Description
The meta Description Tag contained in an HTML document describes the content of a page in one or two sentences. Search engines may display the contents of this tag in their search results. A meta description should reinforce the page title (tag), be relevant to the page content and include offers and secondary keywords (phrases) to support the page title message.
Code for a meta Description Tag:
<meta name="Description" content="Your meta description here. " / >
The Free Meta Tag generator (http://tools.seobook.com/meta-medic) - offers a free formatting tool and advice on creating meta Description Tags.
(Source: SEOBook.com)

Meta Tags
Meta-information about the content of a page placed in the source code of an HTML page. See 'Description Tag', 'Keyword Tag' and 'Title Tag'.

Organic Results – Organic Search Listings - Organic Search Results
"Listings on SERPs (Search Engine Ranking Pages) that were not paid for; listings for which search engines do not sell space. Such sites appear in organic (also called "natural") results because a search engine has applied formulas (algorithms) to its

search crawler index, combined with editorial decisions and content weighting, that it deems important enough to allow inclusion without payment. Paid Inclusion Content is also often considered "organic" even though it is paid advertising because paid inclusion content usually appears on SERPs mixed with unpaid, organic results. [Organic Search Listings are] listings that search engines do not sell (unlike paid listings). Instead, sites appear solely because a search engine has deemed it editorially important for them to be included, regardless of payment. Paid Inclusion Content is also often considered "organic" even though it is paid for. This is because paid inclusion content usually appears intermixed with unpaid organic results."
(Source: Sempo.org)

Outbound links
Outbound Links to another website.

PageRank
Google describes PageRank as:
" PageRank (PR) relies on the uniquely democratic nature of the web by using its vast link structure as an indicator of an individual page's value. In essence, Google interprets a link from page A to page B as a vote, by page A, for page B. But, Google looks at more than the sheer volume of votes, or links a page receives; it also analyzes the page that casts the vote. Votes cast by pages that are themselves "important" weigh more heavily and help to make other pages "important".
(Source: Google)

Pay-For-Performance
see 'Affiliate Programs'

Pay-Per-Click (PPC)
PPC is an advertising model used on websites, in which advertisers pay only when their ad is clicked. With search engines, advertisers typically bid on keyword phrases relevant to their target market. See Google Adwords (http:// adwords.google.com)

Phrase Match
Phrase Match is a form of keyword matching where the user's search query includes the exact phrase, even if the query contains additional words. "If you enter your keyword in quotation marks, as in "tennis shoes," your ad would be eligible to appear when a user searches on the phrase tennis shoes, with the words in that order. It can also appear for searches that contain other terms as long as it includes

the exact phrase you've specified. Phrase match is more targeted than broad match, but more flexible than exact match." (Source: Google)

Quality Score
The Quality Score is a number assigned by Google to paid ads that, together with Cost per Click (CPC), determines each ad's rank. Quality scores reflect an ad's historical Click Through Rate (CTR), keyword relevance, landing page relevance, and other factors proprietary to Google.

Query
The keyword or keyword phrase a searcher enters into a search field.

Rank
How well positioned a particular web page appears on Search Engine Results Pages (SERPs).

Reach
In statistics, advertising and media analysis, "reach refers to the total number of different people or households exposed, at least once, to a medium during a given period of time. Reach should not be confused with the number of people who will actually be exposed to and consume the advertising, though. It is just the number of people who are exposed to the medium and therefore have an opportunity to see or hear the ad or commercial. Reach may be stated either as an absolute number, or as a fraction of a given population (for instance 'TV households', 'men' or 'those aged 25-35'). (Source: Google)

Reciprocal Linking
The practice of trading links between websites resulting in links going 'both ways'.

Referential Integrity
This is a definition of the indexing technique that some SEO experts believe Google uses to get a better understanding of the meaning of the content on a web page or blog: "Referential Integrity is a property of data which, when satisfied, requires every value of one attribute (column) of a relation (table) to exist as a value of another attribute in a different (or the same) relation (table)".
(Source: The Web Division)

Referrer

A web page that refers visitors to your site or blog.

Relevance
In the eyes of a searcher or a search engine, the probability that a certain web page will be of interest or useful to a searcher.

Robots.txt
A file in the root of a site that tells search engines which files not to crawl. However some search engine robots will still list your URL even if you tried to block them using a robots.txt file. Don't put files on a public server if you do not want search engines to index them!

RSS - Really Simply Syndication - Rich Site Summary
A variety of web feed formats used for distributing frequently updated digital content usually originating on blogs.

Search Term
A keyword or phrase used in a search engine query.

SEM – Search Engine Marketing
"SEM, is a form of Internet marketing that seeks to promote websites by increasing their visibility in search engine result pages (SERPs) through the use of paid placement, contextual advertising, and paid inclusion. The industry peak body Search Engine Marketing Professional Organization (SEMPO) founded by Barbara Coll in 2003, includes search engine optimization (SEO) within its reporting, and SEO is also included in the industry definitions of SEM by Forrester Research, eMarketer, Search Engine Watch, and industry expert Danny Sullivan. The New York Times defines SEM as 'the practice of buying paid search listings".
(Source: Wikipedia)

SEO
Search engine optimization (SEO) is the process of improving the volume or quality of traffic to a web site from search engines via 'natural' ('organic' or 'algorithmic') search results. Typically, the earlier (or higher) a site appears in the search results list, the more visitors it will receive from the search engine. SEO may target different kinds of search, including image search, local search, and industry-specific vertical search engines. This gives a web site web presence. (Source: Wikipedia)
SERP

Akronym for Search Engine Results Page: the page returned to your browser after submitting a search.

Siloing
Siloing (also known as Theming) is a site architecture technique [also called Silo Structure,] used to split the focus of a site into multiple themes. The goal behind siloing is to create a site that ranks well for both its common and more-targeted keywords. (Source: Bruce Clay)

Social Search
Social search or a social search engine is a type of web search method that determines the relevance of search results by considering the interactions or contributions of users. When applied to web search this user-based approach to relevance is in contrast to established algorithmic or machine-based approaches where relevance is determined by analyzing the text of each document or the link structure of the documents.
Social search takes many forms, ranging from simple shared bookmarks or tagging of content with descriptive labels to more sophisticated approaches that combine human intelligence with computer algorithms.
The search experience takes into account varying sources of metadata, such as collaborative discovery of web pages, tags, social ranking, commenting on bookmarks, news, images, videos, podcasts and other web pages. Example forms of user input include Social Bookmarking or direct interaction with the search results such as promoting or demoting results the user feels are more or less relevant to their query. (Source: Wikipedia)

Spam
Any search marketing method that a search engine deems to be detrimental to its efforts to deliver relevant, quality search results. Some search engines have written guidelines on their definitions and penalties for SPAM. Examples include doorway landing pages designed primarily to manipulate search engine algorithms rather than meet searcher expectations from the advertiser's clicked-on ad; keyword stuffing in which search terms that motivated a click-through are heavily and redundantly repeated on a page in place of relevant content; attempts to redirect click-through searchers to irrelevant pages, product offers and services; and landing pages that simply compile additional links on which a searcher must click to get any information. Determining what constitutes Spam is complicated by the fact that different search engines have different standards, including what is allowable for

listings gathered through organic methods versus paid inclusion (referred to as spamdexing), whether the listing is from a commercial or research/academic source, etc. (Source: Webmaster World Forums)

Static Web Page
A Static Web Page that was created and saved as a HTML file not created dynamically from a database.

Submission
Submitting a web site to search engines and search directories. For some search engines, this is performed simply by submitting the home page URL, directories usually request descriptions of the web site submitted.

Tagging, Tags
(see Bookmarks)

Target Audience
The target audience is the market in which advertisers wish to sell their product or service to. Target markets are defined in terms of demographics, psychographics, purchase behaviour media or product usage.

Technorati
Search engine for blogs.

Themes
A theme is an overall idea of what a web page is focused on. Search engines determine the theme of a webpage through analysis of the density of associated (key-)words on a certain page.

Title
The title element is used to describe the contents of a document. The title is one of the most important aspects to doing SEO on a web page. Each page title should be:

- Unique to that page: Not the same for every page of a site!
- Descriptive: What important ideas does that page cover?
- Not excessively long: Typically page titles should be kept to 8 to 10 words or less, with some of the most important words occurring near the beginning of the page title.

Page titles appear in search results as the links searchers click on. In addition many

Glossary

people link to documents using the official document title as the Link Text / Anchor Text. Thus, by using a descriptive page title you are likely to gain descriptive and are more likely to have your listing clicked on.

Title Tag
The Title Tag can be found in the source code of a page and in the <head> tag of a web page. The page title should be determined by the contents of that web page and is generally displayed in a search engine result as a bold blue underlined hyperlink.

Unique Visitors
Unique visitors is the number of individual users who have accessed your web site. The "user session" metric however does not provide an accurate unique visitor count, as multiple user sessions can be generated by one unique visitor.

URL – Uniform Resource Locator
This acronym stands for Uniform Resource Locator and means basically the same as website address.

User Generated Content
User-generated-content gets created and published by the end-users, typically on social media sites. Examples are content sharing sites such as Facebook and YouTube.

Viral Marketing
The buzzwords viral marketing and viral advertising refer to marketing techniques that use pre-existing social networks to produce increases in brand awareness or to achieve other marketing objectives (such as product sales) through self-replicating viral processes, analogous to the spread of pathological and computer viruses. It can be word-of-mouth delivered or enhanced by the network effects of the Internet. Viral promotions may take the form of video clips, interactive Flash games, advergames, ebooks, brandable software, images, or even text messages. The basic form of viral marketing is not infinitely sustainable.
The goal of marketers interested in creating successful viral marketing programs is to identify individuals with high Social Networking Potential (SNP) and create Viral Messages that appeal to this segment of the population and have a high probability of being passed along. (Source: Wikipedia)

Web 2.0

Web 2.0 is a term coined by O'Reilly Media in 2004 (http://en.wikipedia.org/wiki/Web_2) to describe blogs, wikis, social networking sites and other Internet-based services that emphasize collaboration and sharing, rather than less interactive publishing (Web 1.0). It is associated with the idea of the Internet as platform.
(Source: Sempo.org)

Weblog
see 'Blog'

Wordpress
Wordpress is a popular blogging software platform, offering a downloadable blogging program and a hosted solution.

Wordtracker
(see also 'SEO Tools')
Wordtracker is a popular keyword research tool to assist search marketing professionals and webmasters in identifying important keywords and phrases relevant to their website. It provides detailed information on the number of searches, predicted number of daily searches, competing pages and KEI data.

The list above covers the majority of the terms used in this book but if you can't find what you are looking for, have a look on our site for most recent updates at www.Internet-Experts-Live.com/members/resources/seo-glossary. The Internet, Google, Bing and everyone else constantly introduce new terms to the Internet.

Sources

- Boykin, Jim. "Jim Boykin's Blog." <http://www.webuildpages.com/jim/>
- Callen, Brad. <http://KeywordElite.com>
- Chaudry, Gauher. "The Insider's Guide To CPA Marketing Profits." <http://www.cpahotspot.com/>
- Dr. Williams, Andy. "Creating Fat Content", "Creating Fat Affiliate Sites", "Wordpress for Affiliate Sites Course."<http://ezseonews.com/>
- Duz, Michael. "The LSI Myth." < http://www.seo-blog.com/>
- Eisenberg, Bryan; Ochman, B.L.; Lee, Kevin; Mahaney, Stephen; Mc Gaffin, Ken; Alexander, John; Davidson, Neil; Good, Robin; Usborne, Nick. "Keyword Research Guide." <http://Wordtracker.com>
- Fishkin, Rand. "Search Engine Ranking Factors V2.", "Beginner's Guide to Search Engine Optimization", "Website Analytics vs. Competitive Intelligence Metrics" <http://SEOmoz.org>
- Gorman, Paul. "The Game Of Business And How To Play It", "Take Your Business To The Top", "Copywriting Interview." http://www.paulgorman.com
- Green, Jason; deGeyter, Stoney. "Keyword Research and Selection" < http://www.polepositionmarketing.com>
- Hodgson,Brent; Ware,Eugene. "The Niche Marketing Black Book." <http://www.NobleSamurai.com">
- Jenkins, Andy; Fallon, Brad; Thies, Dan; Rohde, Leslie. "STSE2." <http://www.stomperblog.com/>
- Kaushik, Avinash. "Google – Average Number of Words Per Query have Increased!" <http://www.beussery.com/blog/index.php/2008/02/google-average-number-of-words-per-query-have-increased/>
- Lee, Chris & Nagy, Goran. "The Keyword Master's Course." <http://www.keywordsanalyzer.com>
- LeFever, Lee. "Social Bookmarking in Plain English." <http://www.commoncraft.com/store-item/bookmarking-plain-english>
- Liron, Mac. "Hands On Guide: UK Local Search, Summer 2009" <http://www.marcliron.co.uk>

- Mc Gaffin, Ken. "Why Keywords Matter."

Sources

<http://www.wordtracker.com/academy/why-keywords-matter>
- McDougal, Colin. "The VEOReport." <http://veoreport.com/>
- McGlynn, Matt. "SERP Rank Traffic Calculator." <http://seo-greenhouse.com/2008/11/serp-rank-traffic-calculator/>
- McPhearson, Michelle. "The Social Media Slap." <http://www.michellemacphearson.com/the-social-media-slap/>
- Pierce, Stephen. "Free Article Marketing Checklist." <http://www.dtalpha.com/talkback>
- Rhodes, John; Rhodes, Matt. "Why Would Anyone PAY For Free Information?"
- Ruppert, Peter. "YouTubeReport." Entertainment Media Research, <http://youtubereport2009.com/>
- Schoeffel, JP. "Beyond Silo Structure and LSI" <http://howtoturnsitesintomoney.com>
- Silver, Yanik. "Is There a Business Model to 'Free'?" <http://www.surefiremarketing.com/>
- Stockwell, Jay. "Introduction to Keyword Research", "Different Tools, Different Reasons", "Keyword Research Concepts" <http://KeywordWorkshop.com>
- Wall, Aaron. <http://SEOBook.com>
- Wright, Russel. "The 12 Biggest Missed Opportunities In Profitable Website Development." <http://www.themezoom.com/>

Index

"framed" pages, 146
'natural' search engine listings, 8
'organic' search engine listings, 8
Aaron Wall, 127, 136, 208, 264
Advertisers, 30
Adwords, 44, 195, 198, 250
Alt text, 88, 242
Amazon, 199, 204, 207
analytics programs, 25
AOL, 31, 51, 53, 204, 248
AOL's leaked data, 31
article, 21, 43, 44, 93, 115, 120, 156, 157, 158, 160, 161, 162, 163, 164, 165, 205
Article marketing, 155, 157
Article Writing Roadmap', 158
authority sites, 125
Avinash Kaushik, 9, 9, 179, 188, 194, 203, 204, 263
Bing, 30
blog, 9, 21, 25, 30, 37, 43, 51, 53, 55, 61, 88, 90, 99, 106, 107, 108, 110, 111, 115, 117, 119, 120, 122, 143, 144, 145, 146, 155, 156, 158, 161, 162, 163, 165, 166, 195, 205, 210, 215, 218, 219, 242, 243, 244
blogging, 108, 261
Bookmarking Demon, 152
Breakpoint, 51, 52
business, 7, 8, 19, 20, 23, 24, 26, 29, 32, 43, 47, 52, 74, 81, 110, 115, 156, 165, 166, 174, 182, 209, 217, 218, 219, 242, 243
Businessweek, 163
buzz.yahoo.com, 153, 203
Call to Action, 87
Chris Anderson, 35, 36, 181, 254

click through, 86, 162
Compete, 197, 198, 210
competition, 19, 20, 23, 25, 26, 28, 29, 35, 43, 47, 51, 53, 60, 74, 75, 76, 83, 108, 110, 115, 125, 182, 195, 200, 209, 217, 219
competition analysis, 74
Competition Analysis Tools, 197
competition, 33, 47
competitors, 20, 28, 33, 35, 47, 51, 76, 107, 159, 173, 189, 197, 198, 202, 207, 209, 215, 217
Comscore, 30
Conversion, 32, 245
Conversion Rate, 32
Copyright, 88
Copywriting, 158, 159
Cost-per-Click, 28, 31
CPC, 26, 27, 28, 29, 31, 32, 33, 35, 47, 246, 256
CPM, 246
CR, 32
customers, 4, 8, 9, 19, 20, 21, 22, 23, 24, 31, 33, 37, 44, 45, 47, 76, 81, 84, 86, 93, 107, 110, 115, 117, 146, 156, 157, 159, 160, 164, 165, 166, 174, 179, 182, 215, 216, 217, 218, 219
David Ogilvy, 159
Del.icio.us.com, 163
delicious.com, 153, 205
Description Meta Tags, 86
Digg, 163, 204, 205, 206
digg.com, 153, 205
DMOZ, 248
Duplicate Content, 163, 248, 249
Earnersforum, 51

Index

EBay Pulse, 207
Elisabeth Osmeloski, 57
email, 90, 163, 201, 241, 242, 245
embedded links, 146
Emotional Writing, 159
Empathy, 89
Flickr.com, 120,181
freebies, 87
Freemium, 181
Gary Halbert, 22
Google, 8, 15, 19, 20, 22, 25, 26, 28, 29, 30, 31, 33, 35, 37, 43, 44, 47, 51, 53, 55, 56, 63, 74, 81, 83, 86, 88, 99, 100, 101, 107, 108, 110, 115, 117, 118, 119, 122, 125, 143, 144, 145, 150, 161, 162, 163, 166, 190, 201, 202, 204, 209, 210, 215, 216, 217, 218, 241, 242, 244, 245, 249, 250, 255, 256
Google Keyword Tool, 26, 28, 29, 33, 47, 217
Google Adwords, 86, 133, 189, 190, 244, 255
Google Analytics 25, 31, 179, 188, 250
GoRank, 199, 200
guarantees, 87
headline, 76, 83, 97, 110, 159, 217
Hitwise, 30
Hubpages.com, 120
hungry crowd, 7
inbound links, 56, 144, 243, 250, 253
indexed pages, 146
initial keywords, 26
Internet, 19, 26, 32, 35, 47, 51, 55, 115, 156, 173, 179, 188, 209, 252, 261
J P Schoeffel, 107
John Caples, 159
Ken Evoy, 93

Keyword Density', 93
Keyword Discovery, 196
keyword formulas, 29
keyword lists, 26
keyword phrases, 22, 28, 35, 43, 44, 45, 46, 47, 217
Keyword Popularity Tools, 189
keyword research tool, 26, 261
Keyword Selection Tools, 189
Keyword Spy, 200
Keyword Suggestion Tools, 189, 190
keyword theme, 44
keyword tools, 19, 26, 64, 190, 198
keyword value, 26, 31, 33, 47, 217
KeywordElite.com, 195, 196
KeywordSpy, 200
Latent Semantic Indexing, 44
leadership, 19
leverage, 19, 163
Link building, 145, 146, 253
Link Farms, 146
link popularity, 253
link texts, 158
links campaign, 21
long tail, 35, 43, 44, 46, 47, 130, 110, 158, 216, 217, 251, 254
long tail keywords, 83
low profit products, 23
LSI, 44
Market Samurai, 195
market value, 29
Marketing, 4, 22, 51, 55, 156, 188, 209, 260
marketing campaign, 19, 21, 22, 47
marketing skills, 32
Match, 43, 244, 255
Matching, 143, 216, 252
meta tag, 76, 97, 110, 217, 254
Michelle McPhearson, 162

Index

Microsoft, 30, 90
mixx.com, 153
modified, 19, 46, 47, 83, 100, 216, 217
modifier, 35
MSN, 30, 83
natural listing, 8, 9
Navigation, 88, 122
Nielsen Netrating, 30
Noble Samurai, 108
no-follow, 144
non-reciprocal, 144, 146
offline, 21, 163, 246
online, 4, 7, 8, 9, 19, 20, 21, 23, 27, 29, 35, 51, 76, 83, 107, 115, 118, 146, 164, 182, 195, 201, 215, 243, 245, 246, 260
PageRank, 81, 107, 118, 144, 145, 150, 162, 199, 210, 249, 253, 255
paid advertising, 8, 255
Pay-per-Click, 8, 22
Penn State research, 8
PPC, 8, 9, 22, 30, 45, 189, 198, 200, 246, 248, 255
PPC Web Spy, 199
PR, 119, 125, 144, 145, 161, 209, 255
press releases, 21
price, 22, 24, 32, 35, 180
primary keyword, 33, 46, 47, 93, 158, 217
profession, 23, 165, 166, 218
profit margins, 23, 24
profit potential, 26, 30
profitability, 45, 115
profitable keyword, 23
Rand Fishkin, 40, 55, 89, 126, 210, 236
ranking, 15, 21, 30, 45, 47, 55, 56, 63, 76, 83, 90, 101, 107, 108, 110, 117, 122, 143, 150, 155, 156, 157, 161, 162, 178, 183, 210, 215, 217, 242
Rational writing, 159

Ray W. Intkins, 160
reddit.com, 153
redirected pages, 146
Referential Integrity, 44
related keywords, 19, 26, 44, 46, 47, 100, 101, 158, 216, 217, 252
Resources, 26, 108, 185
return on your investment, 31
robots, 93, 163, 257
ROI, 31, 246
Rosalind Gardner, 99
RSS feeds, 164, 242
sales agent, 20
sales letters, 21
search engine optimization, 8, 19, 43, 53, 55, 107, 111, 215
search engine rankings, 30, 150, 189, 195
search engine results, 21, 55, 76, 89, 111, 217, 256
Search Funnels, 194
Search Keyword Tool, 108, 244
Search Volume', 27, 29
Searched Based Keyword Tool, 25
secondary keywords, 26, 46, 47, 97, 110, 145, 158, 216, 217, 254
seed list, 23
Seed List, 23
Semiologic, 108
SEO, 8, 19, 56, 63, 79, 83, 90, 93, 111, 115, 120, 163, 173, 188, 189, 195, 197, 199, 207, 257, 259
SEOMoz, 204
SEOToolbar, 208
SERPS, 58
server logs, 25
Shoulders of Giants, 161
Silo, 61, 63, 105, 106, 107, 109, 110, 122, 216, 218, 258

Index

Silo Structure, 43, 63, 105, 106, 107, 108, 109, 110, 122, 216, 218, 258
Sitesell.com, 93
Social Bookmarking, 150, 151, 152, 153, 204
Social Marker, 151
Social Media Sites, 115
source code, 85, 243
Spamming, 97
specific keywords, 197
Sponsored Listings, 8
Squidoo.com, 120
Static, 90, 259
stumbleupon.com, 153
sub-headline, 76, 86, 97, 110, 217
tags, 58, 85, 88, 150, 151, 153, 204, 205, 242, 243, 254, 259
target market, 22, 23, 37, 45, 156, 162, 179
technorati.com, 153, 210
Ted Nicholas, 157, 159
The Economist, 163
The Financial Times, 163
The Wall Street Journal, 163
Theme, 60, 61, 99, 103, 110, 143, 217
Themezoom, 15
Theming, 43, 45, 63, 99, 101, 107, 258
Title Tag, 85, 260
Toolbars, 189, 207
Top Ten, 144
Topix, 204, 206
Traffic, 30, 150, 156, 162
Trellian, 197
Trend Analysis Keyword Tools, 189, 201
Trendy Commercial Keywords, 207
trusted resource, 20
Twitter, 21, 141, 180
unidirectional, 146
unique selling proposition, 23

Unpaid advertising, 8
URL, 76, 83, 88, 89, 90, 97, 110, 120, 151, 199, 217, 243, 253, 257, 259, 260
USP, 23
video tutorial, 28
Visitor Value, 30
Web 2.0, 120, 144, 161, 162, 261
web pages, 26, 27, 101, 144, 199
WebSpy, 198
Windows Live, 30
Wired, 180
Wordpress.com, 108
Wordtracker, 191, 193, 194, 261, 263
XE "phrase match"', 43
Yahoo, 31, 32, 83, 173, 203, 204, 210, 248
YouTube, 28, 120, 173

Notes

Notes

Notes

Notes

Notes

Notes

Publications by the Authors

Book and Reports

- The Copywriting Roadmap – How to Attract Customers with Great Copy
- How to Attract Customers with Video Marketing
- Insider SEO Secrets - Raise Your Business to the Top of Google Now
- SEO Templates at: www.Internet-Experts-Live.com/members/templates

Webinars / Seminars

For Webinars and Seminars please check: www.Internet-Experts-Live.com

Lightning Source UK Ltd.
Milton Keynes UK
27 September 2010
160414UK00006B/164/P